An Introduction to Theology in Africa and the Kpelelogical Foundations of Christian Theology

An Introduction to Theology in Africa and the Kpelelogical Foundations of Christian Theology

CHARLES AMARKWEI

Foreword by J. Kwabena Asamoah-Gyadu

WIPF & STOCK · Eugene, Oregon

AN INTRODUCTION TO THEOLOGY IN AFRICA AND THE KPELELOGICAL FOUNDATIONS OF CHRISTIAN THEOLOGY

Copyright © 2021 Charles Amarkwei. All rights reserved. Except for brief quotations in critical publications or reviews, no part of this book may be reproduced in any manner without prior written permission from the publisher. Write: Permissions, Wipf and Stock Publishers, 199 W. 8th Ave., Suite 3, Eugene, OR 97401.

Wipf & Stock
An Imprint of Wipf and Stock Publishers
199 W. 8th Ave., Suite 3
Eugene, OR 97401

www.wipfandstock.com

PAPERBACK ISBN: 978-1-6667-1186-8
HARDCOVER ISBN: 978-1-6667-1187-5
EBOOK ISBN: 978-1-6667-1188-2

10/19/21

To the glory of God,
in honor of
Irene Lantsoi Amarkwei
and
in loving memory of
Paulina Naa Amorkor Ankrah,
August 10, 1980 to August 29, 2009

Contents

Foreword by J. Kwabena Asamoah-Gyadu | xi
Preface | xiii
Acknowledgments | xvii
Introduction | xxi
    African Christian Theology and the Kpelelogical Foundation of Christian Theology | xxi
    "Who do you, Africans say that I am?" | xxiii
    The Kpelelogical Method | xxv

Part 1: Defining African Christian Theology | 1
    Introduction | 1

1. African Christian Theology as Universal and Concrete | 3
    Definition of African Christian Theology | 3
    The Universal and Concrete Expression of African Christian Theology | 14
    The Characteristics of African Christian Theology | 28

2. The Kpelelogy of Faith | 31
    The Kpelelogy of Christian Faith | 31
    African Roots of Paradox in Christian Theology | 37
    Faith and Love: A Theological Significance of Kpelelogical Paradox in Contemporary African Christianity | 43
    The Significance of Kpelelogical Paradox in Formulating Contemporary African Christian Theology | 48
    Conclusion | 50

Part 2: The Nature of Contemporary African Christian Theology | 53
    Introduction | 53

3. Contemporary African Christian Theology | 55
    The Kpelelogical and Kpelelogical Background of
        Contemporary African Christian Theology | 55
    Inculturation Christologies | 69
    Liberation Christologies | 81
    Cultura-Libero Christologies | 90
    Some Limitations of Theologies from Africa | 92

4. Method and Criteria of African Christian Theology | 100
    Postmodernism and African Christian Theology | 100
    Methods of Doing African Christian Theology | 101
    Criteria for Doing Theology | 110
    The Nature of Christology Today (Postcolonial and Third World
        Christology) and the Criterion. | 116
    Some Critical Issues and the Criteria for Doing Theology Today | 118
    Dichotomies of African Christian Theology | 120

5. The Essence of African Christian Theology as
  Faith in the Absolutely Concrete | 133
    Christian Faith and African Christian Theology | 133
    African Christian Theology Is Not Mere Intellectual Exercise
        but an Interrogation of African Christian Faith | 134
    The Impact of Distorted Christian Theologies in Africa | 135
    Not an Ideology of Identity but a Trinitarian Theology
        of the African Christian Experience | 138
    Not Utopianism but a Trinitarian Theology of African
        Christian Experience and Eschatology | 141
    The Distorted Theology in the New Testament | 143
    The Distorted Theology Addressed by the Early African Church | 145
    The Call to Engage the Sources of Tradition in the
        Context of African Christianity | 147
    Meaningfulness Is Based upon the
        Connection of *Logos* and *Logoi* | 150

Meaningfulness without the Absolutely Universal
   or Absolutely Concrete? | 155
Conclusion | 166

Part 3: A Kpelelogical Theology: *Kpele* and the Kpelelogical Theology of the *Okpelejen Wulormor* | 171

6. The Concept of *Okpelejen Wulormor* in the *Kpele* Traditional and Religious Institution of the Ga People of Southern Ghana | 173
   An Antecedent of Jesus Christ the *Okpelejen Wulormor* | 173
   Kpele Religious Thought in Ga Life | 176
   The *Wulormor* of the *Kpele* Institution | 179
   The *Wulormor* as Priest | 182
   The *Wulormor* as a King | 186
   The *Wulormor* as Prophet | 189
   Homowor Festival | 191
   The *Okpelejen Wulormor* | 203

7. The *Munus Triplex* and the Theology of the *Okpelejen Wulormor* | 207
   The *Munus Triplex* | 207
   The *Munus Triplex* of John Calvin | 209
   Karl Barth's Trinitarian Approach to the *Munus Triplex* | 211
   An Examination of the Critique of the *Munus Triplex* by
      John F. Jansen, Albert Ritschl, and Wolfhart Pannenberg | 213
   The Priest/Prophetic/Potentate African Theological Paradigm | 216
   Is Jesus *Okpelejen Wulormor* or *Osorfonukpa*? | 218
   Jesus the *Okpelejen Wulormor* | 220
   Conclusion | 222

Conclusion | 225
Bibliography | 231

Foreword

WE HAVE IN THIS volume a bold attempt by a budding African theologian, Rev. Dr. Charles Amarkwei to revisit some of the key elements, ideas, idioms, and thoughts within which the discipline, African theology, has been fashioned within postcolonial Africa. He begins the story from the Church Fathers. Dr. Amarkwei is at an age in which one may conveniently say that he relates to some of the names he writes about and whose theological ideas he engages with as ancestors. In other words, as a young theologian, he brings into the postmodern context ideas that were originally fashioned within the modern African religio-cultural context to interrogate their relevance or otherwise for current generations. That is the reason for my referring to this work as a bold attempt in theologizing. Dr. Amarkwei has not pulled punches, but nevertheless has very carefully and systematically engaged with the theological thoughts of scholars whose work span generations.

We encounter in this work not only names like Origen, but also John S. Mbiti and Kwesi Dickson who laid the foundations for theology in Africa. One of the most significant names in this light is Kwame Bediako who carved a niche for himself in the study of African Christianity as one of the most innovative thinkers of the late twentieth century as far as Christian scholarship is concerned. The interest of Dr. Amarkwei in the theological ideas of Paul Tillich would not be lost on those who read this volume. African theology, Dr. Amarkwei argues, flows from the depths of African spirituality, a spirituality that continuously seeks to experience the Divine. To illustrate this experiential nature of African Christianity in concrete ways, the book works with the oral theological expressions of the older independent church movements and the more contemporary Pentecostals to bring to the fore the dynamism that has characterized African theology when understood from the viewpoint of those at the grassroots.

This work is refreshing in the way it brings together the works of generations of theologians—Church Fathers, modern and even postmodern—to interrogate the key themes that have emerged with the rise of new Christian religious movements on the continent. The various elements of objective and subjective knowledge of God, as Dr. Amarkwei argues, are expressed explicitly and in depth by traditional theologians as Paul Tillich and whose works marked the transitions between modernism and postmodernism. The experience of African Christianity does not only emphasize experience of conversion he notes, stating that they go beyond to assert other experiences associated with the subjective reality of God in them. These realities, conspicuously missing from Protestant theology as Dr. Amarkwei further notes, are the miracles, healing, prophecy, and exorcisms. He calls for the integration of these pneumatic realities in theologizing in Africa because they are bedrocks of Christian soteriology found in the accounts the New Testament and the tradition of the Church Fathers. Hence, African Christian experience of the Divine through grace and by faith in Jesus Christ in the Spirit is a critique and further, an enrichment and affirmation of Christian tradition itself.

This is a useful volume that opens new vistas in the study of theology in Africa and it is hoped that emerging theologians will find in it the needed inspiration to take the study of theology in Africa to a new level.

Rev. Prof. J. Kwabena Asamoah-Gyadu PhD., DD (HC). FGA
President, Trinity Theological Seminary, Legon, Ghana

Preface

SURELY, IT IS A joy to have this work published when I remember the context of the opportunity to study in Hanil University and Presbyterian Theological Seminary in the outskirts of the city of Jeonju, South Korea for the degree of Master of Theology (ThM) in 2012.

Firstly, it was unexpected, and I never had a plan in mind to travel outside of Ghana to study. But lo and behold, I saw the great potential it had for me, so I took the opportunity.

Secondly, whatever it was, it made me to think more and more about God and through my lecturers particularly Koo Choon-Seo who insisted that I should stick to African Christian theology finally led me to think about doing theology from the Ga ethnic group of the southern Ghana context.

Thirdly, I believe my experiences at Hanil was somehow orchestrated by God to bring me to deeper faith and to further bring me to understanding in different ways that has become for me something that is mind-blowing. Particularly, the three years I spent studying for the PhD degree in systematic theology, I had to bring to bear my being theological to do this theological work. My understanding and my experience as a Christian in the various encounters I had both in life and in my readings/debates were effectively synchronized. Thus, like other Africans before me and other theologians before me, I came to the realization that theology is not just a matter of praxis like an empty barrel making a lot of noise, rather it ought to arise out of being theological that is being put in a theological frame by the ultimate concern that is encountered through the love of God in Christ and in the Spirit.

Then I also realized that this is very true of traditional theology itself with regards to John Calvin, Friedrich Schleiermacher and Karl Barth and Paul Tillich whose theology possessed my being. This too, is true of what Christianity is for Africans today. The experience of conversion toward the end of my secondary school and the fellowship that was enjoyed with the Christians in my neighborhood (mostly Presbyterians who were now Charismatic Christians) accentuated my theological ontology. The non-denominational fellowship which I attended in the Labone-Cantonments area of Osu coupled with my involvement in the renewal of my local church and other numerous encounters brought me to the understanding that, being theological must be absolutely true of African Christianity.

Fourthly, I discovered that, this whole idea of being theological is ingrained in the African personality. Thus, the African worldview of possessing a high spiritual sense of existence is an evidence that God has not left himself without a witness (Acts 14:17)—meaning God is universal. And that, graciously it prepares the way for God's love revealed concretely in Jesus Christ, the Son of the Father in the power of the Holy Spirit to be grasped in ecstasy in the African peoples. Furthermore, it is worthy of note that, the concrete experience in the economy of God expressed in the experience, resonates with all other Christians worldwide to affirm our common Lord, faith and baptism (Ephesians 4:4–6).

Fifthly, it struck me that, the person and works of Jesus Christ had a place in the *Wulormor* of the Ga traditional and religious institution in the southern part of Ghana. Moreover, I was fascinated when I discovered it concurred with the *munus triplex* in Christian traditional theology. This led to the development of my Masters Degree Thesis titled "Jesus the *Okpelejen Wulormor*: Doing African Christology in the Ga of Ghana Context".

Sixthly, publishing this work was always on my mind, but when I started to put it together, it became clear that I needed to shape until it got to this stage. I added a definition for African Christian theology that seemed to be not farfetched while I aimed at relating it to the understanding that existed already in Christian theology. Doing this was especially important since there seemed to be a disconnect between local theologies of contemporary theology and Western theology in general. For me, the only way Christianity could be more meaningful is when we connect ideas to affirm our common faith and baptism in our Lord Jesus Christ. And where there are differences, I feel we are called upon to understand the peculiarities and appreciate the uniqueness and the fresh insight and enrichment they bring to bear on Christianity in general. Moreover, for me, isolationism brings to bear the psychological issues or anxieties which underpin most theological reflections today.

Thus, in this book, the focus has also been to understand the paradoxical streak inhering traditional theology and which is pronounced in African Christian theology as Kpelelogy. African Christianity is embedded with faith encounters that may be related to the born-again experience. And both the Reformed and the Lutheran understanding of it essentially, is the same. But the existential exposition of Paul Tillich is what for me highlights the African Christian experience.

And this whole idea I call Kpelelogy is the basis upon which I assess contemporary African Christian theology. The ecumenical spirit as well as the reality of African Christian experience tied together with the objective revelation of God in Christ and in the Spirit in the context of Africa is so important. Moreover, I am wary of the pitfalls associated with utopia and totalitarianism since a Kpelelogical mind is subject to the Trinitarian God's rule in the present, in the past and in the future. It shows the unhealthy dichotomization and fragmentation of African Christian theology today and advocates for and represents a holistic approach to doing theology in Africa.

It is my prayer that, this book will go ahead to reignite the flames of African Christian theology in a new way. It does not attempt to present a theology that is free of corrections and improvements. It is an attempt to present theology in a light that will promote devotional life and commitment to God in new ways that engender a more responsible African Christianity, and which works with God, and under God in Jesus Christ for life in fullness in the power of the Holy Spirit. So that, by so doing, African Christian theology will be a true representation of what Jesus has done in history and which the apostles professed and preached. And further, that, it will remain true to all subsequent Christian understanding that agrees and yet as presented in the uniqueness and grace of the African context.

Acknowledgments

I AM EXTREMELY GRATEFUL for God's sustenance, inspiration, and guidance throughout my period of stay at the Asian Pacific Graduate School of Theological Studies,(APGS), Hanil University and Presbyterian Theological Seminary (HUPTS), Jeonju, South Korea. I thank God also for granting me the grace that saw me through this work successfully.

I owe the former president of HUPTS, Rev. Prof. Koo Choon-Seo, a soothing panegyric and acclamation for being my distinguished theology professor and supervising the entire master of theology thesis, which I have modified and published as this book. To the glory of God, the two works of mine that he supervised have all been published. I thank him for all the lovely recommendations he made on my behalf to have this work published. I am also incredibly happy that he has endorsed this book. I acknowledge and thank him for his extreme tolerance for my wild speculations, questions, and arguments; for his perspicacity, guidance and invaluable contributions that have resulted in the successful completion of this work. *Papa Oyiwaladon! Moksanim Kansaminida!*

I am deeply indebted to Rev. Dr. Chung Chang-Bok, former president of Hanil University, for giving me the honor and privilege to study in Hanil. Through his able leadership we enjoyed a wide range of facilities aimed at making us comfortable and studious for moral, spiritual, and academic excellence.

My sincere appreciation goes to Rev. Dr. Kyung-Sik Pae for being my theology professor in piety and modern theology. His piety will always distinguish him, and I am incredibly happy to study under him and therefore very grateful for all the other contributions he made for my studies and the successful completion of this work.

I am grateful to the former dean of APGS and theology professor Rev. Dr. Yu Tae-Ju for all the academic programs and invaluable contributions put together to equip us effectively in our future endeavors. Many thanks to Rev. Dr. Richard Hamm for his untiring service as a professor and as the director of APGS. Indeed, his immense contribution as a director ensured our good and successful stay in Hanil University. I am highly grateful to him for his pastoral care and teaching which has greatly boosted my confidence in ministry. My heartfelt gratitude goes to the then-registrar Ms. Eun-Mi Cho for all the arduous tasks she needed to undertake to ensure my admission and successful stay in Hanil University. Thank you to all the staff, academic and nonacademic, and all students for making our studies and stay in Hanil and Korea fulfilling.

Many thanks to Pastor Yoon Jae Deok, formerly of Palbok Somang Presbyterian Church, in Jeonju for all the support he rendered to us during our stay in Hanil. He opened his pulpit for me to preach during Sunday worship services; yes, I am very thankful, for he is one out of a million. Indeed, he is a man with a rare kind heart.

I thank the former moderator of the General Assembly of the Presbyterian Church of Ghana (PCG), Very Rev. Prof. Emmanuel Martey, and the General Assembly for giving me this rare opportunity to study in Hanil University. I am also grateful to him for endorsing this book graciously.

I also thank the former clerk of General Assembly, the Very Rev. Hebert Opong, for ensuring that the necessary arrangements were in place for the entire period of my studies. I will always remember his pastoral care and guidance during the period of my studies.

I am highly indebted to the former Ga Presbytery chairperson and the current clerk of the General Assembly of the PCG, Rev. Dr. Nii Noi Odonkor, for ensuring a good care for my family and in addition supplying me with some vital primary sources I have used in the production of this thesis.

A lot of thanks to Brian Heldenbrand and Rev. Dr. Abraham Nana Opare Kwakye for taking time to edit and proofread my work.

I also thank the then–District Session and the Zimmermann Session of Nungua for the support they have provided for me and my family. Rev. Ebenezer Nmai Ollennu, thank you very much.

I express my deepest love and thanks to my wife, Harriet Naa Djanwaa Amarkwei, for her selfless service and sacrifice, which made my studies and this work possible. I also acknowledge the support and cooperation of my children, Nii Amarh, Zimmermann, and Naa Shidaa. A big thank you to my siblings and especially my parents for all their support and for raising me up to serve humanity in such a time as this. A big thank you to my mother-in-law, Gladys Tetteorkor Tetteh (*Imaa*), for her immeasurable support to my family. May God bless all other family relations and friends who contributed to the completion of this thesis.

I also wish to thank the president of the Trinity Theological Seminary, Legon, the Very Rev. Prof J. Kwabena Asamoah-Gyadu, for his constant encouragement that has led to the publication of this book.

I am also incredibly grateful to all faculty, staff, and students of the Trinity Theological Seminary for their numerous contributions that have resulted in the production of this book.

I need to mention that I am sincerely grateful to the current moderator of the Presbyterian Church of Ghana and former president of the Trinity Theological Seminary, Legon, the Rt. Rev. Prof. J. O. Y. Mante, for his consistent and timely support that has resulted in this work. And I thank very much also Rev. Prof. D. N. A. Kpobi for his continuous support and encouragement. May God richly bless them all. Amen.

Introduction

African Christian Theology and the Kpelelogical Foundation of Christian Theology

THIS BOOK ENDEAVORS TO introduce African Christian theology as a Kpelelogy and further help the reader appreciate the Kpelelogical underpinnings of Christian theology itself. It serves as introducing African Christian theology in a critical manner on one hand. And on the other hand, it seeks to provide a Kpelelogical theology that implies that faith in Jesus Christ—*Okpelejen Wulormor* (More than a Cosmic Priest/King/Prophet) is a paradox based upon knowledge and experience of the triune God revealed in history and by grace through faith in Jesus Christ in the power of the Holy Spirit. The interesting point to note is that this way of *being theological* in contrast to *doing theology* and discussed in this book as *Kpelelogy* is fundamental to Christian doctrine.

Kpelelogy, as a hybrid term, is made of the *kpele* word of the Ga religious institution in Ghana, and *-logy* from the Greek *logos*. *Kpele* means all-encompassing and thus holistic, while *-logy* is science, study, or reasoning. So *kpelelogy* (small "k") means the pre-Christian holistic *logos* structure of the mind, particularly of the African. And bringing that to bear in Christian theology is making it Kpelelogical (capital "K"). This is consistent with the all-encompassing reality of God as Father, Son, and Holy Spirit in the *oikonomia*.

This Kpelelogical theology does not emanate from ideological presumptions. To the contrary, it is the outcome of experiencing the reality of God's redeeming power through the knowledge of God's Son in a primal conscience or kpelelogical conscience. Thus, the Kpelelogicality of the theologian throughout this book is a *sine qua non*.

One issue in the history of the church that has really caused stir and contention is the struggle to understand who Jesus Christ is. The identity of Jesus Christ seems to be a challenge wherever the gospel is preached. And irrespective of how we look at it in the times of the apostles and now, the Messiah or Christ as the identity given to Jesus by most Christians (Matt 16:13–16) lingers on. Likewise, although there remains the question of whether Jesus accepted the notion of the royal and priestly Messiah or not, it does not take anything away from it. For so long as Jesus Christ gives his own interpretation as an eschatological agent, be it in the Son of Man or the Son of God,[1] the terminology of the Messiah or Christ could be applicable. Thus, just as Jesus Christ takes on the symbol of the New Being in Paul Tillich, so in this book, the symbol of this eschatological agent is identified as the *Okpelejen Wulormor*.

So then, following the above, Christian history is replete with the aim of giving fresh meaning to the gospel of Christ that is embedded in the person and works of Jesus Christ in different times and places as the revelation of God in the Spirit. Moreover, giving fresh interpretation is the basis of every Christian doctrine or theology. And today, Christians all over the world, including Third World Christians, ask themselves the question which Jesus put to the disciples, "But what about you? Who do you say I am?" (Matt 16:15).[2]

Of utmost concern to the identity of Jesus is the spread of the gospel. This is because in the world of missions, the identity of Christ becomes a concept which ought to be defined as the truth revealed by God (Matt 16:17), and yet that which occurs within a specific context. The confrontation of religions and philosophies and the struggle between cultural and religious and socioeconomic and political ideals has contributed to this challenge in Christian missions. For as long as the gospel continues to engage the future, and the identity of Jesus the Christ remains a question, then theology is dynamic.

The progressiveness of Christology or Christian theology also points to the eschatological hope as a concomitant criterion in the moments of faith seeking understanding. Thus, it is consequential to understand that even in attempting to have a more relevant knowledge of Christ, there ought to be some essential criteria. And it is noteworthy that, different from the theological method, the criteria serve to authenticate the

---

1. Dunn, *Jesus Remembered*, 705–62.

2. Ferm, *Third World Liberation Theologies*; Schreiter, *New Catholicity*; Küster, *Many Faces of Jesus Christ*.

theological attempt to understand the person of Jesus Christ in the mission of the triune God.

This fundamental basis should be held in mind recognizing that there are exclusivist, pluralist, and many inclusivist views of the same issue.³ First, one might safely concede that the inclusivist view is not well defined. Second, there are nuances between exclusivist and pluralist ideas.⁴

"Who do you, Africans, say that I am?"

Following the discussion above, this work is inspired by the question Jesus asked his disciples regarding his identity. Also, it was Peter who gave a contextual answer to the question revealed by the Spirit and which was authenticated by Jesus premised on Jesus' own understanding of the Messiah. Interestingly, the search for the identity of Jesus is one that is significant to the triune God. At the same time, this knowledge is extremely essential to unearthing the function of Christ among the people among whom he is known and experienced. Besides, as this search continues throughout the history of the church, like the Apostle Peter, we get it right and wrong. We get it right when by the Spirit we proclaim the will of God; and get it wrong when we focus first on ourselves (Matt 16:13–20, 21–28).

Typical of the risk involved in identifying Jesus' nature and work is the christological controversies, which today, many Third World theologians have also engaged in a functional way.⁵ Africans constitute a major part of this new functional way of doing theology in its diverse contexts. Consequently, this book, on one hand, seeks to critically engage the African answer to Jesus' question "What about you? Who do you say I am?" And on the other hand, establish the Kpelelogical theology that embraces the being and life in a real encounter in the grace of *Okpelejen Wulormor*.

---

3. Carter, *Rethinking Christ and Culture*; Carson, *Christ and Culture Revisited*; Race, *Christians and Religious Pluralism*; Migliore, *Faith Seeking Understanding*, 306.

4. Knitter, *Introducing Theologies of Religion*; Migliore, *Faith Seeking Understanding*, 306–16.

5. Lowe, "Christ and Salvation," 236; Koo, *Doing Christology in Asian Context*, 25–26.

Important personalities for this Kpelelogical reflection are Carl Christian Reindorf (1834–1917);[6] Margaret Joyce Field;[7] Marion Kilson;[8] Irene Odotei (1944);[9] Philip Tetteh Laryea (1957);[10] and John David Kwamena Ekem (1959);[11] representing the context of being kpelelogical or Kpelelogical. Then, Paul Tillich, John Calvin, and Karl Barth representing major Kpelelogical sources of Christian tradition. Another important person is J. Kwabena Asamoah-Gyadu. His and other contemporary scholars' contributions in African Christianity are certainly critical in understanding African Christian theology in general.

This book has an introduction, followed by seven chapters organized in three parts, and a conclusion. The book examines how African theologians have understood the enterprise, particularly from the definition of John Mbiti in chapter 1.; and further, to understand the principle of paradox as a basis of being Kpelelogical rather than doing African Christian theology, in chapter 2, which ends the first part.

In part 2 (chapters 3–5) there is an attempt to see how African theologians have embarked upon the journey of theologizing or particularly how they have done theology. The criteria and methods for these

---

6. Carl Christian Reindorf was a pastor and missionary with the Basel Mission in the Gold Coast. He was a teacher in Basel Missionary Seminaries and a composer of Ga hymns for the mission. As a typical African, he managed to dialogue in a pragmatic manner his faith with his Ga culture. He is also known as Ghana's foremost historian.

7. Margaret Joyce Field was a British anthropologist who worked in the Gold Coast (Ghana) between the early 1930s and early 1970s. Her work on the medicine and religion of the Ga people is one of most cherished documents about the Ga people.

8. Marion Kilson was an American anthropologist, professor, and academic dean of Emmanuel College (1967), Harvard University, and formerly at the Radcliffe Institute, and associate professor in the Department of Sociology, Simmons College, who focused on *Kpele*, the religion of the Ga people, whose work serves as a gold mine for many unanswered questions about the general Ga conception of reality. She also worked on the social organization of the Ga people.

9. Irene Korkoi Odotei, PhD, is a seasoned researcher and professor / former director of the Institute of African Affairs at the University of Ghana, Legon, and one of the foremost authorities on Ga history and culture.

10. Philip Tetteh Laryea, PhD, is a minister of the Presbyterian Church of Ghana and a professor at the Akrofi-Christaller Institute of Theology, Mission, and Culture, Akropong-Akwapim—Ghana.

11. John David Kwamena Ekem, DTh, is a minister of the Methodist Church, Ghana, and formerly a professor and academic dean of Trinity Theological Seminary, Legon, Accra. He is one of the very few Africans elected into membership of the prestigious *Studiorum Novi Testamenti Societas*, the highest academic body for New Testament Studies made up of all the leading New Testament scholars in the world.

theologians are also critically engaged. And the essence of African Christian theology is then defined as faith in the absolute concrete.

Finally, part 3 looks at the Ga context of *kpele* as a way of throwing light on the concept and essence of Kpelelogy in chapter 6.[12] Here the *Wulormor* who presides over the *Kpele* religious institution as high priest, king, and prophet becomes the typology adopted for Jesus Christ. The typology is adopted, although the *Wulormor* in the office of the *Kpele* institution is limited and thus rejected as a symbol of understanding God in Jesus Christ. However, it is accepted because of its transformation into a typology of the *Okpelejen Wulormor* as the symbol of Jesus Christ, who is the all-encompassing One and as the One who is more than a priest, king, and prophet. And in chapter 7, the *munus triplex* in Christian tradition is discussed in the light of the Ga concepts of *Kpele*.[13] Interestingly, doing this may help us appreciate the mission of God in Jesus Christ in the light of his person as the symbol of *Okpelejen Wulormor*. This leads us to the question of theological method used in Kpelelogical theology. Thus, in the following, the method of Kpelelogy is discussed.

The Kpelelogical Method

The theological method of Kpelelogy employed in this book is an interpretation for Jesus as the *Okpelejen Wulormor*. The method of Kpelelogy is the confluence of the enlightened conscience of the Christian based upon the revelation of God in Christ in the Spirit as attested in the Bible on one hand; and the very being of the African in existence on the other hand. This confluence of two realities occurring at the "moment," "event," or "occasion" interact with each other paradoxically because of the divine presence. Thus, questions are raised in a dynamic fashion, because in *kairos*, the divine illumination itself, is a rejection of the context; yet it accepts it and utilizes it for meaningfulness after transforming it.

12 As shall be seen, Jesus the *Okpelejen Wulormor* is a term comprising *Okpelejen* and *Wulormor*. *Okpelejen* is another name for *Ataa Naa Nyonmor* (Father Mother God or Father Grandmother God) the Ground of Being which means the All Encompassing One. *Wulormor* is the name of the leader or president who is the high priest and prophet of the land (the word *priest* is not sufficient to replace the word *Wulormor*). Jesus the *Okpelejen Wulormor* means, therefore, the All Encompassing One who is more than a priest, king, and prophet and is fundamentally cosmic.

13. The Ga of Ghana is one of the numerous ethnicities in Ghana, who belong to the Greater Accra region located at Accra, the capital city of Ghana. They belong to the same group of the Adangme people and thus commonly called the Ga-Adangme.

The issue of methods for doing theology in Africa is discussed more deeply subsequently in chapter 4 and in part, dealing with the nature of contemporary African theology. However, it should be noted that it is an interpretation between two positions: the Christian traditional view of Jesus Christ and the viewpoint held by the Ga *Kpele* religion. As will be seen, this stance is a *revised* postcolonial hermeneutic position which also employs critical tools of interpretation. At the end of the paradoxical interaction, Jesus, the *Okpelejen Wulormor*, is to be found in-between the fulfillment and mutual positions of the theology of religions. This means it is the fulfillment of the *kpele* conscience, yet the *Kpele* religion enriches and fulfills the meaning of the Christian message. Thus, the *Kpele* religion is viewed with respect, yet as unfulfilled in a mutual critical paradoxical correlation with Christian tradition.

The theological method of Kpelelogy is the paradox of the theology from above and theology from below.[14] Koo Choon-Seo defines the above in christological terms as follows:

> [Christology from above] starts from the divinity of Jesus. The concept of the incarnation has a central place in this approach. This kind of Christology also presupposes the doctrine of the Trinity. [Christology from below] begins from the historical Jesus and recognizes his deity within the humanity. It ends with the doctrine of the Incarnation.[15]

In view of the many inadequacies of the two separate methodologies, it is evident that no Christology can be adequate without having the two methods together. To attain to this status of paradoxical methodology, Koo asserts that one should take seriously the revelatory function of the Bible. Still, the role of the Holy Spirit should be made paramount and ultimately there ought to be a dialogue with church tradition.[16]

In this Kpelelogical theology, Jesus the *Okpelejen Wulormor* tends to be skewed toward a Christology from below because of the work of the historical Jesus in the life of African Christians, *videlicet Christus Patiens*. However, we should not also lose sight of the reality that within African Christologies there exists a Christology from above (*Christus Victor*) paradigm. Thus, this position is an affirmation for the amalgamation of Christology from below and Christology from above. It is a point

---

14. Pannenberg, *Jesus, God and Man*, 33–77.
15. Koo, *Doing Christology in Asian Context*, 18.
16. Koo, *Doing Christology in Asian Context*, 26.

buttressed by the fact that within the African conception of realities, there is no separation between the spiritual and material or religious and secular,[17] nor is there in fact in Christian faith; but for a few theological traditions.[18]

Moreover, since the Kpelelogical method is all encompassing in nature as a matter of *being*, paradoxically, putting those Christologies together is natural to it. And practically, within the *Okpelejen Wulormor*, the elements of king, priest, and prophet make concrete the African amalgamation of the two methods of Christology without confusion, and without separation. And I deem it is fitting to adopt the Kpelelogical method insofar as it is amenable to traditional doctrine, as it engages meaningfully the ontology of the *kpele* conscience.

---

17. Gyekye, *African Cultural Values*, 4.
18. Tillich, *History of Christian Thought*, 301–431.

Part 1

Defining African Christian Theology

Introduction

THE QUESTION "WHAT IS African Christian theology?" may be an existential question with significance for both African and non-African Christians worldwide. Thus, part 1 of this book endeavors to unravel the definition as well as its nature by engaging insights from church tradition. In chapter 1, John Mbiti's definition is brought to the fore and its content is critically engaged with other theological views, such as the views of Kwesi Dickson on the African continent and those outside of it, such as Karl Barth and John Macquarie. This brings the uniqueness of African Christian theology critically to the fore on the basis of the strong link it shares with Christian heritage. Furthermore, certain features that are unique to theology in Africa are critically analyzed.

Chapter 2 deepens the understanding of African theology as it looks at the paradoxical nature it possess as more or less a matter of principle. This paradoxical streak is identified in Origen's theology and then traced in the theology of other African church fathers; and also traced to the present African Christian faith expression of David Olanyi Oyedepo, the Nigerian Charismatic bishop of Living Faith Church Worldwide (Winners' Chapel). The purpose is to show the crucial role paradox plays in the interpretation of the faith of Christians and the contributions African Christians bring to it.

Part 1: Defining African Christian Theology

The part ends with a conclusion that highlights the major insights regarding how African Christianity enables its theology to connect to the traditional heritage of Christianity. The reality of faith experienced in a paradoxical mode is indeed crucial in understanding the Kpelelogical essence of Christian faith itself.

1

African Christian Theology as Universal and Concrete

Definition of African Christian Theology

AFRICAN CHRISTIAN THEOLOGY WAS defined by John Mbiti when he wrote,

> African theologies are the articulation of the Christian faith by African theologians as Christians. They ask themselves what the Christian faith means and try to understand and explain it within the context of their history and culture and of the contemporary issues they face. They look at it through reading and understanding of the Bible. They bring into it the rich cultural heritage, which has evolved over many generations. They bring it in their own liturgies or express it through art, drama and song.[1]

This definition of John Mbiti is really thorough as it establishes the continuity of African Christian theology with traditional theology; and discontinuity as it brings out the uniqueness of African Christian theology.[2] Moreover, his definition sets African Christian theology in a mode of creativity and constructiveness. In other words, John Mbiti presented us with elements that are vital for understanding the task of African Christian theology in our contemporary postmodernism that is also laced with postcolonial struggles.

---

1. Mbiti, "African Theology."
2. Bediako, *Jesus in Africa*, 63.

The Definition of African Christian Theology Reflects Universality with Christian Tradition

Of particular interest regarding the elements of John Mbiti's definition that are in continuity with Christian tradition are "articulation of the Christian faith . . . as Christians," "they ask themselves," "try to understand," "explain," "within the context," "through reading and understanding the Bible." These elements above reveal to us the elements of faith experience, the use of reason and the reliance on Scripture, to articulate or interpret the Christian faith to particular groups of persons in a particular context of history. Mbiti's definition in this regard that may concur with traditional theological reflection is buttressed by another African theologian in the person of Kwesi Dickson.

In his definition of "theology," Kwesi Dickson looks at theology as an issue which "has to do with human existence,"[3] his explanation shows that the purpose of theology and for that matter African Christian theology is to investigate the content of beliefs by means of reason enlightened by faith (*fides quaerens intellectum*) and the promotion of deeper understanding.

Indeed, Kwesi Dickson by stating the essence of reason and faith may be buttressing the fundamental understanding of Christian theology as in tradition. For Christian tradition, theology does not ever arise, or better put, ought not to arise out of the whims of any person. Christian tradition is insistent that theology ought to proceed from faith experience following the first evangelists of the faith. Therefore, by following the famous Anselmian dictum—*fides quaerens intellectum*—the definition of African Christian theology sits well with Christian tradition.

Here again, we should not also loose sight of the reality of African Christians today who place value on knowledge based upon actual faith experience. Thus both African theologians in the persons of Mbiti and Dickson are in harmony with the vibrant and contemporary African Christianity. Their views of theology as that which emanates from faith experience is what traditional theology expounds. A few examples of traditional definitions may buttress the point.

First, from the sociological point of view, Robin Gill defines theology formally as "the written and the critical explication of the 'sequelae' of individual religious beliefs and of the correlations and the interactions

---

3. Dickson, *Theology in Africa*, 22.

between religious beliefs in general."[4] Almost instantaneously one identifies two poles in Gill's definition of theology. The first pole deals with the individual subjective experience and faith emphasized in the existential milieu in question. Again, he brings our attention to the corporate experience without which there may never be an individual experience of faith as the second pole. The African though not discounting the reality and the power of the corporate experience of faith is careful in placing more emphasis on individual subjective experience as crucial for faith to possess an understanding of the total Christian experience.

Second, John Parrat defines "theology as the apprehension of God based upon his self-revelation."[5] In this, we may find again the two poles, howbeit a little nuanced from the above. The first pole to be identified is that God's self-revelation is objective as an event in history. Although the search for the historical Jesus may be in futility, we may say Jesus was a historic figure, in that though the information about him in the Bible is an interpretation, its basis is solidly factual.[6] And Jesus is historic insofar as places, times, other records apart from the Gospels and certain archeological findings together with varied interpretations confirm his historicity.

That Jesus Christ once dwelt on planet earth is the point that is important to the extent that it provides the basis for Christian knowledge about God and God's plan for the world. And insofar as it is able to differentiate Christianity from other religions by insisting that the Divine became concrete in history it is significant. Similarly, it is able to show to a very large extent that Christianity is not a fabrication, as it was falsely portrayed by some scholars, such as Ludwig Andreas Feuerbach.[7] And this is the reality African Christians cannot reject. That Jesus lived among human beings, and for that matter that he lived among the whole of God's creation, is of utmost importance to the understanding of theology to Christians in Africa. And the reality of the African context in which the life of Jesus Christ in the world resides is in daily prayers as well as faith reflections of African Christians.[8]

The second pole of John Parratt deals with the subjective experience of Christians that gives real knowledge of what it is to know Jesus Christ

4. Gill, *Theology and Social Structure*, 2–3.
5. Parratt, *Guide to Doing Theology*, 1.
6. Dunn, *Jesus Remembered*.
7. Feuerbach, *Essence of Christianity*.
8. This is most crucial for African women's theology. Oduyoye, *Hearing and Knowing*, 106.

with the faculties beyond the intellect. For how do we know a reality if we have not really experienced it? Mbiti's words that show that African theology is an explication of the Christian faith by African Christians is indicative of the weight placed on the subjective Christian realism of African Christianity. As may be seen in later discussions in this book, it may be clear that African Christian theology is a contextual theology that focuses on the particular experience of Africans regarding the Christian faith. Most theologians emphasize greatly the ethnographical elements that may indicate the religio-cultural engagement; and other theologians also emphasize socio-politico-economic engagements.

Indeed, the second pole of Parrat relates to part of John Mbiti's definition with the phrase "by African Christians as Africans." This is the subjective experience of Africans. In it, those engaged in the theology ought to be first of all those who possess the Kpelelogical ontology (African Christians), and second of all, those theologians who employ the Kpelelogical ontology to interpret the Christian reality in the time and space in which they dwell.

What actually may authenticate the subjective faith experience of African Christians is the actual ecclesiological disposition of the African churches and the membership. Clearly, encountering the Divine subjectively is important for the churches across the board. And this could be asserted when we take a look at its emphases in African Initiated Churches (AICs), Pentecostal Churches (PCs), and Charismatic Churches (CCs), and the renewal emphasis in the Historic Mission Churches (HMCs) that include the Roman Catholic Church, Presbyterian Churches, Anglican Churches, and the Methodist Churches. Most churches in Africa today may be more inclined to focus on conversion rather than on general membership. Again, most churches continue to engage the power of God to help end the various sufferings of people, including, poverty and disease.

African Christians as individuals are of the type who desire a real encounter with God. Thus they are realists who will have room for the idealism of the Christian faith only when it is connected to actuality. For African Christians, the power of God ought to be seen and felt in real experience with a favorable impact.[9] If Christ saves people from the power of sin and of the devil, it ought not to be cerebral without actual experience.[10] Christians in Africa have a strong yearning for a subjec-

---

9. Oosthuizen, *Post Christianity in Africa*, 206–16.
10. Parrat, introduction to *An Introduction to Third World Theologies*, 1–15.

tive experience in the real act of God's self-revelation. And it ought to be realized in physical and spiritual healing and other forms of freedoms such as cultural, social, economic, and political "breakthroughs."

The point above is supported by Ian MacRobert, when he wrote, "The particular attraction of Pentecostalism in non-Western societies lies in its *black experiential roots* outside of white North America and Europe."[11] In the view of J. Kwabena Asamoah-Gyadu, the experiential faith of African Christians, which he calls "pneumatic Christianity," refers to "any form of Christianity that values, affirms, and consciously promotes the experiences of the Spirit as part of normal Christian life and worship."[12] Today, most African churches, be they Historic Mission or Pentecostal and Charismatic, could be described as practicing pneumatic Christianity.[13] J. Kwabena Asamoah-Gyadu wrote,

> As an enthusiastic form of religion, pneumatic Christianity generally promotes radical conversions, baptism of the Spirit with speaking in tongues, healing, deliverance, prophetic ministries, and other such pneumatic phenomena including miracles and supernatural interventions in general.[14]

It should be said that these elements of objective and subjective knowledge of God are expressed explicitly and in depth by traditional theologians, such as Paul Tillich,[15] and who perhaps marked the transition between modernism and postmodernism. It must be noted, however, that the experience of African Christianity does not only emphasize the experience of conversion. Significantly, it goes beyond to assert other experiences associated with the subjective reality of God in them. These other experiences that are conspicuously missing in Protestant theology are miracles, healing, prophecy, and exorcisms. These other realities, it ought to be noted, are bedrocks of Christian soteriology found in the accounts of the four evangelists, the epistles of the Apostle Paul, and the tradition of the church fathers. Hence, African Christian experience of the Divine through grace and by faith in Jesus Christ in the Spirit is a critique, and further, an enrichment and affirmation of Christian tradition itself.

---

11. MacRobert, "Black Roots of Pentecostalism"; Omenyo, *Pentecost*, 89–90.
12. Asamoah-Gyadu, *Contemporary Pentecostal Christianity*, 1.
13. Omenyo, *Pentecost*, 102–98.
14. Asamoah-Gyadu, *Contemporary Pentecostal Christianity*, 2.
15. Tillich, *Systematic Theology*, 1:111; Tillich, *Courage to Be*.

Another important continuity that may be noticed in both the definitions of Mbiti and Dickson is the element of inquiry. Do Africans actually reflect on their faith as Christians? Mbiti makes use of all kinds of words to emphasize the importance of critical thinking in the scheme of doing theology in Africa. African theologians engage reason as an indispensable part of the endeavor to grasp the meaning of the Christian faith in their particular context. In whatever shape and form, it involves the use of logic by asking themselves questions and trying to understand and explain it as much as their worldview as Africans can aid them. Of course, all the creative endeavors in the colonial and postcolonial times have been done not without reason. And the contribution of African theology in shaping global theological thought patterns cannot be glossed over.

Indeed, Karl Barth in his day saw theology as a special science whose task was to grasp and speak of God.[16] This principle of grasping the essence of God especially through the revelation of the Father in the Son in the power of the Holy Spirit forms the basis of traditional theology, if the early evangelist records are anything to go by. An understanding of theology if it is placed in the context of Greek definition may even buttress the point that it is actually a reasoning about the Divine or of the gods. And though theology may be engaged in as a narrative or storytelling,[17] it represented a creative way of thinking about the Divine and the gods.

Arguably, before the advent of Greek thought, ancient Egyptian myths and legends also represented this level of engaging reason to narrate or appreciate the reality and purpose of the Divine or gods in human life as well as in creation.[18] African theology has in recent times also engaged the thought form of storytelling as a way of understanding the reality of God in the light of their faith as Christians.[19] This form of interpreting the Christian faith in particular contexts may be found as a thought form in the early church as well. Our reading of the Scriptures, we are told, ought to be seen as a report of an event that is being narrated to particular audiences.

If this reasoning ought to be philosophical, African theologians have employed their philosophy according to their various cultural categories

---

16. Barth, *Evangelical Theology: An Introduction*, 9.

17. Richardson, "Theology."

18. Olela, "African Foundations," 43–49; Nkrumah, *Consciencism*, 1–40; James, *Stolen Legacy*.

19. Oduyoye, with the Circle of Concerned African Women Theologians, and other Third World Theologians engage storytelling as a way of doing theology.

in doing African theology.[20] At the time of the church fathers, when most of the theological ideas were spawned, philosophical reasoning involving all the sciences available was employed. In fact, Origen might have engaged his African thought pattern together with the Greek thought forms, which was crucial in developing important creeds of the church.

The continuity of the context, where for Mbiti, the context implies the history, culture, and contemporary issues of Africans, could be related to traditional theological formulations. For example, Karl Barth defines theology in another way, as "the science in which the church in accordance with the state of its knowledge at different times takes account of the content of its proclamation critically that is by the standard of Holy Scripture and under the guidance of its confessions."[21] It is buttressed by the question of Bonhoeffer, "Who is Christ for us today?"[22] Thus, just like traditional theology, where not only the history and culture but the contemporary issues of the particular locality is of great interest to the theologian, so it is with the African theologian.

And that African theologians attempt to locate the knowledge of God through the revelation of the Son in the power of the Holy Spirit in their history and culture is taken for granted. Nowadays, however, African theology, unlike that in South Africa, seems to be stuck in the history and culture without a corresponding contemporary interpretation.

Definition of African Christian Theology That Reflect the Concrete in Africa

Having experienced the plight of Africa during the time of colonial subjugation, it may be fair to make inferences with regards to what John Mbiti meant by the phrase "by African Christians." Perhaps, John Mbiti thought that colonial subjugation represented a unique experience implying that it is only the colonized African who could better understand their own situation. Moreover, independence meant independence through and through. Political independence ought not to be restricted but expanded to cover every sphere of African existence, including theology. Therefore, it is quite significant to note that John Mbiti was of a strong view that Africans must do their own theology.

20. Tillich, *History of Christian Thought*, 54–57; Roukema, *Gnosis and Faith*, 93–95.
21. Barth, *Dogmatics in Outline*, 9.
22. Bonhoeffer, *Letters and Papers from Prison*, 279.

In his definition, Mbiti excludes all other persons from engaging in African Christian theology with the exception of those Africans who suffered under colonialism and its impact. It was a bold statement which sought to assert the conviction that the African can manage his own affairs. Here the undertones of political ideas may be observed in John Mbiti's definition. Clearly, the geopolitical agenda of Africa as Africanization began earlier in the mid-1920s with pressure on the colonial administration to loose its fetters on Africa. Thus, as may be realized in the speech of Rev. Peter K. Dagadu at the Assembly of the World Council of Churches (WCC) in 1954, Africanization of the churches in Africa was prominent.[23] On March 6, 1957, the day of Ghana's independent declaration, the then prime minister of the Gold Coast, Kwame Nkrumah, made that profound statement that keeps reverberating in the minds of many Africans. Part of Nkrumah's speech read,

> And, as I pointed out . . . from now on, today, we must change our attitudes and or minds. We must realize that from now on we are no longer a colonial but free and independent people.
>
> But also, as I pointed out, that also entails hard work. *That new Africa is ready to fight his own battles and show that after all the black man is capable of managing his own affairs.*
>
> We are going to demonstrate to the world, to the other nations, that we are prepared to lay our foundation—our own African personality.
>
> As I said to the Assembly a few minutes ago, I made a point that we are going to create our own African personality and identity. It is the only way we can show the world that we are ready for our own battles.[24]

Thus, this Africanization was also put into sharp focus by Kwame Nkrumah, who had enormous influence on the minds of many people, including the churches in Africa.

Now, was Mbiti's insistence on the "African element" a response or a reaction to the colonial subjugation of Africa? If it is a reaction to the negative notion that African people cannot handle their own issues, it may be granted, while appreciating the context or the frame of mind that has been shaped by the independence struggle.

Moreover, African people learned the lessons out of the distortion of African history by colonialists, which deliberately sought to justify the

---

23. Martey, *African Theology*, 63.
24. Nkrumah, "Full Text: First Independent Speech."

oppression of Africans.²⁵ Certainly, this could have been a good reaction for the strong rejection of non-Africans in doing the theology of Africans. Thus, for Mbiti, African Christian theology is for Africans; and all non-Africans are debarred based upon the suspicion of lies and distortion of the African reality by colonial elements.

Now if it were a response, then questions may be raised as to whether it is impossible for non-Africans to do African theology. Realistically, even before the struggle for independence in Africa, missionaries from Europe had embarked upon translation of Bibles into local languages. The translation of Bibles into local languages were theological insofar as they involved the use of concepts surrounding the words that are chosen for every translation.²⁶ Moreover, as in interpretation, where the right meaning ought to be conveyed, the translation works of the early Europeans may be early theological escapades of contemporary Africa. Today, there are many non-African theologians who have had interest in African Christian theology and have written extensively about African Christianity. Thus, they have become partners in the Lord who together with African theologians try to understand the revelation of God in Christ in the power of the Holy Spirit in the lives of African Christians and churches.

It may be needful to add that Africans trained in the theologies of other countries should be able to contribute meaningfully to the development of theologies in those realms. Thus, restricting or debarring others from an ecumenical engagement with regards to theology in Africa may be seen as a psychological issue.

Moreover, inasmuch as the early contemporary African theological escapades may be justified; and while keeping to it, African theologians may have to be open to ecumenical engagements that also go a long way to benefit both the world and Africa.

We may also share the reality in African Christianity where art, drama, and song capture the depth of understanding Africans possess regarding the triune God as a matter of faith experience and as very particular to their contexts. We should admit, however, that there is continuity in this basic principle of expressing theological understanding according to the times and places in all art forms. Traditional Christian expression of the faith always brought the autonomous Christianity

---

25. Diop, *Civilization or Barbarism*, 11–24, 33–68.
26. Ekem, *Early Scriptures of the Gold Coast (Ghana)*.

together with heteronomous Christianity.[27] A reminiscence of Christian artworks on dining sets or on walls or of architecture and painting in the church's history is replete with many examples. And indeed, the African holistic attitude of faith expression will naturally mean the autonomous experiential faith is concretized in all forms of art forms and expressions.

It should be pointed out, though, that Mbiti fails to underscore the primary importance of language in the expression of African theology. For example, Kwame Bediako espoused his belief that *language as in linguistics* is so fundamental to the African expression of the Christian faith that African Christian theology is, essentially, a mother-tongue theology.[28] What one may realize in the long run is that language, fragmented as it may be, is fundamental and ought to be expressed in its holistic terms.[29] The limitation of language as being fragmentary may be part of what is the discontinuity and particularity of the African expression.

The discontinuity and particularity of the African theological expression is reflected in the form (including the style) and substance of the language.[30] For example, in linguistic expressions, the particular language in question is a language in general, but whose nature and style is shaped by the particular substance or the ground from which it emerges. Hence, it may be said that the Ga language of Ghana is discontinuous and particular inasmuch as it is shaped by the Ga society in Ghana. Having said

---

27. *Autonomous* and *heteronomous* are terminologies culled from Paul Tillich to describe the Christianities of Protestantism and Roman Catholicism, respectively. Protestantism dwells so much on the self rule, i.e., repentance and rule of God in the Christian life. The embrace of other laws governing the world such as in the broad sense of the word *culture* is heteronomy. The distortion of both leads to profanization and demonization, respectively. Autonomous Christianity has the propensity to make no sense of symbolisms, rituals, signs, rites, and thus the creative arts evacuated of Christian life and worship. Thus while idealizing the holy, its lack of concretization in art forms such as vestments and the sanctity of that which is holy, i.e., chapels and ministers of church, leads to profanization. Tillich, *Systematic Theology*, 1:84–85.

Heteronomous Christianity reduces the essence of Christianity into concrete forms of culture as used in the broad sense. Thus Christianity is packaged in symbols, rites, rituals, and art forms. The danger, though, as may be observed in history, is that neither the symbols, rites, rituals, nor various art forms in themselves have any capacity to bring saving grace to anyone. That essence dwells in the Divine Self: hence the overprojection of heteronomy without accompanying it with autonomous Christianity leads to the demonization of the symbols, signs, and rituals. They block the view of the real essence as people get fixated on them.

28. Bediako, *Theology and Identity*.
29. Tillich, *Systematic Theology*, 3:57–61, 253–55.
30. Tillich, *Systematic Theology*, 3:60–61.

that, it should not go without calling attention to the reality that language in all its forms, including the linguistic versions, are ambiguous insofar as they respectively represent richness and poverty upon one hand and universality and particularity upon the other hand.[31] Thus, language itself cannot be absolutized, it is fragmentary and it is in need of redemption. And it can take only that which precedes it and that which is with it and that which goes beyond it to redeem it.

Furthermore, it is important for us here to indicate that Mbiti's mention of art, drama, and song are examples; and therefore, more forms of expressions may be added. One unique expression of African Christianity is the body expressions, gesticulations, and dance as a way by which faith experience is expressed in Africa. It is as if the ripples of faith experience in the centered-self or psyche-animated body movements. Consequently, in most cases dance as an art form is a faith expression of an individual African Christian.

I see dance in the church in Africa as Kpelelogical—the rejection but acceptance and transformation of the kpelelogical African dancing spirit.[32] Moreover, the dance of the individual that is a cascade of the internal spiritual experience is also molded by the unique cultural movements associated with the local community or particular ethnic group of the individual. It is a personal expression, but it is also an expression that is communicating a message to others. It is a testimony of God's dealing with an individual person to other people.

African churches, wherever they are found, may be characterized by various dance forms. Besides, these forms of expression may not be limited to the Pentecostal churches or Charismatic churches because it extends to the Historic Mission churches.

It should be said, however, that unlike the Roman Catholic and Anglican Churches in Africa that have a natural inclination for heteronomy in paintings, symbols, and songs, most African churches, Protestant, Pentecostal, and Charismatic, in particular, have very limited concretization of theology in heteronomy. This is a clear example of blind copying of Western Protestant and Pentecostal ideals. Africans naturally involve symbols, signs, carvings, and sculptures to concretize their religious beliefs. Should African Christian theology engage more of this? How about vestments, musical forms, and liturgy? And to what extent should these

---

31. Tillich, *Systematic Theology*, 3:68–70, 253–55.
32. Welsh-Asante, *World of Dance*, 13–19.

art forms be engaged? These questions point to how urgently theology is needed to shape African Christianity for the better. And in this introductory volume the subject is not discussed, pending further discussion in subsequent volumes, God willing.

Having discussed the definition of African Christian theology in the light of its continuity and discontinuity with traditional theology, we may conclude that African Christian theology is in sync with traditonal theology. Nonetheless, the uniqueness of African Christian theology is a sign of its own limitations that it can claim no absolutist status. In that regard, African Christian theology may be defined as *the interpretation of the Christian faith of Africans in the light of the revelation of God through Jesus Christ in the power of the Holy Spirit to them*. This interpretation is based upon not only the objective testimony of Scripture but the subjective experience of Africans within the worldview of Christian tradition as well as their own African worldview and existential life (Kpelelogy).

In the following discussion we will review in brief the historical perspectives of theology in the light of an African interpretation of Christian faith.

The Universal and Concrete Expression of African Christian Theology

Preparatio Theologica

Is Christian theology of Africa isolated from traditional theology? To what extent does African Christian theology move away from traditional theology? Does the uniqueness of African Christian theology make it so different that it cannot be trusted to transmit useful insights in shaping world Christianity? In this discussion, I embark on a brief survey of the historical epochs of Christian theology and to find out how African Christian theology is linked to them.

Geoffrey W. Bromiley identifies patristic theology, scholastic theology, reformation theology, and modern theology as the four main historical groupings of theology.[33] Also, one may have to add a "pre-theological frame of mind" when it is acknowledged that there is a background theological understanding that forms a *preparatio theologica* of the theologian. For example, it may be interesting to observe that Paul the apostle had his

---

33. Bromiley, *Historical Theology*.

Jewish theological background as his *preparatio theologica*. In a similar vein, most theological traditions such as patristic, scholastic, and modern theology may have relied on the theological frame of the Egyptians, the Greeks, and the Romans. And as such, likewise in contemporary Africa, the African primal worldview forms the *preparatio theologica*.

Again, we may also have to add the contemporary theological endeavors as science and theology, contextual theology and theological emphasis on eschatology and the Trinity. Therefore, we may identify the *preparatio theologica*, Patristic theology, Scholastic theology, Reformation theology, Modern theology, and Contemporary theology as four main historical groupings.

As was stated above, there is always a worldview forming a presupposition that aids a theological interpretation of any reality. This worldview or presupposition of doing theology may have shaped the theological formulations of most theologians in church history. This may be associated with the "new perspective on Paul" that is well articulated in James Dunn's *Theology of Paul the Apostle*. Dunn asserts the Jewish theological underpinnings of Paul as one of the group of factors that shaped Pauline theology.[34]

Furthermore, one cannot ignore the great influence of Greco-Roman worldview in the development of theology to date.[35] Yet, even with this influence of Greco-Roman worldview, there are many primal worldviews that also shaped theological formulations. Therefore, as in the period of Paul the apostle, not only did Greco-Roman viewpoint shape thought, but rather fundamentally, thoughts of theologians may have well been shaped by their local theological worldviews (Jewish background).[36] And for that matter, Christian theologians in Africa may be fundamentally preconditioned by the African primal worldview.[37] The nature of this African primal worldview as *preparatio theologica* is discussed further as *Kpelelogy* in the following.

---

34. Dunn, *Theology of Paul the Apostle*, 1–23.

35. Kelly, *Early Christian Doctrines*, 14–20.

36. Kelly, *Early Christian Doctrines*, 3–28; Tillich, *Complete History of Christian Thought*, 1–16; Turner, "Primal Religions," 27–37.

37. Bediako, *Christianity in Africa*, 91–108.

Patristic Theology and the Ontological Source of African Theology

Christian theology arguably ought to be traced to our Lord Jesus Christ as the author of the Divine Spirit in concrete expression in history. Being the *Logos* as John the Apostle teaches, and being the Mind of God as Paul the apostle teaches, there ought to be no qualms at all with this notion. For sure, the Synoptic Gospels testify of him as the teacher in his days. The Messiah was first and foremost the anointed teacher and a prophet who will teach the world to know and follow the will of God the Father.

As James Dunn points out, the Gospels are interpretations of the faith of the early evangelists. It is about hermeneutics of faith, and so the story of Jesus Christ presented in the Gospels may be said to be the theological reflections of faithful Christians.[38] Thus, although the exact words of Christ may not be captured, a form critical analysis may help one to obtain the essence of those interpretations of the early evangelists.

One cannot discount the great contributions of the early church fathers who may be considered to be "witnesses to the traditional faith rather than interpreters striving to understand it."[39] Yet no matter how embryonic their attempts at doing theology may be, Clement of Rome and Ignatius and others did their own interpretations of the Christian message.[40] This goes a long way to buttress the point that theology is done according to the prevailing situations and the need to address pertinent issues. African Christian theology also cannot despise small beginnings of interpreting the faith of Christians according to the relevant needs of our world today. African theologians may not agree with the notion that African theologies are mere sketches inasmuch as they may not be described as mere witnesses. Moreover, one cannot discount what they do and the relevant needs they meet.

It is out of patristic theology that theology as an interpretation emerged when it was confronted with the need to explain the Christian message while engaging the rational categories of Hellenism.[41] One of the foremost was Justin Martyr (AD 100–165) who deployed the *Logos* and *logoi* to explain the Christian message. Thus Christology and Trinity, among others, emerged out of the efforts of people like him. African Christian theology continues with the way the apologists worked; in

---

38. Dunn, *Jesus Remembered*, 99–136.
39. Kelly, *Early Christian Doctrine*, 90.
40. Kelly, *Early Christian Doctrine*, 90–95.
41. Kelly, *Early Christian Doctrine*, 14–28; Tillich, *History of Christian Thought*, 3–9.

that, for example, African fathers such as Origen and the contemporary Kwame Bediako will engage their contexts.

The fact is that for Africans, theological explication is a matter of "being," shown in the method of interpretation Origen employed in his works.[42] And furthermore, this ontological mode of theological explication is emphasized in Kwame Bediako's theology insofar as the interpretation of the Christian message is done using the *mother tongue*.[43] Emphatically, it should be admissible that African Christian theologies follow that approach, because it is inherently Kpelelogical.

Scholasticism and the Ontological Source of African Theology

One particular trait in interpretation, be it biblical or theological, is bringing on board elements of dialectical thought. For insofar as one may have to agree with or disagree with a theologian on a particular interpretation, there is bound to be a back-and-forth dialogue that will effect an outcome. Perhaps through suspicion there may be effected some useful outcomes. Therefore, in African Christian theology, postcolonial hermeneutics, as well as the hermeneutics of suspicion and trust are all paramount in interpreting the Christian faith.[44]

Another important theological idea worth mentioning in the medieval period was the system of antagonism between the principles of the will and reason. It boils down to voluntarism and nominalism.[45] The two positions represent a Platonic and Aristotelian position, respectively; and they reflect a holistic approach and an empirical approach to doing theology. Ultimately, as Tillich shows, they represent the Franciscans on one hand and the Dominicans on another hand. The reality of these two patterns showed the brokenness in looking at reality. It used to be that holistic and encyclopedic frame of mind was deployed in theology as well as in general thought. But this system broke down.

What should be said emphatically is that early theological works of the church did not look at issues fragmentarily. Theologians such as the church fathers did their work by involving both faith and reason, and then will and mind. This is where African theologians may find convergence

---

42. This is discussed further in chapter 2.
43. Bediako, *Theology and Identity*.
44. Okure, "Women in the Bible," 47–59; Dube, *Postcolonial Feminist Interpretation*.
45. Tillich, *History of Christian Thought*, 141–44; 191–93.

insofar as theology encapsulates not only rational senses but the inner emotions around the heart and will. It is obvious to understand how African church fathers like Tertullian, Origen, and Augustine could espouse their theology in this manner. Therefore, African Christian theology from the holistic worldview of African primal religion, that is, *kpelelogy*, endeavors to take on board all the epistemologies as in a *Wissenschaften*.[46]

Inasmuch as African theologians may start from the experiential faith, which actively engages the will and intellect equally, there is a natural expression of it in their piety, prayers, and songs and music and dance, and they may be engaged in theology. Bediako describes this form of theological reflection as "grassroots theology"; some may term it differently, such as "oral theology," or even, a "spontaneous" or "implicit theology."[47] In fact, Bediako's comments below regarding Christina Afua Gyan's (or Christina Afua Kuma's) prayers support the position further.

> So what is this illiterate woman's place in African theology? Here, I believe, is an illustration of that spirituality which gives a clue to the vibrant Christian presence that we know of, and which forms the true basis of African theology; and which also provides clear evidence that Christianity in Africa is a truly African experience. For this is theology which comes from where the faith lives and must live continually, in the conditions of life of the community of faith, the theology of the living church, reflecting faith in the living Lord as present reality in daily life.[48]

African Christian theology flows from the depths of African spirituality that continuously seeks an experience with the Divine. An experience with the Divine is always a delight; however, a more delightful part is when believers ponder over their experience with God. These may be done consciously or unconsciously by the one who encounters the Divine. And although it is possible that some theologians in Africa may be more rationalistic and thus forget the experiential reflection, African Christian theology needs to reflect the manner in which African Christians reflect on the reality of God revealed in Christ through the Holy Spirit. That the fathers, including Gregory of Nazianzus and Augustine

---

46. *Wissenschaften* means the sciences in the broad sense. They include logic and mathematics, sociology, technological and developmental sciences, sequence sciences such as history and biography, spirit sciences such as aesthetics, language, technical sciences and other creations of culture.

47. Bediako, "Cry Jesus!," 7–25; Bediako *Jesus in Africa*, 8–9.

48. Bediako, *Jesus in Africa*, 9.

of Hippo, started their reflections based upon their redemptive experiences as well as their experience of God in the Christian community is not in question. For it was out of the Economic Trinity (ET) that the Immanent Trinity (IT) was appreciated.[49]

Therefore, African Christian theology cannot have a theology that is without the experience of individual faith; it also cannot have a theology which is not arising from the life of the church. Thus, context, does not mean in this sense, the mere religious, cultural, social, economic, and political situation of the people of Africa. Instead, context means the religious, cultural, social, economic, and political situation of the Christian community. Theology when it has failed to acknowledge its starting point as the church is bound to lead to an ideological scheme aimed at a utopian end if not totalitarian to say the least. This ought to be done having in mind the propensity for theologians to err as they try to fulfill ultimately political ideals. It happened in Nazi Germany as well as in Apartheid South Africa,[50] when theologies where constructed without the eschatological end of the beloved Christian community in mind.[51] And which of course, may be the utopianisms of both liberal American Christianity and American Evangelicalism today.

In another vein, there is also the tendency to be embroiled in cerebral but contextual realities like it happened to Hegel but which never had any existential relevance. Theology in Africa cannot rise out of mere idealism, it should rise out of the faith-full understanding of the lives of African Christians in the churches, and in the light of the revelation of Jesus Christ in the power of the Holy Spirit. As an apologetic kerygma, theology should be able to address the needs of ordinary Christians even though they may be academic in nature. In other words, it should be possible to teach and preach a certain theology because it is relevant to the needs of the Christian community.

And that is why for Mbiti, translating theological concepts into liturgy and into the way of the life of the people becomes prominent. This inculturation is different from indigenizing the gospel; since with inculturation, the gospel enters the cultural milieu and takes on the *appropriate form* to project it self in the light of God's self revelation in Jesus

---

49. Augustine, *Trinity*, 101; Beeley, *Gregory of Nazianzus*, 188; LaCugna, *God for Us*, 225.

50. Boesak, *Black and Reformed*.

51. Horton, "Tillich's Role in Contemporary Theology," 32–33.

Christ and in the Spirit. Taking on the appropriate form points to the double function of inculturation.

First, inculturation has the function of critically engaging the form in which the gospel is presented to the local context to obtain the kernel or the substance of it. Second, it ensures that the Christian message as presented is meaningful to the local context but also critical of it. Indigenization tends to possess a militant attitude of processing the gospel as in-breaking, melting, and molding—a case of forgery for the gospel to bow and conform to culture as it lacks a sense of self-critique. For that reason, it is important for African Christian theologians to be wary of any form of Africanization of theology that expresses a bias based on lack of self-critique.

Again, with reference to nominalism, it should be said that a growing African Christianity does not accommodate nominalism at the extreme. The experiential voluntarism has a greater propensity to promote church tradition insofar as voluntarism is driven by the power of grace to enable African Christians to be obedient. Hence, voluntarism as in autonomy is not lawlessness, rather it is moments of the making of the responsible being. Voluntarism promotes inherent consciousness and conscience that grasps the African Christian to be a responsible being. Having said that, it has to be acknowledged that there may be some churches in Africa, especially the historic missionary churches who may be "nominal." And out of this nominalistic situation a lot of the Pentecostal and Charismatic churches were founded because some African Christians in the Historic Mission churches moved out, out of intolerance. Moreover, the renewals in the historic missionary churches attest to the fact that nominalism is secondary to African Christianity.

Likewise and in addition, it may be interesting to note the conditions that triggered the Reformation. If not mentioned at all, nominalism as theology and practice may have immensely contributed to the Reformation. The Christian community is a community that is positioned to enjoy many encountering God's presence. The regimentation and over-rationalization of the Christian faith and practice was bound to hit a wall. The wall of real experience—the experience of salvation as an act of God the Father through faith in Jesus Christ by the grace of the Holy Spirit. Thus African Christian theology even though it has a place in informing and shaping African Christianity, also needs to be aware of its inherent limitations regarding nominalism. The ossification of nominalism which brought about a strong response in the renaissance as well as the enlightenment culminated in modernism.

Modernism and the Bible as Sources of African Theology

The rise of scientific inquiry and its ramifications for all human intelligence came to a head in modernism. Thus Christian theology was confronted with this empirical epistemology as a crucial feature about human knowledge that needed to be addressed. Theology was confronted first with regards to its biblical sources. And second, it was met by an objective approach as the measure for determining the genuineness of religious claims. This second confrontation was directed at the subjectivism associated with the claims of the Christian faith.

The historical critical method particularly deployed for the search of the historical Jesus led to immensely impacted faith in biblical theology. Insofar as theology depended on the biblical texts to advance its claims, it was bound to be hit by the realization that much of the Gospels could not be scientifically verified. This led to the social gospel that among others shaped the content of pastoral care as well as Christian education.

Perhaps African Christian theology's burgeoning might have coincided with the peak of modernism. Certainly the mode of worship and the expression of Christian faith among the churches in Africa may have employed a modernistic outlook. To date, most Historic Missionary churches tend to bask in the modernistic outlook. Yet, a backlash with the experiential spiritual mode of Africans was lurking. This lurking backlash could be identified with the growth of the African Initiated churches and with Pentecostal and Charismatic churches in later times. Indeed, the history of the historic churches particularly, with the example of the Presbyterian Church of Ghana, showed that there was no room for the "African Christian experience." Many people drifted, many also were sacked, while a couple of others who wanted to join the church, like Sampson Oppong, were repelled. Much has been said about this un-African way of nurturing Christians in Africa.

However, the crucial element in diagnosing such a problem was the source. And though it may be an oversimplification of the problem at the time, the modernistic approach to reality may have fueled it. The modernistic outlook, with its empiricism coupled with the elitism with which it appeared, doused for some time the flames of real encounter with the Divine.

African Christian theology cannot ignore its history and learning lessons from it. African Christian theology ought to pay attention to the contemporary epistemological frame of the world at any given time. This will ensure a proper and relevant interpretation of the Christian faith to African Christians—the most vital aspect of theology. More importantly, the history of modernism and how it shaped African Christian theological outlook needs to be appreciated more. For example, when the nature of doing theology in Africa is assessed, it is difficult to trace directly the elements of African Christian experience as may be identified with say, the AICs.

The study of the AICs and the reasons for the New Religious Movements (NRMs) in Africa was clearly carried out. Nonetheless, the infusion of the lessons on major theological works in inculturationist as well as in liberationist theology was lacking. Such a critical input that spoke volumes about the existential African Christian was missing in action! To the extent that some other ecumenical friends will prefer dialoguing with AICs as they bypassed the African theologies of their own denominations raises questions. Was it that modernistic elitism inhibited the healthy growth of African Christian theology?

Having said that, it is interesting to discover how African Christian theology employed, say, historical critical theory to advance its theology. An observation of theologies in Africa is common reference to the historical Jesus. Although there were a few theologians such as John Mbiti who used the *Christus victor* motif (emphasized Christ of faith as well as Christology from above) in African theology and as well as in African experience, most theologians used the *Christus patiens* that emphasized the historical Jesus. As a Christology from below, African Christian theology continues to engage the importance of the earthly ministry of Jesus Christ and his death on the cross.

At the end of the day, what should be borne in mind is that, for the African Christian, and for that matter African Christianity, being grasped by the divine reality of God revealed in Christ by the power of the Holy Spirit takes the historicity of Jesus as granted. Consequently, a scientific search for the historical Jesus does not arise; instead, it is appropriated. This appropriation of the historical Jesus is so crucial for the African Christian in understanding how Jesus' life is socially, psychologically, economically, religio-culturally and politically related to theirs.

Concurrently, the historical Jesus is the point from which faith comes alive; and Jesus becomes Lord and Savior—the Christ. And at this point, the historical Jesus and the Christ of faith is taken as a whole.

Therefore, in African Christianity, the relationship between the historical Jesus and the Christ of faith is reasoned about in relation to the meaning it brings to the African Christian. It is Kpelelogy—an experience in being in existence, in life, and in history radiating an unrelenting hope for the present and the future. The sense it makes is with regards to the fulfillment of the soul of the African; which naturally is followed by genuine confession that Jesus is the Christ of God. The nature of this reasoning is only possible when the interaction between the historical and the faith is accompanied by a divine grasping of the individual. Thus, the work of the Holy Spirit in understanding the seeming contradiction of history and faith in the revelation of God to the African Christian cannot be overemphasized. And on the contrary, it ought to be said perhaps as a matter of principle that the mere intellectualization of the historical Jesus in juxtaposition with the Christ of faith without a real interpretation from the Holy Spirit is liable to negate faith itself.

An appreciation of the African faith interpretation of the Christ event may be achieved when we examine the outlines of James D. G. Dunn. Dunn's elucidation may be affirming of the African understanding, insofar as it embraces the work of the Holy Spirit together with the Christian message as faith generating. And inasmuch as faith is not the evacuation of the mind of thought, but on the contrary, the filling of the mind with knowledge and with the working power of the Holy Spirit,[52] it is possible for the African Christian to find meaning, fulfillment, hope, and comfort in the here and now; and anticipate its fullness as not yet.

This paradoxical frame of mind enabled by the Holy Spirit especially informs greatly the understanding of the historical Jesus by many African theologians. It means that these theologians have the capacity to deploy both scientific reasoning, say in historical criticisms, together with their faith without any qualms at all. For the African theologian, there ought not to be dichotomy between faith and knowledge. And both postcolonial biblical criticism and feminist hermeneutics of suspicion as aspects of the historical criticism of biblical texts has been employed by African theologians.[53]

---

52. Dunn, *Jesus Remembered*, 1:99–136.
53. Okure, "Women in the Bible," 47–59; Dube, *Postcolonial Feminist Interpretation*.

Modern theology essentially in the form of historical criticism has shaped African Christian theology differently from the way it did in the Western world. African Christian theology continues to embrace faith issues as those which place responsibilities on African Christians to live lives in fullness (John 10:10). Therefore, it does more than recognizing the gospel as a means for enhancing social well-being. Inasmuch as the gospel should have strong ethical foundations for highly improved social well-being for African communities; it embraces the divine power that removes their prevailing ambiguities; as it gives meaning, fulfillment, and hope in both the present and the future.

In other words, the individual, insofar as is grasped with the power of the historical Jesus as a matter of faith, at once believes in the existential power of the Divine in bringing prophetic directions, teaching, and preaching for deliverance and healing both psychologically and socially. In African Christianity, therefore, faith and history of Jesus Christ is the foundation for the expectation of supernatural healing in a holistic way, i.e., psychologically, physically, spiritually, economically, culturally, and politically.

Likewise, the theologian vigorously pursues this holistic vision through faith in the historical Jesus, whose deeds become benchmarks for their contemporary lives and world. Fundamentally, both what is known as inculturation and liberation in African theology derives much from the historical Jesus, as said earlier. It ought to be observed, however, that African theology is still in parts. If so, could it be truly said to be African, since African theology ought to have a holistic approach as part of its foundations? As may be gleaned from the above, the theology of African Christianity and African Christian theology are a dichotomy. And the approach of this introduction to African Christian theology is to put the parts together. In the end, the faith in the historical Jesus as the Christ of God, both as subjective and objective experience, is translated into supernatural "breakthroughs" as well as taking pragmatic steps for its realization.

What about contemporary theology? Since the modernist era, the world has shifted into what is known as postmodernism. What are the tenets of postmodernism and does it have any impact on African Christianity and thus African theology? These topics and many more will be addressed in the following discussion.

Contemporary Theology and a Postmodernist African Theological Outlook

Contemporary theology may be viewed as theologies that ensued just after the modern period of history. The postmodernist mind, like the modernist mind, is first of all skeptical. But unlike the modernist mind that wishes that certainty, if it exists, should be grounded on scientific facts; the postmodernist challenges the basis for any certainty. Thus all subterfuges of certainty, including religions, political institutions, as well as epistemological institutions, are challenged with regards to any inherent certainty.

Furthermore, there is a constant deconstruction of religious institutions themselves and thus, the authorities of these institutions become irrelevant to society. In this way, the sources of doing theology become easy targets, and the foundations of theologies become targets of deconstruction, relativism, and pluralism. African Christian theology is not immune from postmodernist context of doing theology insofar as we live in a globalized world. The ubiquitous media that is full of disinformation has now compounded the challenges that postmodernism brings to Africa. The significant issue to note is that Africa can no longer live as if it were an island. Even apart from the pervasive media, the postmodern setup of both our public and private tertiary education is modeled on the current philosophical reasonings that underpin every thought action of contemporary Africa. African Christian theology, therefore, must acknowledge its place and understand the dangers as well as the advantages it brings to the table. This will certainly enable theologians to address the relevant issues regarding the faith and practice of the churches that may be endangered by the postmodernist Africans of today and in the future.

Furthermore, since the postmodernist world has become an arena for doing theology, the interpretation of the Christian faith arising from the milieu has engendered theological discussions that have become a challenge to classical theology. Postmodernist theology has raised issues regarding the theistic God, who has limited the freedoms of the creature into a robotic creature and yet held the creature responsible for evil in the universe. The postmodern theologian is a panentheist whose symbol of God is the One that suffers, as against the theist's God who does not suffer. Has the African theologian a say in interpreting the symbol of God in our contemporary world? If the African theologian has a say, at least from the African worldview, where is the African voice?

It may be needful to scribble down the point that African contemporary theologians may be right when they insist that questions of theology are a matter of context. Because as a matter of postmodernism, African Christian theology itself deconstructs orthodoxy by insisting on its particularity. Moreover, there is a need to raise questions that are germane to Africa. Known as the scandal of particularity,[54] African theology among other Third World theologies insists on their context or their particular situation as the crucible of theologizing.[55] This leads to relativism of thought since every locality has its unique context that shapes theology. Today, there is a pluralism of theologies. Hence, though for now, African theologians have not engaged the Western theological issues of contemporary theology much, they have raised pertinent questions of African existence and they keep answering these questions.

The questions raised in the African context include religio-cultural (inculturation) and socioeconomic and political issues (liberation). These questions tend to address the being and dignity of the African soul or personality. It is a theological response to the pragmatization of salvation inherent in the African psyche. How can we have life in fullness as an experience in our life today? Therefore, for the African, there is no room for abstractions that have no direct connection with the questions that they raise. Moreover, even if they do, the truth of those abstractions remains outside their reality until the truth is experienced by their being. The African keeps the quest of encountering the truth of spiritual healing and then physical healing as the goal of existence. Hence, African Christianity cannot but to engage faith in Christ as a means of resolving their spiritual as well as their physical difficulties.

Nonetheless, it may be useful to also note that in African societies, explanations to address the myriad questions of "why" may also be mediated through inquiries from various sources. These inquiries are made from the wise, the elderly in society, leaders, and the council of chiefs, as well as from ancestors, deities, and God via the activities of priests and priestesses. Therefore, the primal mind has a lot of room for abstractions, as well. It should be stated that the notion that the religiosity of the African mind prohibits and limits it from abstractions, and cerebral reasoning may be far from the reality. For example, there are works of

---

54. Migliore, *Faith Seeking Understanding*, 166.

55. Ferm, *Third World Liberation Theologies*; Küster, *Many Faces of Jesus*, 24; Schreiter, *New Catholicity*, 1–4, 16–19.

ancient African kingdoms of Egypt, Ethiopia, Songhai, Ghana, and Mali that span all the sciences, i.e., *Wissenschaften* as a whole.[56]

Accordingly, the quest for the Africanization of Christian theology cannot remain oblivious of the *Wissenschaften* with which the African mind operates even today. It is a shot in the foot anytime theologians in Africa limit the scope of epistemology in African theological reflections. By default, any epistemological restriction or fragmentation of the holistic logos structure of the African mind in African theology is fundamentally flawed. Subsequently, to make a categorical statement that logic, mathematics, the physical sciences, biological sciences, and psychology on one hand have no bearing on African Christianity is inconsistent with the holistic logos structure of the African mind. On the other hand, to also state categorically that the epistemological realm for African theology is the social sciences, political sciences, and religion and cultural sciences will be slighting the holistic logos structure of the African mind.

As of now, contemporary African Christian theology is made of deconstructing the colonial, racial, and patriarchal structures in the overall understanding of the African Christian. It also aims at reconstructing the overall understanding of the African Christian by rereading and reconceptualization/reconstruction of the Christian faith. These are typified in the inculturation and liberation theologies in Africa. The contemporary studies in African Christianity where phenomenological analysis of African Christianity is a unique way of doing African Christian theology also cannot be glossed over. Studies in African Christianity open the door for appreciating the holistic worldview of Africans in concrete. Thus, studies in African Christianity are a theological paradigm as phenomenological African theology whose theology also forms the major source of doing theology in Africa.

In the interpretation of the Christian faith, African Christian theology has always made mention of the AICs as a source of doing authentic African Christian theology. Though perhaps the AICs were ignored in the process of doing theology in Africa, today, studies in African Christianity ought to be the source instead. In the studies of African Christianity, one sees the concretization of the holistic logos structure of the African mind in so many ways. And the way and manner the Christian

---

56. Adams, *Paul Tillich's Philosophy of Culture*, 145; the reality is actually embodied in Imhotep, the great ancient Egyptian. See Editors of Encyclopaedia Britannica, "Imhotep"; James, *Stolen Legacy*.

faith of Africans is exposed in their quest of experiencing the truth is in their religio-cultural, socioeconomic, and political lives.

Meanwhile, this scenario shows the continuum of contemporary theology of other realms with the African Christian theological paradigm. Though African Christian theology, like many other Third World theologies, has deconstructed orthodoxy and done theology as an orthopraxis, the concerns tend to be converging. This may be found especially when Jürgen Moltmann[57] and other contemporary theologians from the Western perspective deal with issues about relationships and the need to care for every creature of God as a Christian responsibility.[58] These Western theologies attempt to address disability, race, gender, poverty, and other injustices, including ecological issues.[59] And insofar as these issues are common to the world today, there is a continuum, though approaches may be different in nature.

The Characteristics of African Christian Theology

Paul Tillich has opined that ultimate concern must grasp the theologian before any theological discourse.[60] This is a subjective encounter which gets one embroiled in the reality that one seeks to understand. To possess faith is to be grasped, possessed, or enchanted by ultimate concern. So, the distinguishing character of Christian theology from other ultimate concerns is that the theologian is found within the inner circle of theology. The others, though, like the philosopher of religion, may be grasped by the reality that ultimately exists outside the inner theological circle. The philosopher of religion, therefore, looks at the ultimate concern without the grasping of that *concrete* reality from the outside.

This implies that, in understanding Christian reflections as in theology, the experience of the Truth ultimately revealed by the symbol of the One God, Mother/Father, Son, and Holy Spirit by grace through faith is a distinguishing reality. This distinguishing factor is necessary in view of the pluralism existing in philosophy and religion in particular. Thus,

---

57. Moltmann, *Crucified God*; Moltmann, *Coming of God*; Moltmann, *The Trinity and the Kingdom*.

58. Baik, *Holy Trinity*; Migliore, *Faith Seeking Understanding*; Peters, *God as Trinity*; Peters, *God—The World's Future*.

59. Chopp and Taylor, *Reconstructing Christian Theology*.

60. Tillich, *Systematic Theology*, 1:9–11.

though all, including scientists, philosophers, professionals, and religious leaders, may be ultimately concerned; and though they may employ biblical texts, the context and human reasoning, their works may not be classified as Christian theology.

If that were the case, then the phenomenology of the theology of African Christianity,[61] as well as that of African Christians, popularly known as grassroots theology,[62] becomes fundamental to African Christian theology. It ought to be reiterated that faith seeking understanding, as per the African theologian, means employing the African faith in the triune God together with the African contextual categories Kpelelogically.

In other words, the African Christian experience with the Logos itself is a concrete expression unlike the universal *logos* concerns of others. In the same way, the African theologian's work is distinguished from the philosopher of religion; because the former is a member of the faith community which is the concrete expression of the *Logos* and thus the ultimate concern is specific. In other words, the kpelelogical mind becomes Kpelelogical. Kpelelogy is then the main characteristic of African Christianity and of African Christian theology.

What then is the distinguishing feature of African Christian theology since it may share the same principle of the subjective experience of the Truth which is the triune God with other theological traditions? Here the difference may be derived, first, from the Kpelelogical experience where the holistic thought of the African theologian is engaged. This obviously determines the fundamental method underlying the whole thought processes of the African theologian. Second, since the subjective experience of the divine reality is indispensable and it is manifested Kpelelogically, the categories of thought may be based upon the initial experiences and knowledge of the theologian.

These initial experiences may be consciously or unconsciously engaged as presuppositions inherent in the theologian, and which seeks to bring meaning to existence through interpretation of reality and experience. The third distinguishing feature of African Christian theology is based upon the first and second distinguishing features, namely, kpelelogy, and Kpelelogical categories. And it is the African context within which the theologian's subjective experience is made concrete. This necessarily involves the autonomous experience, as well as the impacting of

---

61. Omenyo, "Charismatic Churches in Ghana," 266–68; Kalu, *Power, Poverty and Prayer*, 105.

62. Bediako, *Jesus in Africa*, 8; Kuma, *Kwaebirentuw Ase Yesu*.

heteronomous categories in the mind that are also embedded in the local community or the local situation or the local context.

The impact is made upon the autonomous and heteronomous, in that Kpelelogical experience, all at once, engenders internal and external expressions. These internal and external expressions in African Christianity may be best found in the African Independent Churches (AICs).[63] To date, it is very clear that the African Christian's original expression of autonomous and heteronomous Christianity is located in the AICs. While the AICs are keen on the transformation within the African Christian leading to liberated lifestyles free from the control of demons and immorality, these are also expressed in the concrete through other laws, ceremonies, liturgies, rituals, vestments, dance, art, signs, and symbols.

Pentecostal and Charismatic churches today in Africa who are a significant part of African Christianity are yet to be free from the Protestant repudiation of signs, symbols, and Christian art. Roman Catholic Christianity and to a very large extent Anglican Christianity in Africa have maintained and deepened both autonomous Christianity and heteronomous Christianity. The other Protestants are yet to employ these heteronomous categories of expressions in their churches. Originally, Roman Catholic Christianity is more heteronomous than autonomous.

African Christian theology is, however, important in drawing attention to these realities. This is so, especially having in mind the Kpelelogical experience of African Christians and how that should shape the manner in which African Christianity grows and develops, for the benefit of the church of Jesus Christ worldwide.

---

63. Akinade, "African Christianity in the Twentieth Century," 343–55.

2

The Kpelelogy of Faith
A Cardinal Theological Principle of African Christianity

The Kpelelogy of Christian Faith

THERE IS A DIFFERENCE between the paradoxical primal worldview of Africans (*kpelelogy*) and the paradox in African Christian thought (*Kpelelogy*). And in this case, the inherent paradox in both *kpelelogy* and *Kpelelogy* is the cognition of seemingly opposing epistemological realities into one whole thought—forming the *logos* and Logos structure of the mind, respectively.

Another way by which it may be viewed is that one is universal paradox and the other is the Paradox of absoluteness.[1] The former is occasioned by the universal *logos* (reason) while the latter is informed by the absolutely concrete Logos (Reason).[2] The impact of the universal *logos* on the psychological and religious ontology of Africans may be quite significant in driving them to naturally anticipate and participate in the absolutely concrete Reason. Faith in and spiritual participation in the absolutely concrete who is Jesus Christ—the revelation of God—is a *manifestation* of the *oikonomia* of the triune God in Africa. And this is expressed by the early African Christianity,[3] as well as the contemporary

---

1. Kierkegaard, *Philosophical Fragments*, 35.
2. Tillich, *Systematic Theology*, 3:254.
3. Iliffe, *Africans*, 6–61; Falk, *Growth of the Church in Africa*, 7–60; Isichei, *History of Christianity in Africa*, 1–73; Oden, *How Africa Shaped the Christian Mind*, 46–60.

African Christianity. Thomas Oden shared with me the goal and passion of this particular discourse when he wrote,

> Is it not fitting for Christians of the African South to appreciate and express gratitude for the many generations of sacrifice that Christians of the African north have made to the preservation of Christian scriptures, ancestral traditions, and liturgical practices for all of Africa?
>
> This is the fitting time to encourage black Africans to understand the inestimable value of their own larger African history. Their active empathy can now reach out for those courageous and forbearing intentions from the north[4]

An understanding of the theological insights provided by Origen, Tertullian, and Augustine, for example, shows the paradoxical sense of progression from the particular and universal to the absolutely concrete. The background of Origen as an Egyptian was most important in promoting the idea of participation in the absolutely concrete who is the Christ as salvation.

The mystery religions, specifically the influence of Egyptian religions such as the cult of Isis and Osiris, may have had a direct influence on Origen. Similarly, the traditional religious worldview of contemporary Africa had similar impact on the African Initiated Churches (AICs), Pentecostal churches, as well as the Charismatic churches. In fact this may even be said of the essence of the renewals in the Historic Mission churches. And bishop Oyedepo is one of the Charismatic leaders in Africa whose reflections may be characteristic of Kpelelogy.

African Christian theology is therefore called upon to reflect on the African Christian reality in a manner that is consistent with the primal worldview and also with the traditional worldview of Christianity. Paradoxical or Kpelelogical reflection calls for a holistic approach or multidimensional approach in doing theology. It raises questions from existential realities of Africans as a whole and endeavors to resolve them with the Christian message holistically and paradoxically.

Although it may not be plain that the African primal worldview is paradoxical, it is so. The reality is that the African mind is multidimensional, i.e., kpelelogical because, it views reality in wholes and in totality. It is typical of African minds today and other Africans in the past such as

---

4. Oden, *How Africa Shaped the Christian Mind*, 80.

the ancient Egyptians to not dichotomize between realities.[5] The ancient Egyptians practiced all their sciences within the interpretation of their religious institutions without separation. The whole cosmos was viewed as a religious reality, such that sacred and profane were held together, just as the physical/material and the spiritual were held together without confusion.[6]

Certainly the Egyptian idea of the mound and the waters are the mythical indications of the reality of the material and the spiritual respectively. And Kwame Nkrumah shows how progressively the idea moved into the realm of physics through Thales and other Greek philosophers who followed.[7] The notion that Greek philosophy emerged out of Egyptian philosophy and religion, implied by scholars such as Nkrumah has firm support. Indeed for George James, it is a "stolen legacy."[8] Moreover, that form of philosophy which may have been epitomized in the life of Imhotep makes the position concrete.[9]

Furthermore, the holistic worldview of Africans is affirmed by many contemporary African societies, including the Ga and the Akan of Ghana. Research done by Margaret Field and Marion Kilson about the Ga religious institution and worldview is emphatic. For example, the Ga believe that all creatures owe their existence to God who is Spirit and Supreme. And that their very lives could be influenced primarily by the spiritual and secondarily by the material realities of existence respectively.[10] Kwame Gyekye buttresses the point that

> religion—the awareness of the existence of some ultimate, Supreme Being who is the origin and sustainer of this universe and the establishment of constant ties with this being—influences, in a comprehensive way, the thoughts and actions of the African people. . . . It would be correct to say that religion enters all aspects of African life so fully—determining practically every aspect of life, including moral behavior—that it can hardly be separated.[11]

---

5. Olela, "African Foundations," 43–49; Oden, *How Africa Shaped the Christian Mind*.

6. Nkrumah, *Consciencism*, 1–40.

7. Nkrumah, *Consciencism*, 30.

8. James, *Stolen Legacy*.

9. Editors of Encyclopaedia Britannica, "Imhotep."

10. Field, *Religion and Medicine*; Kilson, *Kpele Lala*.

11. Gyekye, *African Cultural Values*, 3.

The existential[12] worldview of African peoples that may be incurably religious and paradoxical is asserted by John Mbiti when he described it in the following terms:

> Because traditional religions permeate all the departments of life, there is no formal distinction between the sacred and the secular, between the religious and non-religious, between spiritual and the material areas of life. Wherever the African is, there is his religion: he carries it to the fields where his is sowing seeds or harvesting a new crop; he takes it with him to the beer party or to attend a funeral ceremony; and if he is educated, he takes religion with him to the examination room at school or in the university; if he is a politician he takes it to the house of parliament.[13]

Mbiti goes further to establish the existential and paradoxical conception of reality as he shows the categories and their relationships as highlighted below:

> Africans have their own ontology, but it is a religious ontology, and to understand their religions we must penetrate that ontology. I propose to divide it up into five categories, but it is an extremely anthropocentric ontology in the sense that everything is seen in terms of its relation to man. These categories are:
>
> 1. God as the ultimate explanation of the genesis and sustenance of both man and all things.
> 2. Spirits being made up of superhuman beings and the spirits of men who died a long time ago.
> 3. Men including human beings who are alive and those about to be born.
> 4. Animals and plants, or the remainder of biological life.
> 5. Phenomena and objects without biological life.
>
> Expressed anthropocentrically, God is the Originator and Sustainer of man; the Spirits explain the destiny of man; Man is the center of this ontology; the Animals, Plants and natural phenomena and objects constitute the environment in which man lives, provide a means of existence and, if need be, man establishes a mystical relationship with them.

---

12. It is noteworthy that John Mbiti describes the African worldview in existential terms, and especially when he uses the words *being*, *existence*, and *ontological*. Mbiti, *African Religions and Philosophy*, 15–16.

13. Mbiti, *African Religions and Philosophy*, 2.

This anthropocentric ontology is a complete unity or solidarity which nothing can break up or destroy. To destroy or remove one of these categories is to destroy the whole existence including the destruction of the Creator, which is impossible. One mode of existence presupposes all the others, and a balance must be maintained so that these modes neither drift too far apart from one another nor get too close to one another. In addition to the five categories, there seems to be a force, power or energy permeating the whole universe. God is the Source and ultimate controller of this force; but the spirits have access to some of it. A few human beings have the knowledge and ability to tap, manipulate and use it, such as the medicine-men, witches, priests and rainmakers, some for the good and others for the ill of their communities.[14]

Again, it cannot be overemphasized that the multidimensionality of the African worldview referred to in this book as kpelelogy is a system of relationality. This is certain insofar as it connects the secular to the holy, and the physical to the spiritual, and so on, it is also paradoxical with reference to God as the symbol of the ground of being.[15] Thus wise sayings of Africans like the Ga and Akan are replete with paradoxical statements. These statements which may seem absurd or unreasonable or irrational ought to be viewed as rational in the light of the meaningfulness attached to them. A few of these wise sayings are as follows:

> God pounds the one-arm person's *fufu* for [them]. God drives away the insects from the tailless animal.[16]

In these wise sayings, one may observe the way and manner in which the power of the ground of being is invoked to address the predicament of humanity. This form of reasoning is rational insofar as it is full of meaning and provides fulfillment or relief in the midst of pain and suffering. If logic (reasoning of the logos) is making sense of reality,

---

14. Mbiti, *African Religions and Philosophy*, 15–16. This paradox of being whereby all realities relate to the human person and vice versa (correlation) is quite strongly affirmed in the Ga religious institution of Kpele as an all-encompassing phenomenon. Kilson, *Kpele Lala*, 7, 18; and regarding the role of *ta panta* of the *archiereus* in the Ghanaian context, John Ekem engages the *Wulormo* in the exegesis of Heb 2:10; 9:11; Ekem, *Priesthood in Context*, 160–65, 196.

15. Wendell, *On the Resolution of Science and Faith*, 3–6.

16. Gyekye, *African Cultural Values*, 10; in one *Kpele* song of the Ga people, *Opkosansa*, a fish, laments about the protrusions in its front and back and yet tends to accept the situation by linking the situation to God. Kilson, *Kpele Lala*, 46.

it is also meaningfulness.[17] The notion of paradox in Christian belief is reflected upon by Paul Tillich as follows:

> When Paul points to his situation as an apostle and to that of Christians generally in a series of *paradoxa* (II Corinthians), he does not intend to say something illogical; he intends to give the adequate, understandable, and therefore logical expression of the infinite tensions of Christian existence. When he speaks about the paradox of the justification of the sinner (in Luther's formula, *simul peccator et iustus*), and when John speaks about the Logos becoming flesh (later expressed in the *paradoxa* of the creed of Chalcedon), neither of them wishes to indulge in logical contradictions [as in the theology of Emil Brunner].
>
> They want to express the conviction that God's acting transcends all possible human expectations and all necessary human preparations. It transcends, but it does not destroy, finite reason; for God acts through the Logos which is the transcendent and transcending source of the *logos* structure of thought and being. God does not annihilate the expressions of his own Logos. The term "paradox" should be defined carefully, and paradoxical language should be used with discrimination. Paradoxical means "against the opinion," namely, the opinion of finite reason. Paradox points to the fact that in God's acting finite reason is superseded but not annihilated; it expresses this fact in terms which are not logically contradictory but which are supposed to point beyond the realm in which finite reason is applicable. This is indicated by the ecstatic state in which all biblical and classical theological paradox appear.[18]

Therefore paradoxical reasoning may be viewed as reasoning beyond reasoning or reason above reason. It is finding meaning in our ground of being who the Logos (meaningfulness) is, while solving also, the problem of the human predicament. Though it is a universal reality in African Traditional Religion (ATR) as *logos* it is not absolutely expressed as Logos. The absolutely concrete, which is universal, resides only in Jesus Christ through the *oikonomia*.

Two African theologians apart from the African Christian fathers like Origen[19] whose mind may be associated with paradox are Prophet

---

17. Tillich, *Systematic Theology*, 1:56–57; 2:92; 3:165–72, 223–28.
18. Tillich, *Systematic Theology*, 1:56–57.
19. Bediako, *Jesus in Africa*, 80.

Harries[20] and Ephraim Amu.[21] Philip Laryea presents the paradox embedded in the mind of the Apostle Paul and the thought of Amu. He quotes explicitly the mind of Amu as follows:

> I wonder myself how I was able to get through those difficulties. I gave a number of lectures, and today I read some of those lectures over, and see the ideals that I cherish in those lectures. And I am astonished that all those ideals came to me and how I was able to stand up to the opposition against me in various ways. So I couldn't say that I had any particular gift for this sort of thing, but I think its God's own way of doing things. He always provides some means of doing some important work anywhere in the world, and I just happened to be that tool. And that's why I was able to do this, not because of any particular credit of my own. I don't think so.[22]

From the above, it is clear that paradox is a fundamental principle of Kpelelogy embedded in the African psychology. It is the source of power for the Christian to engage every reality by the standard of God through Jesus Christ, God's only Son begotten for meaningfulness and fulfillment.

African Roots of Paradox in Christian Theology

Origen (AD 184–254)

Kwame Bediako made an assertion when he mentioned Origen as one African theologian possessing the Kpelelogical mind due to his existential and paradoxical African worldview.[23] Certainly, the contribution of Origen as an Egyptian Christian and for that matter an African cannot be glossed over by any theologian. And it is obvious why Jürgen Moltmann hinges his theology of the cross partly but fundamentally on Origen;[24] when Moltmann acknowledges Origen as the first to recognize the suffering of God and thus the mutability of God.

Indeed, some fathers held to the theology that the materiality and soul of Jesus as a full human was taken off as in a garment at the

20. Bediako, *Jesus in Africa*, 85–87, 92–96.
21. Laryea, *Ephraim Amu*, 142–49.
22. Laryea, *Ephraim Amu*, 149; see also the appendix A.
23. Bediako, *Jesus in Africa*, 80.
24. Moltmann, *The Trinity and the Kingdom of God*, 24; Moltmann, *Way of Jesus Christ*, 179.

resurrection; thereby rendering Christ pure divinity.[25] Others also held to the theology that the presence of the humanity of Jesus Christ in the Divine though present is suffused and united with the Logos.[26] And Origen, who in accordance with the traditional account of the resurrection maintained the full humanity and full divinity in Jesus Christ, may have followed the latter. Nonetheless, it is important to state that Origen's position does not imply that he embraced the idea of change in God as asserted by Moltmann. Kelly, firms the point in this manner:

> With the resurrection the deification of Christ's human nature really began, his body of becoming of a consistency midway between that of natural flesh and that of the soul freed from bodily ties; and the Christian can say that; "although the Savior was a man, He is now no longer one." The exaltation of the Son of Man consists precisely in this that He has ceased to be other than the Logos and has become identically one with Him.[27]

Moreover the paradox above found in the "suffering God" in the Origenist sense does not imply an actual change in God, inasmuch as there can be no confusion, division, and separation in the divinity and humanity of Jesus Christ.[28]

In the Origenist sense, God revealed the Self through Jesus Christ in order to demonstrate infinite wisdom and power to overcome the problem of being in existence.[29] And in paying a tribute, it may be said that Origen's theology is immense as it corroborated the theology of the Western Church on one hand. And on the other hand it was a major source of creativity in the Eastern Church including the Greek Church. Contributions of Origen with respect to the allegorical interpretation of Scripture; and his theological understanding of the person and work of Jesus Christ are full of paradoxes.

It has been taken for granted that the early African church fathers like Origen was influenced by Neoplatonism. And we need bear in mind that Origen was a student of Ammonius Saccas, together with Plotinus,

---

25. Moltmann, *The Trinity and the Kingdom*, 152–54, 161–62, 213, 214–18.
26. Kelly, *Early Christian Doctrines*, 157–58.
27. Kelly, *Early Christian Doctrines*, 157–58.
28. Origen, "*De Principiis*"; Kelly also states that Origen "did not regard the Son's participation in human nature as either permanent or essential." Kelly, *Early Christian Doctrines*, 157.
29. Origen, "*De Principiis.*"

indicating the influence of Neoplatonism on him.[30] Admittedly, the application of Neoplatonic ideas might have empowered Origen to explicate or communicate the Christian faith to other people persuasively. Nonetheless, what is not mentioned often, is, the African and Egyptian background of Origen and how that motivated him and inspired his creative imagination.[31]

Again, admitting that Greek philosophy is a branch of Egyptian philosophy and religion, it may be safe to surmise that Neoplatonism may be a cross fertilization. And the cross fertilization may be between Egyptian philosophy and religion on one hand; and Platonism on the other hand. In fact, Tillich gives a hint of this idea of cross-fertilization when he described the Alexandrian scheme of thought that "in the highest ecstasy there happens what Plotinus calls the flight of the one to the One, that is, of us who are individual ones to the ultimate One who is beyond number. What is the *telos*, the inner aim, the goal, the purpose, of humans' being? Plato had already given the answer: *homoiosis tou theou kata to dynaton*, which is, becoming similar to God as much as possible. This was also the aim of the *mystery religions*, in which the soul was supposed to participate in the eternal One."[32] It is strikingly important to underscore the point here that the mystery religions when mentioned connoted most often the Egyptian religions, especially those associated with Isis and Osiris.[33]

Furthermore, the participation in the Divine with regards to Greek philosophy differs from the Christian participation in the Divine. On one hand, Tillich says that for the Greeks, philosophizing is the means of participation. And the means is through the Logos, "a *logikon* life"; perhaps we could translate this as a "meaningful life," a life in terms of objective meanings."[34] On the other hand, the Christian mode of participation is through faith; that is a state of being or living in or participating in New Being, which is the realm of the church. Therefore, real participation needs *gnosis*, which is a "cognitive faith, a faith which develops its contents cognitively."[35] Biblical gnosis is found in the theology of Paul in the New Testament. This gnosis is that God can be known in Jesus Christ,

30. Tillich, *History of Christian Thought*, 55.
31. Tillich, *History of Christian Thought*, 57.
32. Tillich, *History of Christian Thought*, 54.
33. Roukema, *Gnosis and Faith*, 93–95.
34 Tillich, *History of Christian Thought*, 55–56.
35. Tillich, *History of Christian Thought*, 56.

who was crucified and rose again. Biblical gnosis admits of an incomplete knowledge of God, therefore it is eschatological.[36] And it is the same biblical gnosis that developed in Alexandria but particularly fueled by the mystery religions of Egypt.[37]

The striking issue here is that the African theologians of Alexandria loathed faith of nominal Christianity devoid of meaningfulness or substance. For them, meaningfulness in God ought not to be irrational or devoid of reason or be by force. It should be a point of meaningfulness and sense of fulfillment that should lead to the acceptance of God enthusiastically. They were thoroughgoing compatibilists and non-interventionists. Therefore, participation also meant reasoning beyond the realm of being or reasoning in the realm beyond reason. This paradoxical idea of the African theologians in Alexandria perhaps took shape in the allegorical method of biblical interpretation. And the chief exponent was Origen.

Porphyry from Tyre, also a Neoplatonist as Origen, saw himself differently from the Egyptian theologian. And the reasons he suggests are not only because Origen was a Christian, but because "Origen would live in a barbaric and irrational way."[38] Porphyry therefore reveals to us that Origen engaged his African ethnic background together with Neoplatonism to explain the Christian faith in an irrational (paradoxical) manner. Moreover, it may be right to suggest that it was the traditional Egyptian worldview, including the religious, cultural, socioeconomic, and political, that was engaged. And it cannot be farfetched that it was a paradoxical worldview.

Furthermore, this paradoxical ontological mode permeated and underlay all the classical doctrines and creeds.[39] One identifies the paradox of finding meaning beyond the realm of being in the allegorical interpretation. For example, Origen says that "there are two classes of Christians: [first] the many simple ones, who accept on authority the biblical message and the teachings of the church without understanding them fully. They take the myths literally . . . they prefer the healing miracles to [second] the story of Jesus going with his three apostles to the mount of transfiguration, which is an allegorical or metaphorical expression for

---

36. Roukema, *Gnosis and Faith*, 151.

37. Pearson, *Gnosticism, Judaism, and Egyptian Christianity*, 196–97.

38. Tillich, *History of Christian Thought*, 57. "Barbaric" in the Greek *barbaros* or *barbarikos* means "foreign." And it is precisely the sense in which it has been used to show Origen's ethnic background.

39. Tillich, *History of Christian Thought*, 58.

those who go beyond the literal meaning to a transformed interpretation of it."⁴⁰ Meanwhile, the church cannot extricate itself from allegorical interpretation, because almost all the Old Testament appropriations of the Christ are allegorical.⁴¹

Following the above is obvious in locating Origen's theology of God that has the elements of the paradox of the Trinity.⁴² For example, Kelly analyzes Origen regarding the subtle plurality and yet the oneness of God as follows: "The true teaching, in [Origen's] view, is that the Son is 'other in subsistence than the Father' or even that the Father and the Son 'are two things in respect of Their Persons, but one in unanimity, harmony and identity of will.' Thus, while really distinct, the Three are from another point of view one; as he expresses it, 'we are not afraid to speak in one sense of two Gods, in another sense of one God.'"⁴³ This meaningful paradox attested by Origen's strong courage is achieved only beyond the realm of human thought but not against it.⁴⁴

Tertullian

It should not be forgotten that in the Western church, Tertullian, also a great African theologian from Carthage (Tunisia) and for the church in Rome laid the solid theological foundation.⁴⁵ The contribution of Tertullian to all orthodox creeds cannot also be glossed over in that respect.⁴⁶ His contributions to the doctrines of Trinity, Christology, and Soteriology are likewise paradoxical. The doctrines had their essential realities correlated with the existential realities. Hence his doctrine of the Trinity is immanent and economic, respectively.⁴⁷ The implication is that reflection on the Trinity is done not according to the divine essence alone or to the salvific event in which the Trinity is revealed alone. Rather, having the knowledge of the revelation as faith, contemplation is done from both sides in complimentary manner. On one hand, contemplation of the

---

40. Tillich, *History of Christian Thought*, 58–59.
41. Tillich, *History of Christian Thought*, 58.
42. Tillich, *History of Christian Thought*, 59–61.
43. Kelly, *Early Christian Doctrines*, 129.
44. Tillich, *History of Christian Thought*, 56.
45. Kelly, *Early Christian Doctrines*, 110.
46. Tillich, *History of Christian Thought*, 46.
47. Kelly, *Early Christian Doctrines*, 110.

Divine in immanence is understood in the economy and the contemplation of the Divine in economy is understood in immanence.

Furthermore Tertullian emphasized that the Divine essence is one with a plurality of three *persona* associated with economy or dispensation.[48] Tertullian posits that "we believe in one only God, yet subject to this dispensation, which is our word for economy, that the only God has also a Son, his Word, Who has issued out of Himself . . . which Son then sent, according to the promised, Holy Spirit, the Paraclete, out of the Father."[49] This means that there are "three characteristic expressions of the divine, in the process of divine self-explication."[50] The absurdity of the singular *substantia* which is also the plural *personae* is clear. Nonetheless, this Trinitarian doctrine is for Tertullian the reason or the meaning or the fulfillment of all existence. Thus the idea of the Trinity is no longer a contradiction but a paradox in which reason is not suspended but overwhelmed by the reason beyond it *ad extra*.

Significantly, the contributions of Tertullian which are reflected in the Augustinian theology of the Latin Church and Protestantism is not farfetched. And the significance of Origen from Greek Africa and the two of Latin Africa above regarding the theology of the sacrament is the grand symbolism of Christology and Soteriology. This grand symbolism of the sacrament cannot be divorced from their African mind and experience.[51] And as shown elsewhere, the correlations between the material and the spiritual and or existence and essence are fundamental to the classical theologies of salvation, the church, and the sacrament.[52] What needs to be added at this point is that such correlations found in the theology of the African church fathers who shaped classical theology are inexorably paradoxical.[53] And that paradox is attested by Paul the apostle.[54]

---

48. Kelly, *Early Christian Doctrines*, 110.
49. Kelly, *Early Christian Doctrines*, 110.
50. Tillich, *History of Christian Thought*, 47.
51. Amarkwei, "Sacrament and Symbolism."
52. Amarkwei, "Sacrament and Symbolism," 105–16.
53. Tillich, *Systematic Theology*, 1:56–57.
54. Tillich, *Systematic Theology*, 1:56–57.

Augustine of Hippo

Augustine of Hippo also, by teaching how the Christian faith is gained and exercised, showed the paradox inherent in the grace of God. Evidently, much space may be needed to show this. Nonetheless, his teaching that there is prevenient grace, cooperating grace, sufficient grace, and efficient grace may be helpful.[55] In prevenient grace, Augustine shows that since humanity is incapacitated through the fall of Adam from divine aid, it needs the grace that gives the will the capacity to aspire for the good. Cooperating grace is the power of God that assists and cooperates with the human will. Sufficient grace was the grace associated with Adam's relationship with God before the fall. And efficient grace is the power of God that enables the believer or the Christian to succeed.[56] This idea that it is God who is the only answer to the predicament of the fallen universe has many questions that could not be answered here.

Nevertheless, it is clear that like the Church in Alexandria, there is the belief that without participation in the divine, spiritual, and invisible reality, there cannot be an end to the predicament of the universe.[57] Whether this participation was mystical or spiritual or natural, it is the basic worldview of these Africans. And it is upon that, amplified by the truth of Scripture, that these great African theologians worked. Typically in Africa today, even in sub-Saharan Africa, there may be no doubts at all that it is the worldview that the paradoxical participation in the Divine is the only true way of having a meaningful life.

Faith and Love: A Theological Significance of Kpelelogical Paradox in Contemporary African Christianity

The pith of this paradoxical principle which essentially borders on the courage to be through participation in the Divine is without doubt expressly demonstrated in African Christianity today. Africa has time and time again demonstrated this courage of confidence more clearly in the ministry of the African Indigenous churches (e.g., Prophet Harries),[58] Pentecostal churches (e.g., Church of Pentecost, Ghana), and

---

55. Kelly, *Early Christian Doctrines*, 367.
56. Kelly, *Early Christian Doctrines*, 367.
57. Tillich, *History of Christian Thought*, 54.
58. Shank, *"Black Elijah" of West Africa*.

Charismatic churches (e.g., Benson Idahosa,[59] David Olanyi Oyedepo, and Nicholas Duncan-Williams) and the impact of the renewals in the mainline churches.[60]

Studies on the faith audacity of contemporary African Christianity as may be profoundly expressed in Pentecostal and Charismatic churches is epitomized by their leaders. Following for example, the faith exploits of David Olanyi Oyedepo, founder and bishop of the Living Faith Church (Winners' Chapel) Worldwide, is a concrete reality of the paradoxical faith as a profound manifestation of the African Kpelelogical mind. Bishop Oyedepo's faith has been shown to be founded on his African background which I have termed *kpelelogy*.[61]

In his own account of how he moved to Canaanland in Ota Nigeria, he reflects on the irrationality of moving into an uninhabited forestland to establish a new church from the human point of view. He states in that regard that it is utterly senseless for anyone called by God to establish a church in a virgin forest that has no human existence on sight. And it is because, for him, the best way to preach the gospel was to move into areas where people lived. The gospel is not to be literally preached to the flora and fauna but for human beings to be saved in Christ. Therefore, the voice of God he heard to move to Canaanland was a defiance of human reason on one hand.[62]

On the other hand, according to him, this seeming denial of human reason made sense to him more because in God or in the Holy Spirit he found fulfillment and meaningfulness.[63] His testimony is that participating in God, i.e., total empowerment by God and total obedience to the voice of God, is the key to success. And it is evidenced today by the reality that the forest church has a fifty-thousand-capacity church building that is crowded on Sundays or any other day of worship. This audacity of faith in Bishop Oyedepo and other contemporary African Christian leaders may be seen by Tillich as the courage of confidence. Oyedepo believes and endeavors to demonstrate this courage of confidence with the metaphor of the lion for the Christian. It is a faith which does not suspend reason, because it analyzes the encounter of faith logically and

---

59. Garlock, *Fire in His Bones*.

60. Kalu, *African Pentecostalism*; Asamoah-Gyadu, *African Charismatics*; Gifford, *Ghana's New Christianity*; Larbie, *Pentecostalism*.

61 Wariboko, *Nigerian Pentecostalism*, 34–35.

62. Oyedepo, "Bishop Oyedepo Unveiling the Stronghold of Faith Pt. 2."

63. Oyedepo, "Bishop Oyedepo Unveiling the Stronghold of Faith Pt. 2."

yet "reason" is found wanting because it is transcended by the absolutely universal and absolutely concrete reason. Nonetheless, these courage of confidences in African Christianity are still of the pietistic type and are yet to move on to the reflection or theological stage.

There are two experiences regarding the Christian religious experience as a personal encounter with God.[64] They are, first, the mystical union, and second, the "personal communion with the source of courage."[65] Accordingly, "faith embraces both mystical participation and personal confidence."[66] The end product with regards to the Divine-human encounter that involves both the mystical union and personal confidence is termed the *courage of confidence*.[67] It is a way in which reason is denied and accepted at the same time in ecstatic reason, as may be seen in the example of Bishop Oyedepo.[68] The person-to-person relationship between God and human being, like in contemporary African Pentecostal and Charismatic Christianity, was the emphasis of the Reformation that was stoked by Luther.[69] Characteristically, it is a firm break away from the "mediation through the [Roman] church, an indirect and partial meeting between God and the soul."[70] Tillich asserts the position firmly:

> When the Reformation removed the mediation and opened up a direct, total and personal approach to God, a new non-mystical courage to be was possible. It is manifest in the heroic representatives of fighting Protestantism, in the Calvinist as well as in the Lutheran Reformation, and in Calvinism even more conspicuously. . . . The courage of the Reformers is not the courage to be oneself—as it is not the courage to be as a part. It transcends and unites both of them. For the courage of confidence is not rooted in confidence about oneself. The Reformation pronounces the opposite: one can become confident about one's existence only after ceasing to base one's confidence on oneself. On the other hand the courage of confidence is in no way based on anything finite besides oneself, not even on the church. It is based on God

---

64. "Personal encounter" as used by Tillich is a common phrase used by contemporary African Pentecostal and Charismatic Christians to describe a faith experience particularly of the subjective soteriology and other experiences.

65. Tillich, *Courage to Be*, 152.

66. Tillich, *Courage to Be*, 152.

67. Tillich, *Courage to Be*, 152; Hamilton, "Paul Tillich," 452–54.

68. Tillich, *Systematic Theology*, 1:53; Emmet, "Epistemology," 212–14.

69. Brown, *Ultimate Concern*, 114–24.

70. Tillich, *Courage to Be*, 154.

and solely on God, who is experienced in a unique and personal encounter. The courage of the Reformation transcends both the courage to be a part and the courage to be as oneself. It is threatened neither by the loss of oneself nor by the loss of one's world."[71]

What may be noted further is that the Divine-human encounter providing the courage of confidence empowers the individual to accept the acceptance of God in spite of the individual's guilt. Therefore, justification through faith which is "accepting acceptance though being unacceptable is the basis for the courage of confidence."[72] For Tillich, "it is the *paradoxical* act in which one is accepted by that which infinitely transcends one's individual self.[73] Hence, the Reformers experienced the acceptance of the unacceptable sinner into judging and transforming communion with God."[74] The idea also concurs with the destiny of the Christian which is divinely transformed into an eschatological hope.[75] Again, in the bid to have the existential courage "to take meaninglessness into itself pre-supposes a relation to the ground of being which we have called 'absolute faith.'"[76]

Tillich demonstrates that the "content of absolute faith is the 'God above God.'"[77] The meaning is that absolute faith which takes into itself, the doubt of God can only be by transcending the theistic idea of God. The courage to be is simply based upon the encounter between an individual who is a being against non-being and God who is beyond being.[78]

In other words:

> Paradox is essential for considering the meaning of "Christ" as the bearer of the New Being in his relation to God, [humanity], and the universe . . . they are the result of an existential interpretation of both *pre-Christian* ideas and their criticism and fulfilment in Jesus as the Christ. This corresponds to the method of correlation, in which questions and answers determine each other, and the question about the manifestation of the New Being is asked both on the basis of the human

71. Tillich, *Courage to Be*, 154–55.
72. Tillich, *Courage to Be*, 156.
73. Tillich, *Systematic Theology*, 1:150–53.
74. Tillich, *Courage to Be*, 156.
75. Tillich, *Courage to Be*, 158–62.
76. Tillich, *Courage to Be*, 172.
77. Tillich, *Courage to Be*, 172.
78. Tillich, *Courage to Be*, 172–80.

predicament and in the light of the answer which is accepted as the answer of Christianity.[79]

Therefore, Jesus Christ is the Mediator, bearing in mind that he is the Son of God but fully God and fully human; and by destiny discharging the duties of reconciling humanity to God as assigned by the Father. Moreover, strictly speaking it is God who asks humankind to be reconciled to God, and God effects the same through Christ's work (in the power of the Divine Spirit).[80] Therefore, the work of Christ is accomplished through another paradox called the incarnation (objective revelation). It is a paradox of the Christian message because God became human.[81]

Pragmatically (subjective revelation), and as may be expressed in African Christianity (e.g., bishop Oyedepo's story) the presence of faith and love are elements or features of the working power of the Divine Presence or the Divine Spirit in the human.[82] Faith and love are not separable. Faith is "the state of being grasped by the transcendent unity of the unambiguous life-it embodies love as the state of being taken into that transcendent unity."[83] Precisely, Bishop Oyedepo concurs when he makes the following remarks regarding faith and love:

> The Holy Spirit injects the love of God into [people's] hearts. Love is what determines your access to revelation, as well as the level you enjoy; . . . Love is the platform on which the laws and commandments function. When it is out of place, don't expect scriptures you have accumulated to produce.
>
> This means that the love of God cannot be acquired through human means. It is the ministry of the Holy Ghost to inject love into the hearts of men; otherwise, it will be mechanical, out of duress, by force and out of necessity, not willingly. By this act of the Holy Ghost, you come into the covenant fulfilment of Matthew 6:33. . . . What can be more comfortable than to have all the things that men are struggling for added to you just because the love of God is supreme in your heart? It is this kind of love— a gift from the Holy Ghost that prompted Paul to ask, "What shall separate us from the love of God?"

---

79. Tillich, *Systematic Theology*, 2:93.
80. Tillich, *Systematic Theology*, 2:93.
81. Tillich, *Systematic Theology*, 2:93–94; Tillich, *Eternal Now*, 115–21.
82. Tillich, *Eternal Now*, 89–91.
83. Tillich, *Systematic Theology*, 3:129.

> There is a way you love God that blinds you totally to your needs and circumstances. I met one of our daughters in Canada some time ago, and she tried to cast my mind back to our early days in ministry. She said, "I know how much you suffered when this church was starting." It sounded like news to me, because I did not know that I suffered at all. Me suffer? I couldn't see what I went through as suffering. . . .
>
> However, I couldn't see those contrary circumstances, because there was something driving me on the inside. I would so often kneel down and thank God for giving me the privilege of serving as a worker in his vineyard. Until this daughter of mine mentioned it, I didn't know that I went through such "hardness." The Lord told me that it was because of the love I have for Him.
>
> The Love of God in the heart is a bedrock; and it is a gift from the Holy Ghost. The Bible talks about "faith which worketh by love" (Galatians 5:6) This means that whatever you speak, believe or act, without love it is futile; and when faith fails to work, it results in frustration.[84]

Accordingly, paradox is attested when the power (Holy Spirit) of the *Okpelejen* (Symbol of God the Father, Feminine Monarch)[85] is activated in the *Okpelejen Wulormor* (Symbol of Christ) through the Christian message thereby producing faith and love in the human person. It gives the power of confidence to labor or suffer with Christ freely and faithfully without regrets.

The Significance of Kpelelogical Paradox in Formulating Contemporary African Christian Theology

On one hand, it is quite obvious in Africa that women are the majority of those frequenting prayer camps seeking solutions for various reasons. These women may also not pay attention to the fact that their real needs could be met by various professionals, including medical doctors, psychiatrists, teachers, and politicians. Their frequent movements in droves to spiritual healing centers as well as prophetic ministries seem to be

---

84. Oyedepo, *Anointing for Exploits*, 61–63.

85. The use of the symbolic language of Paul Tillich accommodates feminist positions of both the fatherhood and the motherhood of God. In the Ga religious institution, the paradoxical symbolism of *Ataa Naa Nyonmor* projects the fatherhood and motherhood respectively of God unlike the implicit Tillichian symbol of God which is the ground of being.

fueled by church leaders who may be oblivious of the connection between faith and professional skill or expertise. The question is, how can African Christian theology address this lack of good balancing between spiritual and secular knowledge and their "powers" in addressing the African predicament?

On the other hand, it may be borne in mind that the context of the population of Africa within which the early theological issues emerged has changed. The population of Africa today has increased tremendously and is more educated. The advancement of Information and Communication Technology (ICT) coupled with growing economies has exposed Africans to the wider world.[86] And it has also led to a growing young middle-class population. It should also be borne in mind that the secularization and formalization of African life over time may douse the holistic worldview or fragment it gradually. Moreover, it is highly important to notice that Western culture once harmonized all the realities but lost it.[87]

Meanwhile, J. Kwabena Asamoah-Gyadu has shown how African spirituality permeates the "multidimensional reality" of African life.[88] What then is the future of African Christianity if increasingly, the distorted and extreme African religiosity on one hand, and the growing secularism among middle-class Africans on the other hand, pull each other apart?

If African church fathers such as Origen and Tertullian endeavored to answer the questions of their time and they were highly successful, Africans of today can do no less. The answer to the question of the relevance of religion or Christianity to the multifaceted life of Africans ought to be addressed by shaping the way Africans utilize their gift of a worldview (kpelelogy/Kpelelogy) that harmonizes all realities through religion. How is this reality possible and how is this reality articulated in African Christian works, such that it can facilitate the attempt to answer the questions of Africans regarding their predicament?

This brings our attention to the need for African Christian theology to engage all realities multidimensionally.[89] Consequently, it may be

---

86. African Development Bank, "Middle of the Pyramid"; Jackson, "Africa's Many Middle Class"; Chimhanzi and Gounden, "Deloitte on Africa."

87. Amarkwei, *Paul Tillich*, 82–111.

88. Asamoah-Gyadu, "Christianity and Sports," 239–59; Asamoah-Gyadu, "Therapeutic Strategies," 70–90; Asamoah-Gyadu, "Religious Pluralsim," 238–44; Frederiks, "Congruency, Conflict or Dialogue," 123–34.

89. Tillich, *Systematic Theology*, 3:20–24.

worthy to state that the emerging issues of theology today ought to be additions to the existing *cultura-libero*[90] African Christian theology—an amalgamation of the inculturation and liberation dichotomy. The amalgamation of inculturation and liberation African Christian theologies is a true reflection of the African primal worldview. The African primal worldview is Kpelelogical (all-encompassing in nature), and thus fundamentally paradoxical. And it is also fundamental in addressing the perennial issue of methodology[91] in African Christian theology at large.

Conclusion

In concluding this part of the book, we note that African Christian theology commits itself to Christian tradition and thus shares the same ideals of faith interpretation. There remain certain critical areas, including who qualifies to do African Christian theology. African theologians are called to engage more in relevant theological issues that affect church and society today.

Furthermore, in the discussion it is quite clear that insofar as the parameters for engaging in African Christian theology remain open, anyone who is grasped to do theology and irrespective of their origins may be welcome. Such a person ought to both enjoy and suffer what Africans go through; that is, they must be thoroughly immersed in the African reality. Apart from this, theologians elsewhere ought to have the boldness to share ideas with African theologians as a way of enhancing each other's theology. This will enable us to appreciate theology from different perspectives and its attending self-critique.

As a matter of principle, African primal worldview engenders a certain paradoxical frame of mind that helps to build faith and aid theological interpretation of Christian experience. The paradoxical frame of mind is seen in the testimonies and works of Origen, Tertullian, and Augustine. It is also seen as a Christian principle in contemporary African Christianity in the light of Bishop David Oyedepo's ministry and from the insights drawn from Paul Tillich's view of Christian paradox. The phenomenon may also have been captured by scholars of African Christianity such as Wariboko and Asamoah-Gyadu, howbeit indirectly.

---

90. This terminology is couched by this author to enhance the categorization of theologies in Africa.

91. Maluleke, "Half a Century," 4–23.

Thus, we realize that faith as an experience of the divine power of Christ is very important for African Christians, and thus has direct implication for being theological and doing theology in Africa. And understanding this mode of being theological and doing theology is embedded in the paradox of faith or the paradox of grace as a matter of principle. It must be said that these paradoxical modes of appreciating reality underlie the Christian faith. If so, then African Christian theology cannot ignore certain principles of tradition anymore. And the fear of certain Western theological views that may be presumed to be inimical to African theology should not even prevent theologians in Africa from engaging traditional theology, irrespective of its origins. Moreover, African theologians need to appreciate even the African roots of Western theology itself and redeem it in today's interpretation of the Christian faith in the context of Africa that exists not without the rest of the world.

Part 2 of the discussion follows from here; and there we will discuss the contemporary state of African Christian theology (chapter 3). Thereafter, the methods, criteria, and dichotomies for doing African Christian theology are examined (chapter 4). Finally, the essence of African Christianity theology being a derivative of the absolutely concrete in Africa viz-à-viz the absolutely universal is discussed (chapter 5).

Part 2

The Nature of Contemporary African Christian Theology

Introduction

IN PART 2, WE will focus on the nature of contemporary African Christian theology as in concrete examples of what theologians have done. And this part has three chapters.

Chapter 3 reviews African Christologies and evaluates them. It starts by examining the background of contemporary African Christian theology. It critically reviews contemporary African Christian theology that includes inculturation, liberation and *cultura-libero* and Kpelelogy. It is important to state that pursuant to the review, issues of critical concern including ultimate concern, contextual and ecclesiological identity and eschatological concerns and intercultural dialogue and the Trinitarian concerns and the Christ event will be critically engaged.

The critical engagement will show that Nyamiti's ancestral theology is important for African Christianity as a whole, and in particular the Roman Catholic Church in Africa. But since the African and the Roman Catholic milieu is the stage from which Nyamiti's theology is formed it seems to have ended there. As to the relevance of the theology of Nyamiti in meeting the needs of African Christianity in general, very little can be said. Finally, the chapter will look at the subject of the theology of African Christianity and its emphasis on ethnography. It will seek to understand ethnographical concerns in both African Christian theology and African Christianity in view of Kpelelogy.

In chapter 4, the methods, criteria, and the issue of dichotomies are discussed. Furthermore, the dichotomy of African Christian theology and theology of African Christianity are discussed. Then the African theological methods of identity/continuity and discontinuity, praxis and kerygma and phenomenology/narrative are also discussed. The Kpelelogical method and the method of correlation are also clarified. The criteria for doing theology is to ensure that African Christian theology stays true to its faith and stays relevant to needs of the church. It is also to ensure that it stays true to African communities and the world as a whole. Examples of the criteria explained are, Trinitarian explication, eschatological explication, ecclesiological identity and relevance, contextuality and intercultural capacity.

In addition, the concerning matter of African Christian theology's dichotomization into inculturation and liberation is raised and discussed. It emphasizes the point that an African Christian theology which is fundamentally Kpelelogical cannot be compartmentalized or dichotomized as it is found in contemporary African Christian theology. Moreover, the seeming confusion existing between African Christian theology and theology of African Christianity is critically appraised in view of a Kpelelogy.

Chapter 5 critiques African Christian theological endeavors in recent years that have placed academic priorities over those of faith. It also tackles the problem of essence by connecting Kpelelogy and the kpelelogy of African Christian theology in view of the *Logos* and the *logoi* connection. It finally raises the question as to whether there is any proper sense of meaning in theology if it concerns itself with the particular without any universal connection or if it does not concern itself with the concrete.

I have introduced the *Okpelejen Wulormor* as a theology which addresses the critical issues of methodology and criteria which seem to have bedeviled the theological enterprise in Africa. It is a Kpelelogical way of affirming the threefold office of Jesus Christ posited by both African Christology and Christian heritage.

3

Contemporary African Christian Theology

The Kpelelogical and Kpelelogical Background of Contemporary African Christian Theology

THERE ARE TWO MAJOR strands of thought regarding the background of African Christian theology. The first strand is the kpelelogical being, upon one hand and the second strand, the Kpelelogical being, upon the other hand. The kpelelogical mind is the one which acts constantly as the *preparatio evangelica*, and which is, first, rejected by the gospel by the advent of the Kpelelogical mind paradoxically because, second, it is accepted, transformed, and utilized by the One who is *Kpetenkplele* or *Okpelejen* (The all-encompassing one who is beyond us) for the redemption of the cosmos including Africa on earth. It is represented by the African Traditional Religion (ATR) which encapsulates the African worldview as described by some scholars. The focus on this strand will emerge when we discuss the sources of contemporary African Christian theology.

Nonetheless, it is important to mention the significance of African traditional religious conscience (kpelelogy) which led to the political, religious, cultural, social, and economic assertion of the African peoples. These holistic self-assertion of African people may be found in the various wars, conflicts and uprisings against the colonialists. In Ghana, many tribes, particularly the Ashantis, the Fantes, the Gas and Adangmes showed their sense of independence when culture, religion and social life were threatened. Adu Boahen had indicated how the indigenes of Africa were almost portrayed as people who did not participate in the struggle against colonial injustice. He wrote, "These views are clearly the products of the old colonial, or Eurocentric African historiography, which seeks to explain most events and developments in Africa in external terms, and in this case, in terms of the frustration of the foreign educated elite. But these views are totally erroneous."[1] Adu Boahen demonstrated how the various classes possessed ample awareness of African nationalism, or some sort of consciousness in three periods. The consciousness which he traced among the traditional people started from 1890 to about the end of the First World War, then from 1919 to 1935, and finally from 1935 to the 1960s.[2]

Boahen continued to show how the kpelelogical consciousness was aroused as it manifested itself in rebellion and insurrection.[3] These disturbances, stemming from the agitated kpelelogical conscience of the traditional African, as Boahen explained, were triggered by "either taxation, land alienation, compulsory cultivation of crops, tyrannical behavior of colonial officials, or the introduction of Western education and with it the condemnation of African culture and traditional ways of life."[4] The role of African traditional religion itself that engendered a kpelelogical being in Africans was also significant.[5]

The *Fante Amanbuhu Fekuw* (Fante National Political and Cultural Society) which was formed in 1888,[6] however, seemed to have been the earliest culmination of all the various self-assertions. And, the Fante Confederation's formation showed that the only way for the liberation of a religion and culture under siege was a self-assertion that was inevitably political. Adu Boahen suggested that the local contribution against colonial oppression was widespread on the African continent. And that includes the formation of the South African Native National Congress by Pixley Izaka Seme in 1910. Additionally, in 1907 local Egyptians led by Sheikh Ali Yusuf formed Hizb al-Islah al-Dusturi on one hand and a nationalist party led by Mustapha Kamil on the other hand. And in

---

1. Boahen, *Perspectives on Colonialism*, 62–63; see also Crowder, *West Africa*, 356–71; Diop, *Cultural Unity*, 356–71; Mudimbe, *Idea of Africa*, 1–37.
2. Boahen, *Perspectives on Colonialism*, 63.
3. Boahen, *Perspectives on Colonialism*, 64.
4. Boahen, *Perspectives on Colonialism*, 64–65.
5. Boahen, *Perspectives on Colonialism*, 64–65.
6. Boahen, *Perspectives on Colonialism*, 68.

Madagascar the North Ngasa Native Association in 1912 and Vvolvy Vata Sakelike were formed in 1912 and 1913, respectively.[7]

Another example whereby the kpelelogical conscience was aroused was when in 1942, the Presbyterian Church of the Gold Coast (PCGC) sent a theological response with Christian Gonçalves Kwami Baeta when existential questions regarding identity were raised by the State Council of Akyem Abuakwa.[8] Here, the quest to dialogue on the part of African traditional institutions with Christianity in Africa was a genuine search for identity. Moreover, Parson notes how the Akyem Abuakwa State Council had indicated the need of this mutuality in 1954.[9] A detailed response from the traditional council to the PCGC showed that Christians should have nothing to do with *abosom* (*wojii/ Jemanworjii*) to which the church agreed. However, the church was silent on *sumai* and *samanfo*.[10] As an example, the above represents the kpelelogical background for contemporary African Christian theology.

Having dealt with the kpelelogical background, we turn now to look at those Christian activities or those activities that emerged out of the Kpelelogical African experience to see how they form the background of African Christian theology.

The Kpelelogical African experience is based upon the subjective and objective revelation of the triune God to the African Christian. And knowing that this is not without the registered holistic experience of the African in the mind, illumination activates a conscience that sees the African predicament in the perspective of Christian truth. Obviously, it might have led to the "theological independence movement" or the Africanization of the Christian enterprise. The material and political corollary is what Kwame Nkrumah describes in his *Consciencism*.[11] Nkrumah's words below, even if political, carried at least the impetus, essentially, for the African Christian theological enterprise.

> The history of Africa, as presented by European scholars, has been encumbered with malicious myths. It was even denied that we were a historical people. It was said that whereas other continents had shaped history, and determined its course, Africa

---

7. Boahen, *Perspectives on Colonialism*, 71–72.

8. Parsons, *Churches and Ghana Society*, 29–30.

9. Address of Welcome by Nana Ofori Atta II to the Synod of the Presbyterian Church in the Gold Coast, 1954, 4–6, in Parsons, *Churches and Ghana Society*, 30–31.

10. Parsons, *Churches and Ghana Society*, 29–31.

11. Nkrumah, *Consciencism*.

had stood still, held down by inertia; that Africa was only propelled into history by the European contact. African history was therefore presented as an extension of European history. Hegel's authority was lent to this a-historical hypothesis concerning Africa, which he himself unhappily helped to promote. And apologists of colonialism lost little time in seizing upon it and writing wildly thereon. In presenting the history of Africa as the history of the collapse of our traditional societies in the presence of the European advent, colonialism and imperialism employed their account of African history and anthropology as an instrument of their oppressive ideology.

Earlier on, such disparaging accounts had been given of African society and culture as to appear to justify slave trade and slavery, posed against these accounts, seemed a positive deliverance of our ancestors. When the slave trade and slavery became illegal, the experts on Africa yielded to the new wind of change, and now began to present African culture and society as being so rudimentary and primitive that colonialism was a duty of Christianity and civilization. Even if we were no longer, on the evidence of the shape of our skulls, regarded as the missing link, unblessed with the arts of good government, material and spiritual progress, we were still regarded as representing the infancy of humankind. Our highly sophisticated culture was said to be simple and paralysed by inertia, and we had to be encumbered with tutelage. And this tutelage, it was thought, could only be implemented if we were first subjugated politically.[12]

Like Nkrumah, Cheikh Anta Diop, the physicist and the great African archeologist, has demonstrated how the history of Africa was distorted by European archeologists and historians.[13] Moreover, Diop underlines the point that if Greek metaphysics has a lot to give to modern science, so should reference to Egypt ought to be that important to todays African in all the sciences.[14] The point here is that Africa has every right to expose the falsehood associated with the Europeans who told the story of Africans to the world.

Therefore, what Emmanuel Martey describes as Africanization in the mid-'20s of the twentieth century stemming from Governor Guggisberg may have appropriately been occasioned by resistance against colonialism and missionary Westernization or secularization by some

12. Nkrumah, *Consciencism*, 62–63.
13. See Diop, *Civilization or Barbarism*, 11–24, 33–68.
14. Diop, *Civilization or Barbarism*, 309.

African elites or Christians.[15] The Gold Coast Aborigines' Rights Protection Society (ARPS) founded in 1897 laid the foundation for the Africanization project. The Christian elite included J. W. de Graft-Johnson, Jacob Wilson Sey, J. P. Brown, J. E. Casely Hayford, and John Mensah Sarbah (cofounders), and then other prominent leaders in the persons of Rev. J. B. Anaman and Kobina Sekyi.[16] Incidentally, the formation of the ARPS led to the founding of Mfantsipim School in Cape Coast as the first secondary school in Ghana. This society was to influence Ephraim Amu as a Christian Nationalist. In the 1920s, Amu composed *Yen ara Asase ni* (This Is Our Native Land), which became the "second national anthem" in postcolonial Ghana. President Nkrumah is said to have made up his mind to honor him but for "certain extenuating circumstances."[17]

There is therefore no doubt that the consciousness aroused in some African Christians after the *Kpelelogical* encounter[18] might have percolated political realms as well as the philosophical realms by the self-assertion of African arts and culture.

In spite of the above, however, the *kpelelogical* resistances cannot be ignored at all, since it has the capacity to recognize dehumanization and injustice. It should be recalled that the ARPS consisted of two groups, first, by traditional leaders, and second, by the elite. The contribution of the traditional leaders as *kpelelogy* means that they might certainly have had their consciences aroused to challenge the undignified manner their peoples were treated. In the long run, the background of contemporary African theology is a melting pot of both *kpelelogical* and *Kpelelogical* realities that rose up against anything that sought to demean or douse African dignity and life. This *Kpelelogical* consciousness,[19] whose ideological corollary may be "Consciencism," resulted in a holistic (political, philosophical, sociological, psychological, and moral) assertion of Africans, and reflected itself in their creative arts and entertainment.[20]

---

15. Martey, *African Theology*, 63–65; Laryea, *Ephraim Amu*, vii, 17–26.

16. Laryea, *Ephraim Amu*, 17–18.

17. Laryea, *Ephraim Amu*, vii.

18. Kamau-Goro, "Rejection or Reappropriation?," 67–83; Nkrumah, *Consciencism*, 70; he talks about the "idea of the accountability of the individual conscience introduced by the Christian religion."

19. Laryea, *Ephraim Amu*, 1–4, 25; see also Williams, *Achimota*, 21; Laryea, *Ephraim Amu*, 25.

20. Laryea, *Ephraim Amu*, 28–43.

The difference between *Kpelelogical* consciousness and Consciencism as portrayed by Nkrumah and other theologians such as Pobee and Laryea may be the starting point.[21] The starting point for *Kpelelogical* consciousness is the divine revelation of the triune God through Jesus Christ.[22] And the starting point for Consciencism is scientific materialism. Consciencism is, however, neither *kpelelogical* nor *Kpelelogical*, because, first, it fails to acknowledge spirit as the primary essence of being and matter; and second, sees matter as the primary reality of existence and spirit as secondary.

The African *Kpelelogical* consciousness may have two main strands. The first is the one that may be associated with the advent of the Europeans into Africa. And the second may be associated with the African Independent Churches (AICs).[23] The former began with the arrival of the Europeans, including the missionaries on the continent of Africa. Their arrival brought chaplains, who together with certain governors, sought to teach and preach the gospel first to the mulattoes and second to the indigenous people. This work led to the attempt by many chaplains to translate certain liturgical and biblical texts into the local languages.[24] Any *Kpelelogical* endeavor, moreover, ought to proceed with the translations of biblical texts, as it interprets the person and work of Jesus Christ according to the local context. Hence, the religio-cultural milieu as well as the socioeconomic and political situations and languages of the time may have been employed. In the Gold Coast, Philip Laryea writes how the missionaries used the "conservative contextual" language to identify the person and work of Jesus Christ.[25]

Nonetheless, it is important to recognize the efforts of many African theologians, such as Kimpa Vita, a young lady noted to be the first black theologian in the eighteenth century, and other grassroots theologians, like Afua Kuma, who may be unnoticed.[26]

And here, mention must be made of those that predated the works of early contemporary philosophical works in Africa. For example, the

---

21. Nkrumah, *Consciencism*; Pobee, *Kwame Nkrumah*, 118; Laryea, *Ephraim Amu*, 34.

22. Laryea, *Ephraim Amu*, 25–26.

23. Akinade "African Christianity in the Twentieth Century," 343–55.

24. Reindorf, *History of the Gold Coast*, 217–22; Ekem, *Early Scriptures*.

25. Laryea, *Yesu Homowor Nuntsor*, 24–126.

26. Bosch, "Converts and Cross-Currents," 1–22; Parratt, *Reinventing Christianity*, 4; Kuma, *Kwaebirentuw Ase Yesu*.

earlier works of Edward Wilmot Blyden, "who attempted to articulate the differences between Africans and Europeans in terms of the former's 'personality.'"[27] Blyden's works include *Liberia's Offering* (1862), *Liberia: Past, Present and Future* (1869), *Christianity, Islam and the Negro Race* (London, 1888; new ed., Edinburgh University Press, 1967), *Africa and Africans* (1903), and *Selected Letters of Edward Wilmot Blyden*, edited by Hollis R. Lynch (New York: KTO, 1978). Kwame Bediako also identifies Blyden as one who seemed to have influenced many Africans home and abroad. He however, indicates that these works and actions instigated by Blyden among others was to deal with the problem of identity.[28]

Therefore, the main problem of African theology was identity. This is understood when the three Cs (Commerce, Civilization, and Christianization) policy of the European missionaries, shown by Lamin Sanneh and John Parrat, for example, are examined.[29] The Christians in Africa saw the negative side of Christianity in the light of the threat the same religion posed to their being and dignity. When civilization in Christianity meant to obliterate and denigrate the being of Africanness, African's realized there ought to be a way out. And the way out was to deal with the "secularization" of African people knowing they were highly spiritual people. David Barrett emphasizes the point when he noted that reasons for the agitation in the churches stemmed from "serious discrepancies between missions and biblical religion in connection with the [African] traditional institutions under attack."[30]

Africans wanted to *realize themselves in essence through the transforming power of the Christian message*. And it is this search for their identity in the triune God that must inspire African Christian theology today. In spite of the favorable and unfavorable sentiments about the missionaries,[31] Africans seem to agree to a large extent and as a matter of principle on the issue of identity as a theological enterprise.

Furthermore, it may be realized in the work of Lucius Outlaw that Pan-Africanism among other identity issues played a crucial role in heightening awareness for the total independence of the African when he stated:

27. Outlaw, "African, African American, Africana Philosophy," 25–39.
28. Bediako, *Christianity in Africa*, 5–6; Bediako, *Theology and Identity*.
29. Sanneh, *Translating the Message*, 105–17; Parratt, *Reinventing Christianity*, 3.
30. Barrett, *Schism and Renewal in Africa*, 268; Hastings, *Church in Africa*, 499–513, 525–33.
31. Parsons, *Churches and Ghana Society*, 23–25.

Pan-Africanism was an organized ideological and political tradtion and movement that emerged in the late 1800s, at the instigation of Henry Sylvester Williams, a Trinidadian lawyer, and, later, W. E. B. DuBois, African-American activist scholar and champion par excellence of the interests of Africans and people of African descent. The principal manifestations of the tradition were a series of conferences (London, 1900) and congresses (Paris, 1919: London-Brussels, 1921, London-Lisbon, 1923; New York, 1927; Manchester, 1945; and Dar es Salaam, Tanzania, 1974—the first Pan-African congress to be held on the continent of Africa), which called upon Africans and peoples of African descent world wide (hence pan-African) to join together in an organized European colonialism, and to free African peoples everywhere from domination and the invidious discrimination of racism.[32]

It should be said that concurrently, there were other movements such as the 1912 African National Congress by black Christian leaders against Apartheid that had support from the Dutch Reformed Church.[33] At the time, the Kpelelogical mind of the African within that context, may have been an agitated conscience. This was fueled by the great work of the Lutheran Sol Plaatje titled *Native Life in South Africa* (1913). The book sought to criticize the Land Act which in effect made it impossible for natives to own about 90 percent of South African land.[34] The role of Anglican bishops and priests, including Bishop Ambrose Reeves (South Africa), Tamu Calata (South Africa), and Fr. Theophilus Hmutumpangela (Namibia, 1934), cannot be overemphasized.[35]

This move in southern Africa may have culminated in the black consciousness movement with Steve Biko in the 1960s.[36] This developments presented the theological context for Southern Africa, a matter of identity which is rooted in politics and socioeconomic issues.

In another space, there were many frantic efforts on the part of the World Council of Churches (WCC) to ensure that churches were independent as possible. Mention is made of the contributions of Visser't

---

32. Geiss, *Pan-African Movement*; Outlaw, "African, African American, Africana Philosohy," 39.

33 Ward, "African Christianity in the Twentieth Century—Part Two," 364–65.

34. Ward, "African Christianity in the Twentieth Century—Part Two," 364–65.

35. Ward, "African Christianity in the Twentieth Century—Part Two," 366–67.

36. Martey, *African Theology*, 7–27; Ward, "African Christianity in the Twentieth Century—Part Two," 367–72.

Hooft and Bishop Bell of Chichester, Canon Charles Raven, Pastor Niemollar with theologians such as Barth, Tillich and Kraemer. In addition, Adrian Hastings takes particular note of J. H. Oldham, who was the first editor of the *International Review of Missions* and author of *Christianity and the Race Problem* (1924).[37] It should be understandable that the contributions of these luminaries might have gone a long way to facilitate the Africanization of the Christian faith. Oldham was noted to be very well acquainted with world Christianity in many ways since he also was the secretary to the World Missionary Conference (WMC). The impact of Oldham was felt the more when he made James Aggrey a member of the Phelps Stokes Education Commission. Aggrey's role and presence as a black African on both the committee and in the World Council of Churches (WCC) was far and wide.[38] And in all of this, the catalytic role of the World War cannot go without a mention.[39]

In 1926, the World Missionary Conference was held in Le Zoute to address pertinent issues affecting the missionary work outside of the Western world. These concerning issues pertain to the tension that existed between the African peoples and the missionaries because the Africans were considered not fully human or civilized and at best possessed only a *tabula rasa*. Africans thus started posing resistance to the missions of the Western church.[40] Therefore, at Le Zoute, the missionaries deliberated on the "approach" to mission in Africa. Moreover, it was clear in the meeting that missionary approaches should let the gospel become incarnated in the local material as much as possible. They indicated that the African possessed the Logos structure of the mind (*Kpelelogical mind*). Kraemer noted:

> The Gospel is the fulfilment of that towards which the African groped in the past, for the Divine Logos who lighteth every human being has shone in the souls of Africans; hence no destruction but a systematic use of the African heritage is demanded. The life of the African being essentially social, while based upon tribal conditions and apprehensions, everything good in the African heritage should be conserved, enriched and ennobled by contract with the Spirit of Christ.[41]

37. Hastings, *History of Christianity*, 41–42.
38. Ward, "African Christianity in the Twentieth Century—Part Two," 357.
39. Ward, "African Christianity in the Twentieth Century—Part Two," 356–72.
40. Kraemer, *Christian Message*, 338.
41. Kraemer, *Christian Message*, 338.

While the above approach was adopted for engaging Africans in Christian Missions, yet, there were others who strongly disagreed. For example, H. Kraemer indicated his strong disagreement with Le Zoute by insisting that Africans ought to be brought up because there was nothing essentially good about them. Moreover, he felt that the Christian message should have an upper hand in those non-Christian nations.[42]

In 1932, Freidrich Hegel wrote that "Africa is no historical part of the world, it has no movement or development to exhibit."[43] Hugh Trevor Roper also said, "There is only the history of Europeans in Africa. The rest is darkness."[44] Sadly, the early Thomas Hodgkin who worked for the Nkrumah government thought initially that the Gold Coast was "a country with no past and no history—and no present either—only perhaps a promising future—and that at a kindergarten level."[45] There is no doubt that these false and derogatory statements about Africa provoked Africans to rise to the occasion to give a true account of themselves.[46] Thus, it is fair-minded to understand why the advent of major theological works in the late sixties was preceded by the proliferation of ethno-philosophy, philosophic sagacity, and professional philosophy in general and nationalistic/ideological philosophies.[47]

Thus, one cannot appreciate more the Flemish Franciscan, Placid Tempels's publication, *Bantu Philosophy* in 1945. "On the continent of Africa, the publication in 1945 of Placide Tempel's *La Philosophie Bantoue*, one of the earliest and most influential explicit acknowledgements of African intellectual efforts and achievements as philosophy, marks the initiation of contemporary discussions of African philosophy."[48] Outlaw brings further clarity when he succinctly wrote:

> Emerging during the apex of European colonization in Africa, the discussion, both in form and content, was shaped by this context, and no less so by subsequent anticolonial stuggles. The focus of the discussion was whether African peoples could have or do philosophy. But this was only the surface issue. The

---

42. Kraemer, *Christian Message*, 338.
43. Wolfers, "Thomas Hodgkin," 95–105.
44. Wolfers, "Thomas Hodgkin," 95–105.
45. Wolfers, "Thomas Hodgkin," 951–55.
46. Awoonor, *African Predicament*, 91–93; Nkrumah, *Consciencism*, 62–63; Diop, "Africa," 3–10; Sertima, "Lost Sciences of Africa," 305–30.
47. Oruka, "Four Trends," 13–22.
48. Outlaw, "African, African American, Africana," 24.

deeper and more pressing question was whether Africans were fully human as defined by the reigning Greek-cum-European philosophical-anthroplogical paradigm centered around the notion of "rationality."[49]

It may be noteworthy to acknowledge Placide Tempel's efforts in the *Jamaa* (family) movement which was to propagate the strong position that the African is capable of managing his own affairs.[50] These concepts in African Traditional Religion (ATR) and the natural development and growth of the African society may have influenced to some extent the theological works which followed. For example, it has been suggested that the philosophical work of Alexis Kagame on the ancestors might have influenced some later theologians.[51]

What about the contributions of other African authors such as Chinua Achebe's *Things Fall Apart*?[52] And what can we say about other literary authors such as Ayi Kwei Armah and Ngugi wa Thiongó who shaped and inspired many Africans in the sixties?[53] Obviously, these questions bring to mind, the context of the African liberation struggle and the aftermath as being so inundated in issues that aroused the conscience to reflect on Christianity as an African life. No one even knows the extent to which African theologians were influenced by the songs of the Reggae musician—Robert Marley.

The second *Kpelelogical* consciousness arousing interests in contemporary African Christian theology was the African Independent Prophets (AIPs) and African Initiated Churches (AICs). Perhaps, it may be important to pay glowing tribute to the efforts of AIPs who also raised issues of Africanization by their words and deeds.[54] Garrick Sokari Braide (1882–1918) in the Niger Delta was highly endowed with the power of prayer, preaching, and healing.[55] Prophet William Wade Harris (1860–1929) had the power to convert towns and villages steeped in fetish beliefs into the Christian faith.[56] He had enormous powers to

---

49. Outlaw, "African, African American, Africana," 24.

50. Hastings, *History of African Christianity*, 42.

51. Kagabo, "Alexis Kagame," 13–44, 36–37.

52 Achebe, *Things Fall Apart*.

53. For the role of literary writers, see Jenkins, *Next Christendom*, 40–45; Kamau-Goro, "Rejection or Reappropriation?," 67–83.

54. Sanneh, *Disciples of All Nations*, 189.

55. Sanneh, *Disciples of All Nations*, 189.

56. Sanneh, *Disciples of All Nations*, 197.

punish those he felt were impedances to his mission while operating in the Gambia, Liberia, and Ivory Coast and Ghana.

Particularly, these prophets had their missions clearly cut out uniquely to break down the barriers in missions that may have stymied the work of the European missionaries. It has to be further noted that these prophets were more ecumenical in their approach than the European missionaries as they instructed their converts to go to the missions to be taught and nurtured. Their spiritual authority enabled them to deal with the churches in their own terms. Their authority did not reside in the church as in an institution, rather it laid in their peculiar calling and mission. In other words, they embodied the authority and power with which they worked. These characteristics resonated with the African worldview of traditional priests, healers and prophets. Hence, they represented a genuine African and Christian mission that resulted in converting many unbelieving African people into Christianity. It was the concrete expression of the African Christian that Christianity may flourish the more in Africa, if African faith is understood, acted on and interpreted from an African point of view.

In East Africa, there was the Balokole (Saved People) Movement in the 1930s, led by Simeoni Nsibambi.[57] In Nigeria was Joseph Ayo Babalola (d. 1959), who led the Aladura Church with massive impact on the whole of Nigerian Christianity.[58] Babalola was gifted with powers to heal, preach, and to do mighty things. The advent of the AICs in Africa opened the eyes of the Historic Missionary churches to the concrete reality of Christ in Africa without depending on others such as missionaries from Europe. The feat of the AICs particularly in getting towns and villages that were difficult areas for the missionaries to convert to Christ could not be glossed over. Moreover, the fact that these works of the AICs were done without any assistance from the Historic Missionary churches spoke volumes and continues to speak today. Again, knowing that the AICs did not employ Western theology, Western idea or action, but rather created and deployed their independent grassroots theology, ethics, homiletics, liturgy, vestments, songs and dances proved that inner presence of *Kpelelogical* consciousness aroused at the revelation of Christ in the power of the Holy Spirit. The interesting issue about the independence of the AICs

---

57. Ward, "African Christianity in the Twentieth Century—Part Two," 360–61.

58. Sanneh, *Disciples of All Nations*, 187–215.

was the high success rate of their theological creations in the totality of Christian worship.

Moreover, some prominent African Christian scholars have attested that the titles of Jesus given by the AICs are readily accepted and appropriated by worshippers.[59] Therefore, the engagement of the AICs as a rich source of doing African Christian theology has been overwhelmingly welcomed. Emmanuel Martey says:

> [For example, Mveng approaches these churches as a theological locus:[60] and for Bonganjalo Goba, they not only provide "raw data for theological reflection," they should also be regarded as a point of departure for black theological reflection.[61] For Fashole-Luke, it is necessary to bring the AICs into theological focus because their innovative insights will not merely contribute toward the development of African theology, they will also prevent African theology from "becoming sterile academic exercises divorced from the life situation of Africa" and from becoming a product only fit for Western consumption.[62] According to Muzorewa, the reason for considering the phenomenon as dependable source for defining African theology is contained not merely in the fact that "it draws most of its insights from traditional religion and culture when it indigenizes the faith." but it is as well informed by "both the needs of the African soul and the Scriptures."[63]][64]

Kpelelogical consciousness in both Historic Missionary Christianity as well as those of the AICs may form a crucial underlying motivation for the African Christian theology "movement." Thus, both *Kpelelogical* consciousness have contributed immensely and should continue to contribute meaningfully to the development of African theology. The African mind was ready to do its own reflections.

Nonetheless, John S. Mbiti lamented the situation where the African, as of 1967, had no African systematic theological identity stemming from

---

59. Omenyo, "Charismatic Churches," 266–68; Kalu, *Power, Poverty and Prayer*, 105; Haar, "Standing Up for Jesus"; Akrong, "Salvation in African Christianity," 23.

60. Martey, *African Theology*, 76.

61. Goba, *Agenda for Black Theology*, 76.

62. Fashole-Luke, "Footpaths and Signposts," 401; Martey, *African Theology*, 76.

63. Muzorewa, "Definition of a Future African Theology," 171, in Martey, *African Theology*, 76; Mazorewa, *Origin and Development of African Theology*, 35.

64. Martey, *African Theology*, 76.

the African tradition and culture.[65] Aylward Shorter also lamented that pure African Christologies have yet to bloom.[66] However, John Parratt identified some developments within the theological circles of Africa.[67] He mentions, first of all, Desmond Tutu in 1978 declaring that African theology was inevitable insofar as Western theology "was scratching were it was not itching."[68] In other words, for Tutu, what Western theologians sought to do in their theology did not directly address pertinent issues bedevilling African peoples. Parratt identified the second development to be the position held by Englebert Mveng in 1982 bemoaning that Western theology did not dialogue with African theology.[69] And then third, Parratt makes a point about the efforts of Kwame Bediako to relate African theology to the question of identity in the early centuries of the church's existence.[70] In this trajectory, Parratt gives us an appreciation of the direction of contemporary African Christian theology today.

After a period one sees other developments that seem to divide African theological discourse into different parts. Following the trajectory of Bediako in terms of critically engaging early Christian writings (tradition) on identity, there seemed to have been an emergence of translating the gospel in the process. The translation paradigm has a strong base with Lamin Sanneh, and in particular English World Christianity scholars.[71] The result was the mother tongue theology and now ethnography. This trajectory or school of thought is growing rapidly in the whole of Africa but of particular interest is Ghana.

Perhaps concurrently, there seems to be another trajectory within the southern part of Africa which thrives on theologies that respond to developmental needs of the African people. In doing this variant of theology, there is a craving for African theology to provide solutions to the

---

65. Mbiti, "Some African Concepts of Christology," 51; Moloney, "African Christology," 505.

66. Moloney, "African Christology," 505; Mugabe, "Christology in African Context," 343.

67. Parratt, *Reinventing Christianity*, 2.

68. Tutu, *Voice of One Crying in the Wilderness*, 1–22.

69. Mveng, "Only a Monologue of the Poor" 72–75; Parratt, *Reinventing Christianity*, 1–22.

70. Bediako, *Theology and Identity*. Parrat, *Reinventing Christianity*, 1–22.

71 Walls, *Missionary Movement in Christian History*, 27–28; Sanneh, *Translating the Message*.

myriad problems of African societies.⁷² This kind of theology, i.e., *assuming it is not utopia*, certainly is more development based and holistic and seems to be very relevant to the needs of growing African churches. It does not lose sight of the initial issue of identity which has ramifications on race and politics.

Certainly, moving forward, African Christian theology needs to sit back and do self-reflection. Again, looking at the trajectories, there seems to be some lopsidedness in paying attention to the African predicament. If African Christian theology is holistic in nature, then all trajectories need to give equal attention to all the individual issues that make up the spectrum of the African ontological predicament. And the aim of this introductory work is to point to, as well as present, the holistic dimension of African theology in a Kpelelogical theology of Africa.

In the discussion below, an exploration of the nature of contemporary African Christian theology is pursued. The two main types of African Christologies, as inculturation and liberation, are critically engaged.⁷³ And in addition to the two types above, a *cultura-libero* type is also identified and discussed. The whole discussion culminates in *Kpelelogy* as the African Christian sense of interpreting the Christian experience and the Christian message in its past, present, and future contexts. And particularly in doing this, the essence of *Kpelelogy* is advanced as it is juxtaposed with ethnography.

Inculturation Christologies

Generally, inculturation Christologies base the identity of the person and work of Jesus Christ on the religio-cultural context of the African community.⁷⁴ Within specific ethnic groups, there are various religious and cultural situations which may find congruity with biblical theology and church traditions and it is the interaction between the two that constructs the inculturation Christologies. These Christologies include: Christ as Victor, Christ in Kingship, Jesus as Master of Initiation, Jesus as Healer, and Jesus as the Ancestor. Inculturation Christologies attempt to clarify the essence of African religion and culture. And in so doing, the negative conceptions surrounding the religion is done away with.

---

72. Benkes and van Huffel, "Towards a Theology of Development," 224–40.
73. Nyamiti, "African Christologies Today," 17; see also Martey, *African Theology*, 81.
74. Martey, *African Theology*, 81.

This notwithstanding the above, it also embarks upon a mission to challenge elements of the ATR that tend to prevent the flourishing of humanity and the whole of God's creation. This inculturationists do by using African categories to address the difficulties of the African person and the environment in which Africans live in the light of the work of Christ. It also aims at making African Christologies truly Christian and truly African so that the universality and the concreteness of Christianity is established. Also, it seeks to lead Africans to embrace Christianity as bona fide religion.

The problem with inculturation Christologies is that they lack the potency needed to address political and economic challenges in Africa which is also inevitable. This situation may be attributed to their main uses, which are limited to practical theology, Christian education, and biblical studies. In the coming discussion, some of the inculturation theological works as in the person of Jesus Christ's interpretation in Africa is looked at. The first to be discussed is "Christ as Victor.

Christ as Victor

Many Africans from the African viewpoint of ATR believe in a material but spiritual universe.[75] The spiritual universe is composed of spiritual beings, some benevolent, others malevolent. Any good in the community of the African is thus one which is orchestrated by the benevolent spirits, while any evil is perpetuated by the malevolent spirits.[76] The aim of the worship of benevolent spirits/deities, such as deities (Ga: *Jenmanwojii, Wojii*; Twi: *Abosom*) and the veneration of ancestors (Ga: *Sisai*; Twi: *Saman*), are to ensure that evil is defeated. Receiving blessing and protection from these deities and ancestors against evils such as witchcraft, sorcery, and war and calamities, are major reasons for African traditional worship.

Based upon these facts, John Samuel Mbiti might have been persuaded that for the African, Jesus the Christ is the Victor. Christ is the one who overcomes all forces of evil and even death. Therefore, the resurrection of Christ becomes the issue in the salvific event, which should be of major importance for the African. Charles Nyamiti makes the observation that "Mbiti discovers that the idea of *Christus victor* (Miracle worker and risen Lord) is particularly relevant, for this Christ is the conqueror

---

75. Nkrumah, *Consciencism*, 1–29; Gyekye, *African Cultural Values*, 4.
76. Mbiti, *African Religions and Philosophy*.

of those evil powers (spirits, magic, disease, [and] death) feared by the African and is Guarantor of immortality."[77] The event before Easter exists to be shared by all, but for Mbiti, the crux of the matter is Easter, the resurrection.[78] The resurrection demonstrates that Jesus has conquered all the evil forces and has overcome death. This theme, although not emphasized by many theologians, is one of the main drivers for the AICs and the PCCs in Africa.[79]

It is important, nonetheless, to admit that first, this Christology fails to depict the role of the other issues in the Christ event, which form an essential part of the revelation of the triune God. Notably, the Pentecost, where the ministry of the Holy Spirit is very important, particularly in the African church. Further, Mbiti's Christ as Victor is presented to us without a Trinitarian explication, and the Trinity is necessary for every Christology. Second, such a Christology with emphasis on the victorious Christ is akin to Christology from above, which gives an erroneous impression to the effect that African Christologies may not arise from below. Thus, the weakness of Mbiti's Christology of Christ the Victor is that it is only partly representative of the holistic African christological reflections. The following questions exist: Where is the suffering Christ who identifies himself with the poor and oppressed Africans? And where is the redeeming Jesus who saves the whole of God's creation? This shortfall may be one of the warrants for exploring other Christologies, which may be representative of the holistic African Christologies.

Christ in African Kinship

African societies are made up of the extended family system. The extended family has a leader, but ultimately the chief is the father of all the people in the land. Reference to colonial abuse of the chief has made it a difficult category to use in African Christology.[80] Francois Kabasele indicates to us, however, that in the Bantu parish of *Luba*, where he undertook his study, Christ is seen as the Chief because he is the Anointed

---

77. Nyamiti, "African Christologies Today," 4.

78. Mugabe, "Christology in an African Context," 347; Mbiti "Some African Concepts of Christology," 57.

79. Omenyo, "Charismatic Churches in Ghana," 266–68; Kalu, *Power, Poverty and Prayer*, 105; Haar, "Standing Up for Jesus," 226; Akrong, "Salvation in African Christianity," 23.

80. Nyamiti, "African Christologies Today," 11.

One, *Mulaba*, and even *Luaba*, the Anointed One, who is the Chief for the present and the future (eschatological).[81] Christ is the Chief because he is *Cimankida* (Hero), *Cilobo*—"the hero who never flees before the enemy" and "*Kanda Kazadi*—one who wins victories, whom no one dares to confront."[82] Jesus the Chief is known as such because he is accepted as the Chief's Son, the Emissary, by the reason of generosity and reconciliatory abilities.[83]

The concern against the use of the Chief as typology in African Christian theology is due to the abuse of the office as a colonial tool of oppression.[84] Although John S. Pobee sees a Royal Priesthood from the Akan perspective as appropriate, he concludes by saying it fails to represent Christ, who suffers for all and reigns with all in his kingdom.[85] Moreover, I think this perspective fails to express the Trinitarian way by which Christ is revealed in the Chief. Some critical issues as the suffering, death and resurrection and ascension and Pentecost and Parousia are not engaged in a manner that resonates with the African contexts. Hence, it is difficult for the Chief Christology to have relevance to the worshiping community in Africa.

Harry Sawyer (1909–1986) applies the category of the Elder Brother to Jesus. Jesus for Sawyer is the Elder Brother around whom all things revolve; Jesus is the firstborn among many brethren who together form the church (Eph 2:19). Hence, from the Christian point of view, the blood of Jesus binds all races, ethnicities and nations together and this truth is significantly supported by the consanguinity of the extended family.[86]

Drawing, from the Akan tradition, Pobee continues to support Sawyer's kinship view, howbeit quite differently. As Sawyer emphasizes so much the Elder Brother, Pobee sees the consanguinity sense of Akan community as significant, because it points to the kinship of Jesus.[87] Every member of the extended family must be initiated into the community in

---

81. Kabasele, "Christ as Chief," 103–5.
82. Kabasele, "Christ as Chief," 106.
83. Kabasele, "Christ as Chief," 108–12.
84. Chike, "Proudly African, Proudly Christian," 232.
85. Pobee, *Toward an African Theology*, 81–98; Nyamiti, "African Christologies Today,"7.
86. Mugabe, "Christology in an African Context," 344.
87. Mugabe, "Christology in an African Context," 344.

order to become a legitimate member of the community.[88] And the church as a community of God's children becomes the fulfillment of this sense of community in the Akan society. Emmanuel Asante also affirms the latter's position on the Akan.[89] However, Emmanuel Asante relates this form of kinship to the kingdom of God whereby God's kingdom is universal and not limited to any particular race or ethnicity.[90] Thus the kingdom of God's openness served as a critique of any tribal or racial bias in the community of faith. This belief is also a Christology from below, in that Jesus identifies with the people as siblings. However, Jesus the Elder Brother as a christological elucidation does not show clearly the consanguinity through the economic activity of the Holy Trinity. Furthermore, what may be the roles of Jesus' death, resurrection, ascension, Pentecost and the Parousia in this Christology? This question, and many issues that could be raised, becomes the challenge associated with this paradigm of Christology.

Jesus as Master of Initiation

Anselm Sanon bases his Christology of Jesus, the Master of Initiation, upon the African cultural milieu.[91] The African culture provides for rites of passage at every major stage of life, including birth, puberty (adulthood) and marriage and death. The initiation is from adolescence into adulthood and it is upon these that Sanon draws inspiration for his Christology of initiation.[92] Every initiation rite has symbolisms as well as the spirit of initiation.[93] Thus the authenticity of an initiation rite is not merely based upon the symbolisms, but the spirit behind the act of initiation. To Sanon, Jesus was initiated in his own tradition and the Letter to the Hebrews bears testimony to the fact that Jesus "leads saved humanity to perfection and this in definite manner."[94]

Christ was thus initiated into the humanity of the world by the Holy Spirit. Jesus was born, grew, suffered, died, and was buried. This event

---

88. Mbiti, "Some African Concepts of Christology," 56–57; Mugabe, "Christology in an African Context," 344.

89. Asante, *African Christian Theology*, 80.

90. Asante, *African Christian Theology*, 138.

91. Sanon, "Jesus, Master of Initiation," 8–102.

92. Moloney, "African Christology," 507.

93. Moloney, "African Christology," 95.

94. Moloney, "African Christology," 94.

of his incarnation as great initiation makes him an Elder Brother of the initiation.⁹⁵ Sanon thus portrays Jesus as a mediator who intercedes for his siblings, and rightly so because he is the Eldest Brother and thus the Representative of them. He is thus a Chief yet a Brother, Master and yet a Servant.⁹⁶ The body is a symbolism of the spirit; the symbol of an individual and social person; and the act of the ritual itself indicating the sense of identity, which is common to humanity.⁹⁷

Jesus, according to Sanon, has made the initiation decisive inasmuch as he died for all once and for all.⁹⁸ Moreover, this Christology is relevant insofar as the practice of initiation rites in contemporary Africa, particularly rites of passage from adolescence to adulthood need to be brought to the front burner. It should be noted that others think the rites of passage are no longer relevant in African societies.⁹⁹ Moreover, like the other African Christologies evaluated so far, there is a lack of how this Christology fits in the Trinitarian economy. Other important issues on the Christ event such as resurrection, ascension, Pentecost and Parousia are not tackled. Moreover, this Christology is not reflective of the holistic African worldview.

Jesus as Healer

In many African societies, there are special people whose main task in the community is to provide healing to the community. This African tradition has been engaged by some theologians and writers, notably Raymond Buana Kibongi, Aylward Shorter and Cece Kolie,¹⁰⁰ and Gabriel Molehe Setiloane.¹⁰¹ Though there are many tribal names for these special healers, the most commonly used name is the *Nganga* (traditional healer).¹⁰²

---

95. Moloney, "African Christology," 94–95.
96. Moloney, "African Christology," 95–96.
97. Moloney, "African Christology," 96–97.
98. Moloney, "African Christology," 98–99.
99. Moloney, "African Christology," 507.
100. Moloney, "African Christology," 508; Kibongi, "Priesthood," 47–56; Shorter, *Jesus and the Witchdoctor*.
101. Mugabe, "Christology in an African Context," 345; Setiloane, "Where Are We in African Theology?"
102. The *Nganga* are traditional healers who are not priests or kings. Moloney, "African Christology," 508; see also Kolie "Jesus as Healer," 136.

An evaluation of the work of Cece Kolie is done in order to understand the work of the *Nganga*. Kolie's work demonstrates that he is looking at the entire situation of the traditional African, the concept of death and the practice of healing.[103] He identifies three modes of healing by a healer as confronting destructuring, violence and possession.[104] Destructuring is the alteration of the traditional social setting by the capitalist type. Concerning violence, one may appreciate that violence is the work of malevolent people. Kolie is also concerned about the possession by demons and other spirits of the people. In this sense, the healing has a holistic impact on society.[105] The use of the term *Nganga* allows Kolie to probe and diagnose issues from a wider perspective including the social environment.[106]

So according to Kibongi, the *Ngangas* did their best to save humanity, but it was not enough.[107] Also, Pobee recognizes the work of the traditional healer as that which may be compared to Jesus the Healer. A comparison finds the divinity and life of Jesus as one which is unattainable by the *Nganga*.[108] Gabriel Setiloane[109] and Aylward Shorter[110] both believe the christological title of Jesus as the Healer as adequate. One may agree with the latter as the healing experience characteristic of the AICs, PCCs, has moved into the HMCs.[111] The challenge with this christological title has been the abuse of the powers the *Ngangas* have.[112] Nonetheless, since Jesus as the *Nganga* becomes the focal point, Jesus the Christ overcomes the weaknesses of the *Nganga* insofar as the Christian community dwells in him. Moreover, Christian healing implies vertical and horizontal reconciliation that has solid foundation in the salvific event as the work of the triune God to be accomplished at the end of history.

---

103. Kolie, "Jesus as Healer," 132–35.

104. Kolie, "Jesus as Healer," 135–36.

105. Kolie, "Jesus as Healer," 136–37.

106. Kolie, "Jesus as Healer," 137–38.

107. See Kibongi, "Priesthood," 52–53; Mugabe, "Christology in an African Context," 345.

108. Pobee, *Towards an African Theology*, 93; Setiloane, "Where Are We in African Theology?"

109. See Mugabe, "Christology in an African Context," 345.

110. Shorter, *Jesus and the Witchdoctor*; Moloney, "African Christology," 508; and Mugabe, "Christology in an African Context," 345.

111. Omenyo "Charismatic Churches in Ghana," 266–68.

112. Mugabe, "Christology in an African Context," 346.

Jesus the Ancestor

African society has a philosophy which is similar to Platonism because of the belief in the concept of prior existence.[113] As God is alive, so are those people who proceed from God, which is why in my opinion, it makes sense for Mbiti to call the ancestors, "the living dead."[114] Therefore, in African primal worldview, ancestors are no more, yet alive and active, not dormant because among other things, they serve as mediators of God and humanity.[115] The true qualifications of a person to become an ancestor, has been expressed by Nyamiti.[116] They are the custodians of clans and are the source and enforcers of all laws and taboos.[117] In this way, the society is governed by the ancestors through the elders of the clans and the community. Therefore, ancestors are the embodiment of the entire history and life of the people to whom they belong. No wonder they are specially revered and venerated.[118] In most Ghanaian societies like the Ga, the ancestors are invited to be part of every occasion.[119]

From the perspective of the Ga, the African sees the ancestors to be in a similitude of a "cloud of witnesses." This presence of the ancestors in the life of the people creates enormous "fear" within the people. This "fear" is based upon Ga understanding that the ancestors are "security forces, lawyers, and judges who render instant judgment." It has been suggested that like the Ga people some Africans may fear ancestors more than the spirit beings controlling the community, while others may not.[120]

According to John Pobee, Jesus is *Nana*, namely the Great Ancestor.[121] *Nana* in the Akan scheme of conceptualization, represents a title

---

113. Plato's "forms/ideas" and "matter" give such an idea in African thought because every form of existence is authenticated only by a perfect spiritual source. On Plato's forms/ideas and matter, see Stumpf, *Philosophy: History and Problems*.

114. Mbiti, *African Religions and Philosophy*, 83–84; see also Reed and Mtukwa, "Christ Our Ancestor," 149.

115. Mbiti, African Religions and Philosophy," 67, 82; Reed and Mtukwa, "Christ Our Ancestor," 150.

116. Nyamiti, "African Christologies Today," 11.

117. Field, *Religion and Medicine*, 196–205.

118. Reed and Mtukwa, "Christ Our Ancestor," 151.

119. Field, *Religion and Medicine*, 49; see also Reed and Mtukwa, "Christ Our Ancestor," 151–96.

120. Field, *Religion and Medicine*, 49–59; see also Moyo, "Material Things," 52; Reed and Mtukwa, "Christ Our Ancestor," 151.

121. Pobee, *Towards an African Theology*, 81–98; Nyamiti, "African Christologies

with power and authority to judge, reward, and punish. Since for the Akan, like many other African ethnic groups, the ancestors control almost every facet of life, it follows that *"Nana Yesu"* controls everything in the community. What makes Jesus have such a tremendous ability here is the fact that he is not like the ancestors who are known to be dead but living human beings. Jesus is dead, but a risen God-human and therefore not just one of the *Nananom Nsamanfo* (ancestors), but the *Nana* who is God. Jesus has power and authority over religious, cultural, social, economic, and political affairs of the community.[122]

Francois Kabasele's work takes the worldview of the Muntu and the Bantu people of Africa to advance the idea of ancestral Christology in Africa.[123] He starts by affirming the fact that to the Muntu, the ancestors are the way through, by which they reach God. This is paralleled by Jesus' statement in John 14:6 that "I am the way the truth and the life. No one goes to the Father except through me."[124] Considering the fact that the biblical Adam may be the natural ancestor of the Muntu, there is an appropriation of the Apostle Paul's comparison of Adam and Christ (Rom 5:14b, 15b).[125]

Jesus is then known as the spirit ancestor and Mary is also considered to be an ancestor, i.e., male, female ancestor, respectively.[126] While noting that the nature of the ancestor is complex, Kabasele still tries to break down the nature of the ancestor as life, presence, the eldest, and mediator.[127] He presents Christ as the life and source of abundant life (John 10:10) with the African ancestor. And so, Christ is the Ancestor who gives life beyond measure.[128] African ancestors are also known to offer protection by their presence, driving away evil spirits or leading people away from troubles. Christ, the Ancestor, exhibits all these traits.[129]

Further, for the Luba, the name of God reveals much pertaining to God's nature as ancestor. *Mvidi-Mukulu* denotes "Spirit Elder" in the

---

Today," 7.

122. Pobee, *Towards an African Theology*, 81–98; quoted in Nyamiti, "African Christologies Today," 7.

123. Kabasele, "Christ as Ancestor," 116–27.

124 Kabasele, "Christ as Ancestor," 116.

125. Kabasele, "Christ as Ancestor," 116.

126. Kabasele, "Christ as Ancestor," 117.

127. Kabasele, "Christ as Ancestor," 118–26.

128. Kabasele, "Christ as Ancestor," 120.

129. Kabasele, "Christ as Ancestor," 120–21.

literal sense; however, *Mvidi* refers also to a tree, which signifies life in the Luba community.[130] This tree is evergreen even in drought and produces seeds, which are normally planted in front of houses to signify life in abundance. To Kabasele, the *Mvidi-Mukulu* really means the God who gives life in abundance; hence, God is the Ancestor of life. Kabasele still recognizes in the Bantu Christian life, Jesus the Elder because in the family, the position of the eldest son is almost equivalent to the position of the father. All members of the family owe great respect and allegiance to him. Also the Elder Brother has responsibilities attached to his position, such as prayers and offerings which should be made to the Supreme Being and the ancestors by him on behalf of the rest of the family. In that sense, Christ is the Elder Brother par excellence because, although human ancestors have become failures in some respects, Christ has satisfied both the Father and the people.[131] Another important work of the ancestor is mediation.[132]

According to Kwame Bediako, Christ is the Supreme Ancestor.[133] Christ is the Supreme Ancestor because the rite of passage, which includes birth, initiation, work, death, and ancestorship, points to the salvific event. Bediako says that the African who moves through the vagaries of life ends up in the realm of spirit power. Thus, the salvific event of the Lord Jesus Christ in the African context makes Jesus Christ the Supreme Ancestor, i.e., the one who comes to not only save, but the one who comes to judge all things. It should be noted, however, that the divinity of Christ does not stem from his death and resurrection, but rather from his very nature. This position of Christ moves the ancestors to make room for the Lord Jesus in the realm of the Spirit. Here his higher status establishes him as both the Judge of the living and the dead (Matt 22:32; Rom 14:9).[134] This position as Judge of both the living and the dead places Christ as the Supreme Ancestor. However, this position of Christ elucidates the horizons of the African Christian to understand the human ancestors.[135]

130. Kabasele, "Christ as Ancestor," 121.

131. Kabasele, "Christ as Ancestor," 121–22.

132. Kabasele, "Christ as Ancestor," 117.

133. Bediako, *Christianity in Africa*, 127. See also Reed and Mtukwa, "Christ Our Ancestor," 152.

134. Bediako, *Christianity in Africa*, 218; and see also Reed and Mtukwa, "Christ Our Ancestor," 153.

135. Reed and Mtukwa, "Christ Our Ancestor," 153.

In the similitude of Platonic philosophy, i.e., forms/ideas and matter, Benezet Bujo tries to differentiate his Christology from the rest by insisting on avoiding syncretism.[136] To him, the human ancestors should not be mixed entirely with Christ's ancestorship by acknowledging Jesus as one of the human ancestors who is glorified. Rather Jesus should be seen as an Ancestor from whom all things flow and who the true and original Ancestor is. Thus, the human ancestors are like shadows, images and illustrations of the real Ancestor, who is Christ. Therefore, Jesus is the Proto-Ancestor, who is the first, the Original and the Perfect Ancestor. And so, it becomes very easy for Bujo to discourage the use of the *Logos* (Word) and *Kurios* (Lord) in that the Proto-Ancestor served such a purpose, but in a more adequate and convincing manner because it is in the African context.[137] Obviously this idea of Bujo has stemmed from the fact that he seeks an African Christian ethic.[138]

Charles Nyamiti, the Tanzanian Roman Catholic theologian, presents a Christology based on the fatherhood of God as the Supreme Being and the brotherhood of Christ as the Son of the Father by the power of the Holy Spirit.[139] This clearly brings out the intention of Nyamiti in his writing pertaining to the Trinitarian view of Christology and also the ecclesiological view of Christology, which ought to be made evident in African Christology.[140]

Nyamiti states as follows:

> The Father is the Ancestor of the Son, the Son is the Descendant of the Father. These two persons live their ancestral kinship through the Spirit whom they mutually communicate to as their ancestral Oblation and Eucharist. The Spirit is reciprocally donated not only in token of their mutual love as Gift but also on behalf of the homage to their reciprocal holiness (as Oblation) and gratitude to their beneficence to each other (as Eucharist, from the Greek: *eucharistein* "to thank").[141]

---

136. Bujo, *African Theology*, 77; Reed and Mtukwa, "Christ Our Ancestor," 154.

137. Bujo, *African Theology*, 77; Reed and Mtukwa, "Christ Our Ancestor," 154; see also Bujo, *African Theology*, 49.

138. Bujo, *African Theology*, 71; cited by Reed and Mtukwa, "Christ Our Ancestor," 153.

139. Nyamiti, "African Christologies Today," 11.

140. Nyamiti, "African Christologies Today," 11.

141. Nyamiti, "African Christologies Today," 11.

Ecclesiologically, Nyamiti looks at the consanguinity of the believers and thus, creates a situation where the body of Christ, also the *ekklesia* is represented by the head, who is Christ and the body, which is the church.[142] Christ is the unique Brother Ancestor *par excellence* by the economy of the Trinity in which the Father imputes the ancestorship to God's Son, Jesus Christ. The Holy Spirit is the Medium of relating the Father (Ancestor) to the Son (Descendant) and vice versa. Notably, that unique relationship represents a relationship of the body of Christ, essentially as the Holy Spirit's relationship with the Son.[143]

According to Nyamiti, the activity in the church ought to be Spirit led in fellowship, which is full of prayer and without racial prejudices.[144] By the Spirit of Christ, his works of love are principally expressed in evangelization by both Word and deed. Moreover, this is revealed in caring for the sick and other integral redemptive actions, which are carried out in his body, which is the church.[145] He also makes room for the church triumphant as being the ancestors who are in *Sheol* and who are also a cloud of witnesses.[146]

It is highly important at this juncture to state that the ancestor paradigm of African Christologies form the most comprehensive of the inculturation types. This Christology deals with the suffering and glorified Christ in a genuine manner; hence, it is both a Christology from below and from above. In addition, Charles Nyamiti has demonstrated clearly how the Trinity can be found in the Ancestor Christology. It has demonstrated how Ancestor Christology is connected to the church in this world and in the other world and showing that it is eschatological. Are there any critical issues to be raised nonetheless?

Yes, and first, the issue concerns how ordinary African believers can appreciate the ancestor Christology in church practice. Second, looking at the ubiquitous nature of the ancestral religiosity of the African, its acceptance comes with many risks of moving back to African ancestral worship. Third, practically speaking the ancestral Christology has not shown any appreciable outlook in the African churches and neither can they be identified in the AICs or the PCCs. However, these objections

---

142. Nyamiti, "African Christologies Today," 11–12.
143. Nyamiti, "African Christologies Today," 11–12.
144. Nyamiti, "African Christologies Today," 11.
145. Nyamiti, "African Christologies Today," 11.
146. Nyamiti, "African Christologies Today," 11.

may not be upheld in view of Roman Catholic faith where the connection between the Christ, the saints, and the African church ought to be made. On that score, Nyamiti had contributed immensely to the part of the African church belonging to Roman Catholicism. The fourth critical issue to be raised then is the ecumenical sense in which African Christian theology ought to be engaged.

This means that African Christian theological formulations ought to transcend the barriers of confessions in order to make it truly African and not just the points making a confessional faith. By making the Christian message concrete in Africa, confessions may have to be transcended. Ancestral Christologies in Africa are so important to African theology and church because they reveal the limitedness of African ancestors and the transcending power of Jesus Christ. The idea or fact that human ancestors are limited is pervasive among African Christians shows that Ancestor Christology is vital to African theology but perhaps not the most important; because Jesus Christ obviates all other intermediaries such as the African ancestors.

Liberation Christologies

Liberation Christologies are those which identify Jesus Christ's person and work based on the socio-politico-economic situation. The main branches are Black Christology from South Africa and liberation Christology mainly in sub-Saharan Africa. African women's theology also forms part of Liberation Christologies.[147] These Christologies address teething problems in economics and the development of African nations. African Black Christology has therefore fought to eliminate most conditions, which tended to oppress blacks in South Africa. Similarly, the women of Africa, who are the main sufferers of the economic difficulties, also engage this liberation Christology to have their issues resolved.

The challenge of these Christologies in their efforts to liberate Africans is their tendency to oppose African religio-cultural issues which subjugate Africans. This stance forces inculturation and liberation to seem to oppose each other, which is a great disincentive to African Christologies. It causes African Christologies to become quite fragmented and thus incoherent. Therefore, advancing a more coherent and consistent

---

147. See Ukpong, "Emergence of African Theologies," 523; see also Martey, *African Theology*, 81.

Christology requires a Christology which amalgamates the two and it is the *cultura-libero* and *Kpelelogical* theology which does this. And so, Jesus, the *Okpelejen Wulormor*, as a *Kpelelogical* Christology combines the issues of religion, culture, sociology, economics and politics in a coherent whole. The following section is an evaluation of the liberation Christologies in Africa.

African Black Christology

This kind of Christology is mainly found in South Africa and takes inspiration from the American Black Christology.[148] It leans on the historical Jesus, whose life is an indication of a preferential option for the poor and oppressed.[149] Like the counterpart in America, African Black Christology identifies Christ as the one who takes sides with the poor and oppressed black people in Africa. Just as Christ was crucified, so in the same way, the blacks in Africa are being crucified in the shanty towns of which squalor and backwardness is the stereotype created by the white community.[150] Some people have tried to bring out the differences between black theology of South Africa and black theology of America.[151]

In most cases, the distinction has been drawn by those who are not black theologians.[152] Many black theologians of Africa know the backgrounds of their theology, which is the basis for their actions.[153] Martey shows the background of South African black theology and reveals the significance of the Black Consciousness Movements.[154] Though the contexts may be different, the problem of blacks as a matter of principle may be the same. For what is the difference between Black Power / Civil Rights Movements and Black Consciousness Movements? Or were the

---

148. Boesak, *Farewell to Innocence*, 37; Moloney "African Christology," 513; see also Nyamiti, "African Christologies Today," 12–13; Martey, *African Theology*, 82.

149. Nyamiti, "African Christologies Today," 13.

150. Gqubule, "Theologie noire sud-africaine," 106; Moloney, "African Christology," 514.

151. Nyamiti, "African Christologies Today," 13; see also Moloney, "African Christology," 513.

152. See the work of Mbiti, "An African Views American Black Theology," 382; Nyamiti, "African Christologies Today," 13; Moloney, "African Christology," 513; a response to this approach is given by Tutu, "Black Theology / African Theology," 385.

153. Boesak, *Black and Reformed*; and also Boesak, *Farewell to Innocence*.

154. Martey, *African Theology*, 82.

individual Black South Africans on the front lines during the fight against apartheid not Christians? The point is, one may attempt to articulate an African black theology different from the American black theology as a matter of principle, only if one stays out of touch with actions and realities of African black consciousness.

If indeed ideological differences divide theology in Africa, it is a pity. For the younger generation, none of the ideologies, such as Capitalism or Marxism can save, inasmuch as they are essential tools for understanding the *sitz im leben* of Africa. There is therefore no need to follow credulously, certain principles that cannot be a blessing to Africa.[155] Blacks need to be united and forge ahead with the development to tackle the challenges, which a following portion of Setiloane's poem graphically represents:

> How like us He is, this Jesus of Nazareth, beaten, tortured, imprisoned, spat upon, truncheoned, denied by his own, and chased like a thief in the night; despised, and rejected like a dog that has fleas, for no reason.[156]

Black suffering is not only limited to suffering in Africa or America, but all over the world. Evidently black Christians faced with discrimination, marginalization, and oppression fall on the Jesus of Nazareth, their only hope, their only redemption, and their only comfort in a world that is hostile to them.[157] The suffering Christ is therefore the One who in Black theology is known to be the Black Christ or Black Messiah.[158] The representation of Jesus as the Black Christ rests in the reality that Jesus identifies with black suffering and pain and bears it on their behalf. Black theologians are not oblivious of the fact that their liberation in Jesus Christ today in the world is fragmentary. Therefore, they look forward to the coming eschaton when all creatures including blacks and whites shall experience wholeness.

---

155. All theologies and Christologies in Africa, i.e., inculturation and liberation, agree that foreign cultures and philosophies cannot save the African. Inculturationists believe that African philosophy is the bedrock for the realization of the African true self and identity. In similar fashion, liberation theologians have stated unequivocally, the anthropological impoverishment as race issue, which has ramifications in social, economic, and political life of Africans. There is no reason for Africans to be divided on the two positions above, as division is the bane for self-assertion.

156. Setiloane, "I Am an African," 131.

157. Hopkins, *Black Theology*.

158. Gqubule, "Theologie noire sud-Africanie," 106; cited in Moloney, "African Christology," 514.

Black theology is not an escapist and fundamentalist Christianity that goes to sleep in wait of the eschaton for the new earth and new heaven to come. To the contrary black theology motivates all who are united with Christ Jesus in the Spirit according to the eternal will of the father of bringing renewal and wholeness in the present and in the future in view of what God has done in the past. Thus black struggle continues as black responsibility and a Christian ethic in anticipation of the coming reign of God. The struggle, for example, of Allan Boesak to declare as heretical the theology of apartheid is most ennobling.[159] One also shall not forget Simon Maimela and Buthelezi Manas for their relentless efforts in Black theology.[160] To Buthelezi, Jesus Christ exemplifies it all when he identifies with the victims of oppression, corruption, injustice, and ignorance.[161]

The above Christology is a typical Christology from below and hence partly representative of the general African reflection on Jesus the Christ. It does not reflect the disposition of a typical African church although it has the potential. Its christological treatment is inadequate since it is disinterested in a Trinitarian look at Jesus.

African Liberation Christologies

It may be striking to observe that liberation Christologies in Africa are scattered phenomena in Africa. Although theologians may desire to look at liberation in terms of the Latin American liberation theology, and conclude that much is not done comparatively, one recognizes the existence of a substantial number of people who belong to the African liberation fraternity, contributing to it in many ways. Their main bone of contention is for the liberation of the poor and oppressed of which majority of the African populace are.

Therefore, they engage in political, economic, and social struggles within the religious and cultural milieu. They believe in the historical Jesus who went about doing good, healing all manner of diseases and liberating humanity from the powers of death. Jesus is seen as the man who suffered for the well-being of the poor. Jesus is the one who has taken

---

159. See Leonard, "Moment of Truth," 86.

160. Mugabe, "Christology in an African Context," 349; for details, see Buthelezi, "Daring to Live for Christ," 178–80.

161. Mugabe, "Christology in an African Context," 349; see Stinton, "Christology in the Third World," 8–9.

preferential option for the poor, dehumanized and subjugated. In Ghana, one is yet to see the potency of their position clearly in the public sphere through a proper organizational framework. Their relevance is long overdue looking at the developmental needs of the nation. The development of this group could go a long way to see the developmental vision of Africa become a reality in the now. The utopian ideals associated with this position are a very real danger staring this theology of liberation in the face. Though Africa has no propensity for totalitarianism, it needs to be wary of utopian goals and see that the holistic redemption that includes redemption from poverty is constantly attached to the realization of the coming kingdom of God.

African Women's Christologies

One should also recognize the work of African women liberation theologians, whose contributions can never be overemphasized. The struggle of women like Mercy Amba Oduyoye, Musimbi Kanyoro, Teresa Okure, and Musa Dube et al. have contributed immensely. Nyamiti in 1989 suggested there was a vast amount of hope for African women's theology and today one may firmly emphasize that it is a reality.[162] A look at the Circle of Concerned African Women Theologians (CCAWT) reveals the praxis in the fight for liberation. The founder of the Circle is Prof. Mercy Amba Oduyoye and there is a book titled *Women and Health in Africa* written in her honor. At the inauguration of the Circle, there were seventy women from Islam, Christianity, Judaism, and Traditional African Religion.[163]

Professor Amba Oduyoye talks about Christology in the Jesus of Nazareth and his mother, Mary, in the magnificat.[164] The life of Jesus, according to Oduyoye, is good news to the people of Africa because of his life of good deeds, suffering and death and resurrection.[165] The life of Jesus drives every anxiety and despair away from the people and offers them trust in God. Jesus is the *Agyenkwa*, the rescuer who plucks the oppressed from the ambience of dehumanization and places them in

---

162. Nyamiti, "African Christologies Today," 13.
163. See Circle of Concerned African Women Theologians on the web.
164. Oduyoye, *Hearing and Knowing*, 106.
165. Oduyoye, *Hearing and Knowing*, 106.

a position to grow into an authentic humanity.[166] "The *Agyenkwa* offers your life back you in all its wholeness and fullness."[167]

Oduyoye looks at Christ based upon the Exodus account of the Israelites and uses the Akan religious cultural terms to demonstrate who Jesus is to African women. Using the Hebrew word *Yasha*, Oduyoye explains that God liberates God's people like a great military commander in charge of logistics, both physically and spiritually, of the army. Therefore, Jesus is seen as the *Tufohene* and also as *Osabarima*, the Great Warrior, who saves in battle.[168] Jesus is the Great Friend (*Damfo Adu*) and Guarantor (*Okyirtaafo*).[169] Just as *Yahweh* delivered those tormented of disease, famine and fire, from flood and the deep sea, from disgrace and humiliation in the Hebrew Scriptures, so does Jesus snatch women and men away from domination and death and also reconciles them to God.[170]

Oduyoye boldly and confidently challenges the Anselmnian Christology of satisfaction by employing the Akan terms *Ponfo Kese* and *mpata*, in Fante hymns.[171] She attacks Christologies of privatization in African churches and particularly Byang Kato (1936–1975) on that score.[172] She denounces Christologies which seek to make the sinner and the slave as spectators, to assert a shift from a market place Christology to a battle field Christology in which God fights and breaks the chains of captives, prisoners and slaves.[173] She employs the figurative Hebrew language of *Yasha* and *Padah*, which implies a rescue from the stroke of the sword (Job 5:15; 8–6). Hence, God shall rescue the many African women suffering from political, social, economic, and religious, and cultural oppression with the stroke of the sword with this act of God being undeserved.[174]

The remembrance of this gracious act of God should "make us champions of the principles of the rule of God."[175] Moreover, on their part, Elizabeth Amoah and Mercy Amba Oduyoye (Ghana) reviewed African Christology constructed mostly by males. They agree to most

---

166. Oduyoye, *Hearing and Knowing*, 106.
167. Oduyoye, *Hearing and Knowing*, 106.
168. Oduyoye, *Hearing and Knowing*, 99.
169. Oduyoye, *Hearing and Knowing*, 100.
170. Oduyoye, *Hearing and Knowing*, 101.
171. Oduyoye, *Hearing and Knowing*, 102.
172. Oduyoye, *Hearing and Knowing*, 103.
173. Oduyoye, *Hearing and Knowing*, 103.
174. Oduyoye, *Hearing and Knowing*, 104.
175. Oduyoye, *Hearing and Knowing*, 105.

of the categories and the titles employed; however, their problem exists regarding the inability of those Christologies to locate the feminist concerns adequately.[176] Obviously, they fill in the blanks by engaging the experience of women in Ghana with biblical teachings. For them, Jesus is Victor over all enemies of progress, both spiritual and physical; Jesus is the Anointed One, the Comforter, the Friend, and the Sacrificial Lamb whom a woman anointed (King, Prophet, and Priest).[177]

Nasimiyu-Wasike, in her work, exposes the situation of women in Africa in totality as dehumanizing and highly oppressive.[178] She then samples the views of six ordinary women to show who Jesus is to them. The responses these women gave showed that Jesus is strength, savior, hope, and closest friend and the core of their lives.[179] She examines Jesus' work and the reference to women in his teachings as against mainstream rabbinic pedagogy. Also, Jesus' defense of women both in teaching and deed is acknowledged.[180] Nasimiyu-Wasike challenges the early church and the medieval conception of women as unchristian and the cause of the relegation of women to the background in African churches.[181]

The crucified Christ is eschatological; the anthropological Christ is the one who was concerned with humanity and the relationships of love toward others. The liberating Jesus is the one who liberates the suffering masses of women from their burdens of socioeconomic and political hardships. Also, the cosmological Jesus is the one who restores.[182] Nasimiyu-Wasike's Christology is encapsulated when she writes that Jesus

> meets them [women] in their own cultural, physical, environmental, political, and economic variations. For African women Jesus Christ is the victorious conqueror of all evil spiritual forces; He is the nurturer of life, and a totality of their being. Christ is the liberator of the sufferers, the restorer of all those who are broken, the giver of hope and the courage to be[183]

---

176. Amoah and Oduyoye, "The Christ for African Women," 35–37, 39–42.
177. Amoah and Oduyoye, "The Christ for African Women," 43–45.
178. Namisiyu-Wasike, "Christology and an African Woman's Experience," 71.
179. Namisiyu-Wasike, "Christology and an African Woman's Experience," 71–73.
180. Namisiyu-Wasike, "Christology and an African Woman's Experience," 73–75.
181. Namisiyu-Wasike, "Christology and an African Woman's Experience," 76–77.
182. Namisiyu-Wasike, "Christology and an African Woman's Experience," 77–80.
183. Namisiyu-Wasike, "Christology and an African Woman's Experience," 8–81.

On her part, Teresa Hinga provides defining characteristics of an African feminist Christology which "dismantles the unjust social structures."[184] She sees Christ to women in Africa as a Friend, the Enabler,[185] and a Prophet.[186] Jesus for many African women is a personal friend who comforts, leads and helps in the difficulties of hardships in their lives. Even under the heavy load of cultural and economic oppression, Jesus is the personal Friend who comforts. Jesus is the Enabler because he is the One in whose name divine power is unleashed against all spiritual and physical forces of oppression and it is the African women who love Jesus for this amazing experience of liberation. Jesus the Prophet advocates for the women who are under heavy loads of oppression.

For Teresa Souga, Jesus was incarnated through a woman and lived as a human being and died for the love of showing kindness to the oppressed and, therefore, God has raised him.[187] To her, Jesus' incarnation speaks volumes about the liberation of women and working with them as disciples.[188] Hence, Jesus in Africa is on their side to destroy cultural, spiritual, and socioeconomic encumbrances in their lives.[189] Jesus gives room for women to actively engage and participate in church life.

While unearthing the many oppressive situations of the African woman, Luise Tappa, with an articulate feminist hermeneutics of suspicion, magnifies the love of Jesus for women. For example, she magnifies the willingness and love Jesus has for women who have been relegated by patriarchy.[190] The Christology of Tappa is particularly hinged on Mark 5:21–34, where Jairus's daughter and the woman with the hemorrhage are discussed.[191] Jesus encourages African women's self-affirmation for women as children of God.[192] Thus, Jesus the Liberator enables African women to stand up, show up, and speak up against all odds of patriarchy.[193]

---

184. Hinga, "Jesus Christ and the Liberation of Women," 19–192.

185. Through Jesus, these women, mainly found in AICs but now pervasive, i.e., even in mainline churches, pursue a higher power in the Holy Spirit which enables them to overcome all challenges and to endure hardships.

186. Hinga, "Jesus Christ and the Liberation of Women," 190–91.

187. Souga, "Christ Event," 22.

188. Souga, "Christ Event," 23–29.

189. Souga, "Christ Event," 26.

190. Tappa, "Christ Event," 30.

191. Tappa, "Christ Event," 32.

192. Tappa, "Christ Event," 33.

193. Tappa, "Christ Event," 34.

It is very heartwarming to comment that the women theologians in Africa are women who embrace most of the African christological discourse which inure to their benefit. In such a scheme, they are able to employ such concepts as Christ the Victor and Christ as Priest, King, and Prophet. They are also able to employ categories of the suffering Christ and Jesus the Friend. Therefore, they find it easy to employ both Christologies below and above as their approaches. This again emphasizes the point that African Christologies are both from below and above without separation. Nevertheless, one should be quick to observe that they lack Trinitarian elucidation and Pentecostal appreciation, which is the reason why more work ought to be done on the subject.

Having dealt with inculturation and liberation Christologies, it is important to turn attention to the *cultura-libero* type observed in Jesus the Lord of *Homowor*. Before I proceed further, however, in the above discussion I observe that inculturation and liberation groupings are needless. Surely, in African Christianity, faith based upon Christ the Victor, Master of Initiation and Christ in African Kinship and Christ the Healer and Jesus the Ancestor and Black theology and African women's theology does not make sense without both religio-cultural and socio-economic and political realities put together.

African women's theology in the category of liberation deals with fundamental religious and cultural issues equally as the socioeconomic and political issues. In doing women's theology, culture and religion in African setting that undermine the well-being of women are exposed and confronted in view of Christ's love for them. Likewise, black theologians in Africa cannot declare their freedoms in socioeconomic and political terms only when they are downtrodden on the basis of their skin color, origin and religion and culture.

Again in the realities of the African context, ancestors are invoked on matters concerning religion, culture and hunger and poverty and disease and injustice and oppression. The dominion theology Africans preach and teach in the Charismatic and Pentecostal churches deal with issues of African religion, culture and particularly, social, economic and political issues.

Thus in effect, all African theologies ought to be grouped under a *cultura-libero* category. Nonetheless, by so doing we have been able to show the nature of contemporary African Christian theology.

Cultura-Libero Christologies

Another type of Christology may be identified as that which seeks the identity of Jesus in such a manner that it involves the holistic context. The holistic context of doing theology as mentioned above includes the religio-cultural as well as the socioeconomic and political needs. This Christology allows the gospel to be confronted dialectically by the religio-cultural and socioeconomic and political situation of the people and vice versa.

This *cultura-libero* type of Christology is to uphold the identity and the work of Christ in a manner that is functional in the total reality of the African people. For example, one may classify the work of Philip Laryea, *Yesu Homowor Nuntsor*, in which he identifies Christ as the Lord of *Homowor* (lit. "The Lord of the hoot [war] against hunger"),[194] as a *cultura-libero* Christology. Douglas Waruta's work, *Who Is Jesus Christ for Africans Today? Prophet, Priest, Potentate*,[195] which is another example of *cultura-libero* Christology in Africa, is of great interest to this work because it shows that the *Okpelejen Wulormor* is African. Samuel Waje Kunihyiop from a Western evangelical perspective looks at the holistic reality of Africa as well.[196] Kunihyiop's approach is kerygmatic and tends to throw the hard solutions of the Christian message at the people of Africa. It is a christocentric methodology that hardly raises the questions of the African predicament before providing solution. It is also noteworthy to mention Diane Stinton's African theology in narrative form.[197] Surely it has an all-encompassing approach in addressing African realities in the stories told.

Yesu Homowor Nuntsor Le (Jesus the Lord and Conqueror of all Human Quests)

Homowor is a cherished festival among the Ga people and it is the only festival which is celebrated by all the major groups of the Ga people. Certainly, the length of time apportioned to the festival clearly depicts

---

194. Laryea, *Yesu Homowor Nuntsor*, 127. Bracketed translation mine. Emphasis on the liberation is made by the use of the word *war* to indicate the struggle of the Ga for not only food in abundance, but also prosperity.

195. Waruta, "Prophet, Priest, Potentate," 52–69.

196. Kunihyiop, *African Christian Theology*.

197. Stinton, *Jesus of Africa*.

the importance it has on the life of the Ga people. The *Homowor* has religious, cultural, social, economic and political importance, which is the reason for its massive celebration. It is the celebration of the historical emancipation from famine for the Ga people and thus, *Homowor* (hoot at hunger). Philip Tetteh Laryea may be the foremost Ga theologian to dialogue, in a most revolutionary manner, regarding the Ga religious and cultural concept of *Homowor* with the gospel. In so doing, he attempted to identify theologically who Christ is to the Ga people.[198]

His work is based upon identifying for the Ga, Jesus within the *Homowor*, in continuity with biblical tradition. He chooses the life of Jews and the exodus as reflected upon by the Apostle Paul in 1 Cor 10:1–4, which reads: "For I do not want you to be ignorant of the fact, brothers that our forefathers were all passed through the sea. And they all ate the same spiritual food and drank the same spiritual drink; for they drank from the spiritual rock that accompanied them and that rock was Christ"; and Acts 14:14–18: "Yet he has not left himself without testimony: He has shown kindness by giving you rain from heaven and crops in their seasons; he provides you with plenty of food and fills your hearts with joy" (Acts 14:17).

According to Laryea, certain principles emerge from the teachings of Paul that:

1. God set forth the places, boundaries, generations, and times.
2. God permitted the past generations to go their own way.
3. God never abandoned humanity through various testimonies [provision of rain and abundance of food].
4. The testimonies of God are fulfilled in Christ.[199]

From the principles above, it is inferred that it is God who established the Ga people and allowed their ancestors to go their own way, which is the *Kpele* religion. *Kpele* religion includes the worship of God, the worship of *Kpele Jemaworjii* (*Kpele* deities)[200] and the veneration of

---

198. Laryea, *Yesu Homowor Nuntsor*, 20–39.

199. Laryea, *Yesu Homowor Nuntsor*, 30 (translation mine).

200. "A *Jenmanwon* (singular, plural—*Jenmanwojii*) is a powerful type of intelligent *won* [spiritual power with limited activity], not specialized in his activities but practically omnipotent and omniscient. 'He comes and goes like the wind.' He is called *Jenmanwon* 'because he walks [moves] about the world and the towns' (*jen* = world, *man* = town)." Field, *Religion and Medicine*, 4.

the ancestors. Also concerning this fact, God has a testimony evidenced in the celebration of the *Homowor*, which testifies about the abundant life the people have enjoyed. It is the celebration of good life and good living based upon the religious, cultural and social and economic and political success.[201] This success in the "past generations" was attributed to the *Jemaworjii*.

Therefore, the point that Laryea establishes is that the testimonies of the *Homowor are* never perfect in the ways of the ancestors; rather it is fulfilled in Jesus the Christ.[202] He thus follows the continuity of the rock in Exodus as Christ to appropriate for the *Homowor*, and the Lord behind the supply of rain, a bumper harvest, and the *Homowor as* the same Christ. Laryea authenticates his Christology by locating it within the tradition of the church, citing the celebrations of Easter and Christmas.[203] If Christ in the past was the Lord supplying abundant rain in order to destroy hunger, then the Lord of the *Homowor is* Jesus the Christ. The difficulty with this Christology is that with all its great potential, it is with little explication of how relevant it is to the church, the Christ-event, eschatology, and the Trinity.

Some Limitations of Theologies from Africa

The many works of preceding Christologies indicate to us the many evaluations already completed in the construction of African Christologies.[204] African Christologies have dialogued with each other, thereby enriching the knowledge of African Christologies. As to whom Africans say Jesus is, it can be said that there may be many answers depending on the religio-cultural, socioeconomic, and political positions of the theologian. Honestly speaking, this should not alarm us at all, as in the Scriptures, Jesus has over thirty titles. So in spite of the numerous titles, we still need to examine and reexamine the views of who Jesus is to the African for a good faith knowledge.

If the Jewish views of Jesus were not upheld by Jesus, then the true identity of Jesus is simply not a mere opinion of individuals or a group of persons; rather it is what is authenticated by the Spirit of Christ. Hence,

---

201. Laryea, *Yesu Homowor Nuntsor*, 28–29 (emphasis mine).
202. Laryea, *Yesu Homowor Nuntsor*, 33.
203 Laryea, *Yesu Homowor Nuntsor*, 30–33.
204. See above for the review of the various Christologies in Africa.

it is needful to have a criteria which enables one to discern the identity of Christ in such a manner that is amenable to the Spirit of Christ. The criteria discussed after this chapter attempt to justify the critical evaluation of African theology in this chapter. These points are as follows: ultimate concern, contextual relevance, biblical and ecclesiological identity, and dialogue, location within the salvific event, ecclesiological relevance, Trinitarian uniqueness, and eschatological relevance.

It should be acknowledged that Nyamiti's account on ancestral Christology needs to be commended. Indeed, it stands out as the umbrella Christology for the Ancestor category, and the evaluation of his Christology will assist to appreciate more the Ancestor christological paradigm. He set his own criteria and then attempted to meet them. He indicates that for any African christological scheme to weather the storm, it must be Trinitarian in approach and should also have an ecclesiological relevance. The *perichoresis* of the Trinity allows the Father, who is the Ancestor *par excellence*, to work with the Son who is the descendant, and the sharing of the Holy Spirit as an act of oblation and Eucharist. The economy of the Trinity is revealed in the body of Christ, which the Holy Spirit by the will of the Father and the Son formed. By faith in the Son, who is the Brother *par excellence*, and by the power of the Holy Spirit, the Father gives birth to other children.

As could be realized, Nyamiti does well, but he does not deal with the Parousia of the salvific event, knowing well that the child Jesus was born, went through the rites of passage, and died. The eschatological dimension of the hope Christ gives is not tackled by Nyamiti. Moreover, his Ancestor Christology is not really in the AICs and the Pentecostal churches which have an original way of introducing African categories into Christian churches. Naturally, from the Roman Catholic perspective, such a teaching has a biblical and ecclesiological identity in the veneration of the saints and even exists as quite a slippery road.[205]

Apart from what other theologians have said concerning the Ancestor Christologies, it may be conceded that in many African societies, the *Jemanworjii* really are the controlling forces and their priests are the hope of the community under any circumstance. Thus, although the ancestors seem feared, respected, and venerated, under severe circumstances it is the priests who are consulted. In fact, they are the final authority on both

---

205. See Kabasele, "Christ as Ancestor," 126; see also Nyamiti, "African Christologies," 11.

temporal and spiritual matters and it is this competing element which makes the ancestral Christology unattractive.[206]

Therefore at this juncture, it is possible to choose the *Nganga* (traditional healer) concept as the christological concept of Africa. However, that falls short without a Trinitarian elucidation and an eschatological view, and fails also to deal with the issue of a salvific event, including the birth, life, death, resurrection, and Parousia of the Lord Jesus Christ. Indeed, Christ the Healer has a lot of ecclesiological relevance as in the AICs and the Pentecostal churches, and even in the older missionary churches it is high on demand. But Christ the *Nganga* ought to be understood in terms of the Trinity and should give us hope in the future.

Christ the Victor seems to be very ecclesiological, particularly for the church in Africa. It is true that many feminist theologians see Christ as the Victor. When viewed in the spiritual and the physical realms, it appeals to many theologians and Christians alike. Its ecclesiological identity can be located in Gregory of Nyssa. Biblically, it has a lot of appeal, particularly its focus on the ascended Jesus, who will also be coming to judge the living and the dead. This belief resonates with the African worldview, yet it also lacks the suffering Christ motive, i.e., his birth, life, and death of the salvific event. It also lacks a Trinitarian elucidation, which is very crucial for the identity of Jesus Christ, the Son of God.

Hence, liberation Christologies also fail for the same reasons above. Most of the liberation Christologies have an appeal for the church and hold eschatological views, looking at the Suffering Christ in solidarity with the poor and oppressed. However, it lacks a Trinitarian elucidation. Mercy Oduyoye's Christology, however, addresses all the issues in the salvific event, which is birth, life, death, resurrection, but excludes the Trinity. Although the ascension and the Parousia are not touched explicitly, she deals with the issue of Christ the Victor.

Christ in Kingship and Christ the Master Initiator, although biblical like all the others, lack the Trinitarian explication, and eschatological relevance. Though they deal with most of the salvific event, the ascension and Parousia are not mentioned. Regarding the sacraments and membership within the body of Christ, they are quite helpful because there is no Greek or Jew, male or female, and slave or free. Furthermore, the sacraments of Baptism and the Lord's Supper are well covered by these christological categories.

---

206. This is an African reality which is reflected by the nature of African spirituality. Chapter 4 deals with this issue regarding the *Okpelejen Wulormor*.

Laryea's Jesus the Lord of *Homowor* is biblical; it is contextual, like the other Christologies, yet it lacks the Trinitarian and eschatological explications, as well as the ecclesiological relevance. However, it could be represented by the *Christus victor* in terms of the salvific event, but lacks the remaining points. The *Christus victor* aspect provides it with an ecclesiological identity.

In conclusion, Nyamiti's ancestral Christology is preferable, yet it is also handicapped by factors discussed already. This situation calls for a new approach, by the introduction of the *Okpelejen Wulormor* as a *Kpelelogical* theology. In chapter 5 and 6, the Kpelelogical theology will be introduced through the *Okpelejen Wulormor* as an original concept from the Ga people of Ghana. But before moving on to deal with that, it is crucial to discuss the criteria for doing theology, and also the methods of doing theology in Africa, the themes and other important issues that seek possible ways of moving theology in Africa forward in chapter 4. In the following discussion we would wish to establish the relationship between ethnography and African Christian theology. This will help us to understand what African Christian theology is, and what it is not in view of present currents in ethnography in Africa today.

Theology of African Christianity: Ethnography or Kpelelogy?

Throughout this work, there has been the attempt to define contemporary African Christian theology within a context of African Christianity according to the spectrum of its expressions. The spectrum of African Christianity may be identified as the Early African Church (EAC), the Historic Missionary Churches (HMCs), the African Independent Churches (AICs), the Pentecostal and Charismatic Churches (PCCs) and the Renewing Historic Missionary Churches (RHMCs). It enables us to understand the ecclesiological worth associated with doing theology in Africa. And over the years, many scholars have shown the nature of African Christianity as they engaged different aspects of the spectrum in history. The role that scholars of African Christianity have played can only be hailed as an indispensable and fertile ground for doing African Christian theology. The above assertion is made at the backdrop of the contributions made especially regarding the HMCs, AICs, PCCs and RHMCs.

It is quite intriguing to realize that though there were a few theologians such as Oduyoye, Pobee, and Bediako who did some remarkable work on the African church fathers and their relevance to contemporary Christian theology, very few theologians and scholars of African Christianity have paid attention to the subject. African Christian theology and African Christianity scholarship had dwelt upon the HMCs, AICs, PCCs and RHMCs with tremendous results. And, it is fascinating to ask that if the African Kpelelogical or kpelelogical mind is inundated by the community of the past and present, why not the future, in addition? African Christian theology and the study of African Christianity cannot proceed without an appreciation of the Christian life and thought of African Christians of the past if one were to engage in an "African" study.

Moreover, in the continent of Africa, paying tribute and respect to foremothers and forefathers and those who are distinguished in life and history is of paramount importance. Thus, if ancestor theology is so important to African theologians, why would the life and theology of "ancestor theologians" not be found in the theological works of African theologians and other scholars? The Ga people of Ghana have an adage stated thus: "*blema kpaa no atsaa*" or "*kusum gboo*," which means that the good traditions of the past must be followed. The Akans would say "*amanie wohoi, yen tun twene*" to buttress the point further. If there are ancestors who have done much work in the past to the extent of influencing the whole of Christian thought worldwide, should that not be the starting context of doing theology? How can African theology be done when the traditions of the past African theology and Christian life is not understood? Or how could we understand our present theological disposition and Christian life if we do not have an appreciation of where we have come from?

The above questions lead us to appreciate that African theology and African Christianity of the present context need to be set in the traditions of the past as well as in the future. In this way, the study of theology and Christianity in Africa will be understood holistically and not parochially. Furthermore, in proceeding in the light of the above, African theology becomes more truly African as it moves away from parochial interests. The fact that African church fathers were able to deal with issues that affected Christian theology and Christianity worldwide on one hand, while at the same time they addressed issues peculiar to their local context on the other hand, surely ought to be a guiding principle for contemporary African Christian theology.

The discussion above sets the tone for discussing the issue of what African Christian theology is as against ethnography. Indeed, theology is not ethnography and ethnography cannot be deemed theology. From "ancestor theology" we understand that theology is grasped by a certain frame of mind termed in this discussion as Kpelelogy. And it is this frame of mind with its holistic tendencies that really draws a sharp line between African theology and ethnography. A Kpelelogical mind has a holistic epistemological disposition, which is that it takes information from say both objective and subjective and acts in accordance with its meaningfulness. Ethnography is different in this case in view of the fact that it concerns itself with everything or the whole from an objective point of view. Thus ethnography does not employ the knowledge of intuition or personal feelings of the researcher. Again, ethnography cannot be theology insofar as it does not employ personal experience in the collection and conveyance of information.

The Kpelelogical mind is the mind of faith seeking understanding and thus its immediate context is the Christian community that may be in concrete or latent. The body of Christ which is the church is a sacred community in existence with all its ambiguities. In other words, it is a community that is sacred but living with the secular at the same time. Therefore, both sacred and secular are confronted and addressed in a holistic way. Ethnography in its positivist orientation, though it collects both sacred and secular data, is still fragmentary. It should be said, that due to the secular nature of ethnography it is directly useful more as an academic exercise than in theological formation. Nonetheless, it provides useful information that is needed for better translations of the Bible as well as in the theological interpretation of African Christian faith. Theology partners with ethnography in directly building Christian faith through proper interpretation according to the local context.

As students of African Christian theology, we need to be clear in our minds that theology is not ethnography. Students who are interested in ethnography should be encouraged to pursue it as such. Likewise, theology students should be encouraged to pursue their theological studies without confusing it with ethnography.

Having said this, it should be said that African seminaries ought to pay attention to the fact that Christian theology is paramount in faith building and in ministerial formation. Priority ought to be given theological studies where the focus is on the interpretation of faith and faith building for pastoral duties. If anything at all, there ought to be a great balance between African Christian theology and ethnography. The tendency to skew all theological studies to ethnography means putting the lives of our churches in Africa in danger.

Ethnographical studies done in areas of religion and culture, psychology, sociology, economics and politics cannot be ignored so long as it forms the foundation upon which theological interpretations are made in a given context. Thus directly, from the secular world, ethnography presents the matrix for theology. Again, in the realm of the sacred, ethnography aids the collection of information on counselling, pastoral care, and African Christianity in general. These also are crucial in doing African Christian theology that is relevant to the needs of the African Christians and in mission.

So where do we place African Christianity in the light of the reflections done so far, in view of the fact that chiefly, it engages the ethnographical method in carrying out research? Is carrying out African Christian research the same as doing African Christian theology? In endeavoring to answer the question, it should be said that in carrying out an African Christian research, there is an objective collection of information regarding the African Christian phenomenon under study. If that is so, then the involvement of the personal and subjective faith is strictly forbidden. If the above is the main concern of African Christianity, and it is less concerned with the faith involvement and interpretation of the phenomenon under study, then it cannot be African Christian theology. Furthermore, insofar as African Christian theology, on the basis of its method of praxis as theologizing from subjective experience, is against African Christianity's objective approach, the two cannot be the same. The strong background of African Christianity is scientific and secular in nature while the background of African Christian theology is starkly immersed in faith. Studies in African Christianity like ethnography is neither kpelelogical nor Kpelelogical though it records and transmits African Christian information.

Typically, it is not African since it does not approach its study with the African frame of mind. As discussed earlier, the African frame of mind is either kpelelogical (African primal worldview) or Kpelelogical (African Christian's worldview). Again, kpelelogy and Kpelelogy are subjective, objective and holistic in nature unlike ethnographical studies. And since the approach of African Christianity is not African but deals with information about Africa, it may be said that is both African and not African. African Christian theology both in method and in its object of study remains securely theological and African.

African Christianity today is challenged by many issues regarding the meaning of the Christian faith. And Christian theology ought to be there to resolve these peculiar problems to engender faith in the Christian community. The seminaries and communities for training pastors and other leaders for the growth of the church ought to embrace solid theological training. A theological training that bolsters faith and gives great insight and understanding to ministers and other lay leaders in training. The consequence of understanding the faith better will affect the growth and quality of Christians. And it will surely be the strong basis upon which pastoral ministry and Christian mission in Africa could flourish.

Moreover, ethnographical studies should be seen as an auxiliary tool for the interpretation of the Christian faith in so many ways. Hence, it may be given some space in the seminaries and other Christian institutions. However, ethnographical studies may be quite important in religious departments of other institutions than in seminaries. The call is simply that African Christian theology should never be misconstrued to be ethnography. Additionally, Christian theology in general and in its context of Africa ought to be given a lot of attention it deserves in order to resolve the challenges it is facing in ethics, politics, and science and culture and religion and corporate world and economy and psychology and the well-being of the African person as a whole.

4

Method and Criteria of African Christian Theology

Postmodernism and African Christian Theology

ONE OF THE WAYS by which African Christian theology may well be understood is looking at the method, sources and criteria used in doing it. Postmodernist positions in contemporary theology perhaps as manifested in postcolonial criticisms is to deconstruct some of the traditional ways of doing theology. What ought to be noted in this deconstructive position of theologians is that deconstruction of traditions such as in the church as a matter of principle has limitations. In other words, deconstructive positions in themselves are not absolute in nature. The moment a position of deconstruction becomes absolute, it loses its grounds of deconstruction. Therefore, grounds are still important in the presence of deconstruction in doing today's African Christian theology.

As it is hoped to be discussed, methods, sources and criteria form grounds upon which African Christian theology deconstructs traditional theology and reconstructs it to suit its living reality. As it stands, not every theological escapade may be acceptable and how do we know which theological enterprise is acceptable or not? It is important to ask this question because, without a ground of doing Christian theology in Africa, there cannot be anything that may be described as African Christian theology. John Mbiti's definition of what African Christian theology is, is important in appreciating the salient features required of all African enterprise of theology.

His definition showed the approach, the sources, and criteria of African Christian theology. Mbiti says, African theologians "ask themselves . . . within the context," which suggests a certain method of doing theology. Then he mentions the sources as reason, Bible, history, culture and contemporary context. Perhaps the criteria he suggested was that African theology ought to be done by Africans and ought to be pragmatic. Therefore, it should be reasonable to accept to discuss in principle, the grounds of method and criteria in this chapter. As a matter of approach, the sources have been engaged in chapter 1 and other parts of this book, hence it is not discussed as a topic in this chapter.

Methods of Doing African Christian Theology

In general Christian theology, the use of method is very crucial in defining the nature of theology at stake. Theology defined as faith seeking understanding or the interpretation of the Christian faith may be found among ordinary Christians. As they are known in Africa as grassroots theology, they provide meaningfulness to African Christians as they reflect on their faith and existence. These grassroots theologians may not express these reflections in books, however, they may express these reflections in symbols, songs, dance, and other cultural means of communication. It should be said that inasmuch as the contents of these grassroots theologies may be very insightful and edifying, they may be poetic and lacking in elucidation, consistency of elucidation, syllogism and orderliness and comprehensiveness.

Therefore defining the method of African Christian theology may be helpful in organizing thoughts more creatively, clearly and consistently. J. N. K. Mugambi said in the late '90s of the twentieth century that "African Christian theology is in a methodological crisis owing to the lack of methodological consciousness."[1] This point was made evident during the ecumenical meetings of the Eastern African Theologians in the 1990s.

Mugambi further notes that African theological method of theological anthropology needs a shift toward theological introspection and self-criticism.[2] And he says this on the basis that this shift will help African theologians to frame the cultural foundations of African theological

---

1. Mugambi, "Theological Method," 5.
2. Mugambi, "Theological Method," 5–40.

thought, and creatively build upon those foundations, new theological systems which are attuned to those foundations. In this way, the shift will help African theologians to appropriate the knowledge acquired from other cultural and religious traditions for the edification of African cultural and religious identity.

Again, he suggests, that African Christian theology needs to shift from descriptive and prescriptive methods to postulative methods.[3] However, Emmanuel Adow Obeng suggests a method of praxis as against a synthetic method in order to meet the relevant needs of Africa in the here and now.[4] Other "philosophical" methods include the deductive and inductive methods in doing theology in Africa. According to Mugambi, these two "philosophical" methods yielded different sets of insights in African Christian theology.[5] Mugambi seemed to have put African Christian theological studies into two categorical methods, which are (1) theological anthropocentricism and (2) ethnography.[6] Certainly, Mugambi may have added the study of African Christianity to African Christian theology. And it is important to reiterate the point that if African Christianity is an ethnographical studies, it is difficult to accept it as an African Christian theology.

Mugambi disputes but refers also to the inculturation and liberation methods described by Charles Nyamiti. And looking at the above description of the method of doing theology in Africa, one sees the eclectic manner in which theology is done. Indeed, Emmanuel Martey did not mince words when he stated that

> a student of African theology realizes that the way theologians employ ATR, traditional culture, and philosophy in theological analysis differs considerably, and that it is not all that easy to group theologians into clean, identifiable categories. One theologian may, for instance use more than one methodological approach to the study of ATR. An example is the phenomenological-ontological approach of John Mbiti, not to mention his theological interests. However, a close examination discloses a common approach in the inculturation endeavor and another among the liberation-oriented theologians: While among the

---

3. Mugambi, "Theological Method," 5–40.
4. Obeng, "Synthetic and Praxis Models," 41–54.
5. Mugambi, "Theological Method," 8.
6. Mugambi, "Theological Method," 8.

former, the common approach tends to be phenomenological, among the latter, emphasis is placed on functional analysis.[7]

Certainly, one may have to agree with Mugambi that "these endeavours are important and essential in the growth of the Church but they are not enough to ground the Church in the culture of a community."[8] He said further that, looking at the penetration of the gospel in the communities of the Coptics and Ethiopians, there is a long way to go regarding African Christian theology.[9]

Consequently and at once, the method of doing theology in Africa ought to be one of the greatest interest for the student of African Christian theology. The manner in which African Christian theology proceeds without endeavoring to lay down critical methods of doing theology ought to be discarded. As it is, African Christian theology has all kinds of classifications regarding theological methods which compounds the issue. First, there is the philosophical classification which looks at the method of argumentation. In this case, the inductive and deductive method of argumentation or of doing theology has been deemed theological method.

Second, the philosophical method of doing research has also been appropriated as doing theology in Africa. Emmanuel Martey and Jesse Mugambi both make mention of the phenomenological or the descriptive method and particularly of the African Christianity scholars and the inculturationists. The functional analytical method is seen in African liberation theology. Here again, one sees similarities of Emmanuel Martey's classification to that of John Macquarrie's methods, such as phenomenological, interpretation (analytical) and application methods of theologizing.[10] It should be said, however, that a closer look at inculturation theology will indicate the presence of functional analysis as well. Likewise, liberation theology cannot be done without a phenomenological material. Thus phenomenology and analytical theology both cannot be ignored by any African Christian theology. In other words, both descriptive material and analytical work is needed to do African Christian theology.

Third, there is also a category of theological anthropology and ethnography, which are overarching methods for African Christian theology

7. Martey, *African Theology*, 74.
8 Mugambi, "Theological Method," 10.
9. Mugambi, "Theological Method," 10.
10. Macquarrie, *Christian Theology*, 17–20.

and studies in African Christianity, respectively. And these two tend to represent the prescriptive and descriptive positions howbeit not exclusively.

Fourth, Jesse Mugambi suggests for African Christian theology a postulative method rather than descriptive and prescriptive methods of doing theology in Africa. Meanwhile, fifth, he acknowledges, but hesitantly, the inculturation and liberation paradigms as methods of doing theology in Africa.

Sixth, Emmanuel Obeng asserts the use of praxis for relevant theology in Africa. This comes against the synthetic types that may be analytic be they inculturation or liberation.

Seventh, it is crucial to single out Kwame Bediako for clearly showing his method of doing theology. His method, no less entrenched at Akrofi Christaller Institute at Akropong, Ghana, and as a method of *continuity and discontinuity* or *identity*,[11] employs all philosophical methods of study including phenomenology or description, interpretation or analysis, and induction or deduction. And irrespective of the theological position, be they inculturation or liberation or the *cultra-libero* or that which may be Kpelelogical, the method of continuity or discontinuity is employed.

Kwame Bediako, the father of this method of doing theology in Africa, sees identity as crucial in determining and elucidating the details of African Christian theology.[12] It is finding an identity between the being of the African and the revelation of the triune in God in Jesus Christ in the power of the Holy Spirit. And since the being of the African is more or less encapsulated in the language, translation is key. Thus, the method may be located within the context of translation, which entails a fulfillment position in the realm of the theology of religions. Continuity and discontinuity as a theological method is derived from the early theological works of the church particularly those of the African church fathers such as Tertullian and Origen.

The theological method of continuity and discontinuity is important insofar as it positions itself differently from the indigenizers and biblicists.[13] The indigenizing theology deals with the issue of identity by imposing the religio-cultural as well as other aspects of the contexts of theology on the Christian message. It fights for the identity of the African context including the language, culture and some traditional practices

---

11. Bediako, *Jesus in Africa*, 53–54; 63–76.
12. Bediako, *Jesus in Africa*, 63.
13. Bediako, *Jesus in Africa*, 54–56.

even if they were contrary to the Christian message. The biblicists are on the other extreme of the indigenizers. The biblicists tend to impose the Scriptures on the culture without engagement with African culture.

However, unlike indigenization and biblicism, the method of continuity and discontinuity or method of identity focuses on aspects of the African ontology that agree with the Christian message and those that do not. Those aspects of the African ontology that agree with the Christian message are in continuity and thus affirming. In the meantime, aspects of the ontology that are in conflict are deemed discontinuous and thus rejected.

Defining Method in Doing African Christian Theology

The various categories of theological methods suggests that there is a need to define the meaning or content of the theological method in African Christian theology. There is the philosophical group and the theological groups of methods. Right away, the philosophical methods ought to be subsumed in doing African theology, since philosophy is not theology. And this has been dealt with in the earlier chapters of this work. Furthermore, looking at the theological example of Professor Kwame Bediako, we see that philosophical methods are tools deployed in doing the theology in Africa. However, the act of the faith seeking understanding was engaged as the ontology of the African vis-à-vis the Christian faith. *Therefore, theological methods show which of the two, i.e., African ontology and Christian faith, initiates the theological processes.*

This shows that in the case of the method of continuity and discontinuity, both the African ontology and the Christian faith are held in tension. However, since they are looking for fulfillment in the African ontology the engagement seems to be skewed slightly in favor of the Christian message. The point is buttressed further inasmuch as the African ontology in the engagement is not envisaged to critique the Christian message.

If theological methods show which side of the theological poles of engagement initiate the theological reflection, then praxis is so important. Emmanuel Obeng has shown that the most relevant method for doing theology in Africa is the method of praxis. The poles of engagement are praxis and the Christian message. In the case of Emmanuel Obeng, praxis "is a technical term designating a way to knowledge that bind together action, suffering, and reflection."[14] And in this case the initial step for the theological process is determined by the action and suffering, and then followed by reflection.[15] So though the poles are held in tension like the method of continuity and discontinuity, praxis differs by initiating the theological process. Praxis is the method of doing contextual theology in the Third World as well as among minority and subjugated people in other parts of the world.

Evangelical Christians in Africa may not easily embrace the theological method of praxis as may be compared to the method of identity in view of their background. Certainly, the continuous and discontinuous/identity method shows its evangelical as well as the Roman Catholic leanings.[16] Nonetheless, it is pretty clear that doing theology by postcolonial theologians in Africa show that they critically engage the Christian message and in particular the Bible. Re-reading the Bible in postcolonial hermeneutics and in African women's theology by African theologians be they Evangelicals or not, challenges the above theological method. Insofar as the method of continuity and discontinuity cannot critically engage biblical texts based upon say the language and culture of Africans, it is handicapped within the framework of translation itself and hermeneutics in general.

The opposite is the praxis method although it may have problems with self-criticism, yet it has proven to be liberating for most Christians in the Third World. South African theology in particular has contributed immensely to African theology and to their own national development in this regard. Unfortunately, praxis has not taken root in West African countries like Ghana. Though Emmanuel A. Obeng highlights it, the Ghanaian method of doing theology is that of Kwame Bediako. Taking caution in ensuring that the world does not dictate the Christian message without a critical engagement is also important in faith building communities. And it is important that the method of praxis heeds at all times the need to hold the poles of engagement in tension. Particularly, heeding the pole with the Christian message with the local Christian experience in parity.

It should be said that theological methods viewed from identity and praxis in African Christian theological reflections are linked to the

14. Migliore, *Faith Seeking Understanding*, 17.

15. Guiterrez, *Theology of Liberation*, 9; see also Torres, *Challenge of the Basic Christian Communities*.

16. Knitter, *Introducing Theologies of Religions*.

theological methods in contemporary Christian theology. I have deemed it fit to identify four main methods in Christian theology stemming from which pole of the interpretation of the gospel initiates the dialogue.[17]

There is natural theology that endeavors to establish theology on the basis of what creation and reason inform us. Then, owing to the critique of the above Christian theology as a mere fabrication of the mind, Barth declares that the initiative of the whole theological process is to be taken by the Word of God. Thus the Barthian christocentric method is the second. However, since John Calvin, also the father of the Reformed tradition, has indicated that there is a correlation between the knowledge of God and the knowledge of ourselves, Paul Tillich advances his method of correlation. Tillich's method of correlation is a mutual critical method of engaging questions raised in existence and answering with the Christian message. Though it starts from the realm of existence on one hand, the Christian message has an overwhelming influence. Yet, the pole of existence in the theological dialogue has a critical outlook on the Christian message itself. Therefore, it may be described as a mutual critical method.

Nonetheless, David Tracy has endeavored to advocate for a mutual critical method stemming from what he sees as the weakness inhering the Tillichian method of correlation. Then after the method of correlation, the method of praxis as the fourth method emerged. The method of praxis is similar to the method of correlation; however, the questions raised from existence are questions arising from the human predicament (poverty)[18] that is experienced. Thus a theologian is the one who is thoroughly immersed in the suffering, and pain of the context in which they live.[19]

Moreover, the method of praxis is fragmentary, i.e., not holistic in nature owing to its attachment to the context. It does not also place a premium on deep subjective experience of divine wholeness which is echoed as "life in abundance" (John 10:10). The subjective divine experience of salvation is a cardinal point in African faith expression, and doing theology without it is misleading.[20] The method of correlation has a holistic approach to it because it does not merely involve itself in the theological reflection which is a *sine qua non*, but also listens to the questions or cries of other people posed to the gospel of Jesus Christ.

17. Cf. Migliore, *Faith Seeking Understanding*, 16–19.
18. Bonino, "Latin America," 16–43.
19. Bonino, "Latin America," 31.
20. Parratt, introduction to *Introduction to Third World Theologies*, 1–15.

The Kpelelogical Method

It may be interesting to note that since African Christian theological methods of Kwame Bediako and Emmanuel Obeng fail to hold the poles of the Christian message and the questions of existence in a mutual critical manner, they fail to address the holistic existential needs of African Christianity. Thus, these methods remain fragmentary insofar as they remain divided on religio-cultural and socio-politico-economic existential issues of Africa, respectively, and fail to connect to ecclesiological and faith concerns.

A Kpelelogical method is an all-encompassing African theological method based upon the *Kpele* institution of the Ga people of Ghana. It is a method that brings to bear a way of doing theology as a matter of being grasped by the triune God in today's world, in Africa, and in an active life and reflecting on the meaningfulness of God's grace. This method stems from the divine grasping of the triune God that leads the theologian to bring fresh interpretation of the gospel to the particular in the context of the universal. Accordingly, it is able to interrogate and engage both Christian message and existential issues as a matter of experience in a mutual critical manner.

The Kpelelogical method is useful because it takes into consideration the African Christian experience as crucial in understanding everyday life in the light of the Word of God. That seems to be the African Christian's way of life and it is natural to the Kpelelogical existence where life is interpreted on the basis of the realm of the spirit, and the realm of spirit on the basis of existence. There is a dynamic relationship between the African's existential life and essential life and the two cannot be severed. This method removes the academic tinge on African Christian theology, even the tinge that ossifies it. The method is natural to the African theologian because it flows with the African ontology and Christian ontology that has been united by the subjective experience and knowing of the triune God in an African church context.

The Kpelelogical method differs from natural theology method which derives from creation the understanding of God, because the basis of interpreting the reality of God is the revelation of triune God, the Father through Jesus in the power of the Holy Spirit. Though the Kpelelogical method brings to bear the natural world in the interpretation of faith in God, it is secondary to the African Christian experience on the basis of the church's proclamation. Again, it is not fixated to the realm of the natural order, instead it opens up to the history of the world and its estrangement and seeks for its redemption for today and in the coming kingdom. Therefore, the African estrangement is concerning as a matter of conscience and as a matter of African Christian responsibility. The African estrangement evident in the squalor, poverty, ecological crisis, religion, culture, politics and social values are taken on, in view of the questions and answers they pose and provide respectively to African Christian faith.

In another vein, the Kpelelogical method is divergent in relation to the christocentric method of Karl Barth insofar as it takes on board at the same time the existential situation with the Word of God. Thus, the role of the Kpelelogical method is to provide an Evangelical approach that is highly sensitive and thus relevant to the needs of the people in Africa. Yet it is not an approach that may be found in the African Christian theology of Samuel Waje Kunihyiop. It is not a Word of God that is translated or interpreted to reach the African context. And even if it does, to what extent is the African culture regarded as endowed enough to bring more elucidation of the Christian faith itself? The Kpelelogical method is not merely a "spoon feeding" theology whereby it is assumed that African culture is pure darkness. Far from it, it acknowledges that God has not ever departed from his creation, including those created in God's image in Africa. And this eternal presence of God, though seemingly far away from them has impacted on the cultures with richness of culture that point to the triune God. It involves the African religion and culture and socio-politico-economic context of Africa in a mutual but critical engagement for fulfillment or meaningfulness. Yet, the method is similar to the Barthian method insofar as it takes the Christian message to the same level of the African Christian experience in an ecstatic Kpelelogical conscience.

Paul Tillich's method of correlation that is paradoxical is very close to the African Kpelelogical method. The two methods, namely, the Tillichian and Kpelelogical may be more convergent than divergent, because they take all reality into the realm of the grasping of the triune God. Thus, the difference is found in the "accentuated" African spiritual or psychological experience known as the Kpelelogical conscience that may be manifested physically or in exuberance. Moreover, the two settings are completely different although they are connected by a common principle of the nature of the estranged human being. The exuberance is critical as it leads to actions of advocacy, affirmative action and civil disobedience.

The Kpelelogical method takes seriously both the Christian message and the questions of existence. And the decision about which of the two poles precedes the other resides in the theonomous presence associated with the ontological mode of doing theology known to us as Kpelelogy. Thus the question of which side of the poles initiates the process is not in question because either side is a possibility according to the ecstatic reason of Kpelelogy and paradox.

Moreover, the African methodology of Kpelelogy is natural to their holistic worldview and it is true that most Africans uniquely think this way. Western civilization of science does fragment or compartmentalize the faculties of the human being, but the African in spite of colonization thinks holistically. Therefore, the Kpelelogical method is more original to Africa. Its roots are also the basis for many theological insights in the tradition of the church.

Criteria for Doing Theology

The aim of this chapter is to establish through a brief outlook of the main epochs of the church's history, a criteria for contemporary African Christology. The essential criteria include ecclesiastical identity, contextual identity, Trinitarian identity, eschatological concerns, the Christ event, and the ability to dialogue with other contextual theologies.[21] The purpose is to show that the theology is inextricably linked to the context as well as the nature and work of Christ.

The chapter brings out the necessary criteria, which ought to be addressed in confecting a Christology by observing them in the historical practice of the church. The early church's use of *Christos* and the early and patristic church's Christologies shall therefore be examined. Similarly, it shall extend to the middle ages, the reformation, the modern period and then finally the postcolonial and Third World Christologies. Furthermore, some critical issues pertaining to the criteria in theology will be discussed and conclusions drawn.

---

21. Migliore, *Faith Seeking Understanding*, 187, 22–122; see also Küster, *Many Faces of Jesus*, 15–36.

The Early Fathers, Their Churches, and the Criteria

The word Christology is made up of two words, *Christos* (Christ) and *logos* (reflection). Therefore, Christology may mean reflection on Christ. However, one may then ask who the Christ is? The quick answer may be Jesus of Nazareth. The word Christ is said to have been derived from the Greek word *Christos*, meaning the "Anointed One." It was first used in the Septuagint only twice to mean the Hebrew word "*Mashiach*," at Ps 2:2 and then in Dan 9:26. It would be interesting to understand how the translation was made into the Greek Septuagint as it may enlighten our understanding of the Jewish understanding and the Hellenistic understanding of who Jesus is. The translation for the Anointed One in Hebrew (*Mashiach*), which in the Greek is *Christos*, could have meant for the Hellenists "covered in oil" or "anointed."[22] Thus, the answer for the question "What is Christology?" should be a study to identify who the Messiah is in a given context. And for Hellenists, he is Christ, to wit, *One Covered in Oil*.

Although we could say that Christology began with Gen 3:15,[23] and the translation of the Septuagint, it is safer to admit that the apostolic appropriation and proclamation of the gospel about Jesus of Nazareth was after his death and resurrection. Thus the death and resurrection of Jesus becomes the context within which the early church appropriated the names of the Anointed One. In addition, their proclamation as recorded in the Gospels followed the ascension of the Lord Jesus Christ and the empowerment from on high by the Holy Spirit at Pentecost.

The death and resurrection of Christ is now the power of the gospel. Jesus is seen as the Son of Man, the Son of David, and the Son of God.[24] He was also proclaimed as the Messiah, Anointed One and the Christ as well as about thirty other names.[25] The above statement clearly reveals how contextually relevant the identity of Christ is attached to his function or work. The Anointed One has a special position of saving people from bondage and establishing freedom and justice. Thus, within the name we can identify an ultimate concern and contextual identity because of the languages and meaning of the words used. It contains an ecclesiological and eschatological identity because the church is firmly based on the salvation of Christ whose proof was the death and resurrection (Christ

---

22. *Online Etymology Dictionary*, s.v. "Christ."
23. "And the Seed of Adam shall crush the head of the serpent."
24. Lowe, "Christ and Salvation," 223–25.
25. Sobrino, *Christ the Liberator*, 117.

event). The names appear to have an intercultural element due to the Jewish Messiah and Greek Christos.

The early church fathers also continued within the different contexts they found themselves to identify a more meaningful Christology just as the Apostles did. Therefore, the word *Logos*,[26] which was already an apostolic word, was deeply appropriated. However, in the course of time, it opened a new chapter of doubts. First, that the *Logos* was subordinate to God and second, that the *Logos* was human. This belief led to the beginning of a series of councils, the most significant being Nicaea and Chalcedon.[27] This understanding occurred because the *Logos* was perceived to be subordinate to God.[28] Athanasius rises to the occasion in the Council of Nicaea (325) and argues that the Son is *homousious* with the Father and is thus begotten not created. Also, there was another issue between the Antiochians and the Alexandrians. The Antiochians believed that the divinity and humanity of Christ existed without confusion, while the Alexandrians believed they existed without separation. The Council of Chalcedon (451) therefore agreed that the divinity and humanity of Christ existed without confusion and without separation.[29]

A look at the contexts of the antagonizing actors reveal to a large extent why they opted for a subordinate Jesus and a divine Christ.[30] As long as context has influence on the nature of Christ, it is conjoined with soteriology which is the work and importance of Christ. Since the work of Christ is also connected to the importance or the meaning of Christ, it should possess an ecclesiological and eschatological identity. It is also necessary to note that the divinity of Christ dealt with the Trinitarian identity of Christ, while the humanity dealt with the issues of the Christ event. These debates in themselves are examples of how ecumenical or contextual dialogue was engaged to gain a better understanding of the identity of Christ.

Christ the Victor Christology of Gregory of Nyssa (335–95) expresses how the fears of believers are overcome.[31] Obviously in an era

---

26. The Prologue of the Gospel of John seems to have well appropriated the term *Logos* in the second century, though we see the word in Justin Martyr's apologetics, drawing deeply from the Platonic and Stoic philosophies of "Logos."

27. Lowe, "Christ and Salvation," 226–27.

28. Peters, *God the Worlds Future*.

29. Kelly, *Early Christian Doctrines*, 280–343.

30. Kelly, *Early Christian Doctrines*, 280–343.

31. Migliore, *Faith Seeking Understanding*, 182–83.

of mysticism, the most suitable Christology could only be that which conquers and gives victory to the church. Therefore his Christology is contextual, ecclesial, eschatological, and most probably Trinitarian in view of the Christology from above within the Christ the Victor.[32]

Middle Ages and Reformation and the Criteria

The theory of satisfaction, based on the feudal system of lords and serfs, is another Christology in context of Anselm of Canterbury (1033–1109).[33] Jesus, who is divine and human, is the only way by which human beings could be saved and God appeased.[34] The use of the analogy of the lord and serf apart from penance[35] also suggests the context in which Anselm lived.[36] The self exile imposed by Anselm due to the king's oppression of the church could have been the context.[37] Anselm came face to face with a lord (king) who was so wicked to the extent that exacting taxes arbitrarily was without any human face. Anselm therefore, might have appreciated the satisfaction Jesus the Christ of God gives to all the believers. Here again one recons the contextual, ecclesial, and eschatological and Christ event as essential features of his Christology.

The love affair of Peter Abelard (1079–1142) may be the most probable context in which he wrote his moral influence theory.[38] The moral influence theory is a subjective form of analysis in which the love of God exemplified in the salvific event of the Lord Jesus impels the same kind of love on the ones to whom it is revealed. And even if one agrees that the subjectivity of such a theory may be discrediting,[39] it can still be maintained that without the knowledge of the love of God one can likewise not be able to share with others.[40] Thus, once again, one discerns

---

32. Koo, *Doing Christology*, 24.
33. Migliore, *Faith Seeking Understanding*, 184.
34. Migliore, *Faith Seeking Understanding*, 184.
35. Lowe, "Christ and Salvation," 231.
36. William, "St. Anselm."
37. Sadler, "St Anselm of Canterbury."
38. Lombardi, "Abelard and Heloise."
39. Lowe, "Christ and Salvation," 231.
40. Migliore, *Faith Seeking Understanding*, 185.

a contextual, ecclesiological relevant Christology stemming from his love relationship with Heloise.[41]

Although Martin Luther is said not to have given a coherent treatise on Christology, his idea of justification is very contextual, ecclesiological, eschatological and full of christological and soteriological functions.[42] Volker Küster (1962)[43] sees Luther's Christology as *Crucis patiens*,[44] which is the suffering Christ certainly for the atonement and a blow to the mystic *purgatio*.[45] Truly, the story and life of Martin Luther provides ample evidence for this point. John Calvin systematized a type of soteriological reflection via his *munus triplex*.[46]

A soteriology in which Christ is viewed as the prophet, priest and king, which teaching has the propensity to biblically reflect the moral influence (prophet); satisfaction (priest in rendering the perfect sacrifice); Christ as the Victor vanquishes all foes (king).[47] These two reformers and their works clearly show us the contextual, ecclesiological and eschatological claims of their works in view of the Reformation and the need to clearly state that Jesus Christ is the only Savior whose salvation is sufficient. Hence the Christ event in their works cannot be overlooked.

Modern Christology and the Criteria

Immanuel Kant (1724–1804), with his scheme of rational critique and self-critique moved the noumenal from the phenomenal because the capacity to comprehend the noumenal was not present for the human rationality.[48] Not him alone but people like Gotthold Lessing (1729–1781) had all in the modern spirit made theology an opprobrium because it

---

41. Lombardi, "Abelard and Heloise."

42. Lowe, "Christ and Salvation," 232.

43. Küster, professor of cross-cultural theology at Protestant Theological University, Kampen, The Netherlands, and previously a lecturer in the history of religion, mission, and ecumenics at the University of Heidelberg. Küster's research interests include Christian art and theology in the majority world, interreligious dialogue, and comparative religion.

44. Küster, *Many Faces of Jesus*, 30.

45. Küster, *Many Faces of Jesus*, 30.

46. Calvin, *Institutes*, 2.15.

47. Barth, *Church Dogmatics*, IV.1–3; Also in Migliore, *Faith Seeking Understanding*, 187.

48. McCormick, "Kant, Immanuel"; see also Lowe, "Christ and Salvation," 233.

utilizes ideas without evidence.[49] Responding from all the avalanche of rationalism's attack on the theological enterprise at the time, Friedrich Schleiermacher (1768–1834) comes to the rescue as he makes soteriology a function of Christology.[50]

For him, to experience Christ is to know him. Since higher consciousness makes one aware that life depends solely on God but it is unattainable; yet Jesus Christ presents himself as the higher consciousness.[51] At this stage, one realizes that the christological outlook is most influenced by rationalism and is thus contextual. It is also ecclesiological in that Schleiermacher's *gefhul* is reminiscent of his pietistic roots. This Christian experience at that time must be a great hope to the Christian community.

After the failure of Albert Schweitzer's search for the historical and apocalyptic Jesus, it was realized that the humanity and even the divinity of Jesus was in question. This point implied that the foundation for the argument of Hegel is challenged.[52] Bultmann and his school of dogma came on to demythologize the myth of the gospel and to present the Christ of faith.[53] However, it was Käsemann who understood from the parables of Jesus the opportunity to realize the Christ who is fully divine and fully human.[54] Barth's Christology is Trinitarian, dialectical and soteriological in nature. This stance is crucial in order to avoid a "Christomonism" because Christology works with the perichoresis of the triune God. Barth builds upon the *munus triplex* of Calvin while emphasizing the prophetic office[55]

The above discussion shows that even in the early church, the name apportioned Jesus was indeed contextual and necessarily held a soteriological function. Even within the christological councils one could discern that the nature of Christ provided meaning to the name of Jesus and its relevance to particular communities. Further, reference to the above discussion clearly reveals some essential elements of doing Christology. These include a contextual foundation, which should resonate with the needs and aspirations of the *ekklesia*.

---

49. Lowe, "Christ and Salvation," 233.
50. Lowe, "Christ and Salvation," 233–36.
51. Schleiermacher, *Christian Faith in Outline*, 88, 94; Niebuhr, *Schleiermacher*, 226.
52. Lowe, "Christ and Salvation," 238.
53. Lowe, "Christ and Salvation," 238.
54. Lowe, "Christ and Salvation," 238.
55. Lowe, "Christ and Salvation," 238.

One important factor for meeting the ecclesiological needs is eschatology. The identity of Jesus always carries with it the salvific event. The reflection is Trinitarian representing the act of God in Christ in creation history. It deals with the dialectical relationship between God and humanity.[56] The above discussion was limited to the early church through the modern period which dealt with the critical features or criteria for Christology. It is equally important to now look at contemporary Christology and observe how the criteria are used in post-colonial and Third World Christology.

The Nature of Christology Today (Postcolonial and Third World Christology) and the Criterion.

Postcolonial and Third World Christologies seem to have emerged out of the context of a colonized world after its freedom. It possesses a propensity of self assertion in many ways of which Christology is one.[57] The Third World is mostly composed of underdeveloped and developing countries in the world. It is very striking to note that the contemporary theological enterprise appears to be flooded by the majority of voices within the Third World. Also, it is the postcolonial and Third World context that Christology is being done. This work shall explore the contextual issues and then glean from it the criteria for the Christologies.

According to Küster, the cultural-religious context in the Third World is made up of the accommodation/indigenization/translation models and inculturation theologies. The socioeconomic and political contexts comprise the development/new political and liberation theologies.[58] The context for theologizing in the Third World has been diverse.[59] Members of the Third World accepted the same theme of "liberation" because they all suffer from the same system of domination and oppression.[60]

While Africans and Asians focus primarily on religio-cultural factors of oppression, the Latinos focus mainly on socioeconomic and

---

56. Migliore, *Faith Seeking Understanding*, 187, 221–22.
57. See Sugirtharajah, *Asian Biblical Hermeneutics*, 21–25.
58. Küster, *Many Faces of Jesus*, 24–25.
59. Bimwenyi, "Origins of EATWOT," 19–26; see also Chandran, "Methodological Approach," 95; Rayan, "Irruption of the Third World," 106–27; Martey, "African Theology," 46.
60. Martey, "African Theology," 47.

political issues.⁶¹ From the religio-cultural perspective, African theologians recognized what is called anthropological poverty, which should not merely be defined in terms of material deprivation, but rather "first of all in function of one's conception of the human being."⁶² This understanding comprises everything that constitutes the being and essence of the African. Asian theologians, also on religio-cultural grounds, see poverty as a virtue (choice) or evil (imposed).⁶³ However, it should be noted that the cultures and religions of the Third World may be oppressive and religio-culturally the people must be liberated.⁶⁴ The best form of mediation should be dialogue.⁶⁵ Also, such issues as extreme individualism and privatization, and all cultures of the First World, which compete with the egalitarian societies of the Third World must be confronted.⁶⁶

The current world order of consumerism and a neoliberal economy epitomized in globalization are issues touching on the religio-cultural realities of the Third World, which are causing many difficulties.⁶⁷ Culture should rather be seen as an instrument of God's liberation. The emergence of inculturation and indigenization theologies all point to religions and cultures, which are instruments of liberation orchestrated by God against all manner of oppressive elements. Even today, the qualms that many people all over the world have against liberation theology may be the use of Marxian analysis, which stood as the problem of the African.⁶⁸

The socioeconomic situation as captured by Sergio Torres nonetheless indicates the worsening situations of the poor in the Third World.⁶⁹ There is a widening gap between the rich and poor, although countries working to improve on their economies by creating more wealth within their own countries.⁷⁰ Vandana Shiva (1952) describes this neoliberal economic situation as follows:

61. Martey, "African Theology," 47.
62. Martey, "African Theology," 47.
63. Martey, "African Theology," 47.
64. Martey, "African Theology," 52–56.
65. Bediako, *Jesus in Africa*, 64–75; Martey, *African Theology*, 81–106.
66. Torres, "Irruption of the Third World," 7; see also World Alliance of Reformed Churches (WARC), "Covenanting for Justice," 186; Bediako, *Jesus in Africa*, 54.
67. Torres, "Irruption of the Third World," 7; see also World Alliance of Reformed Churches (WARC), "Covenanting for Justice," 186; Bediako, *Jesus in Africa*, 54.
68. Martey, "African Theology," 55.
69. Torres, "Irruption of the Third World," 6.
70. Torres, "Irruption of the Third World," 6.

> The philosophical and ethical bankruptcy of globalization stems from reducing all aspects of our lives to commodities and shrinking our identities to that of consumers in a global market place. Two thirds of humanity depends on natural resources for their livelihoods and meeting basic needs. They live in an economy with land, water and biodiversity as their primary capital, their means of production their economic security.[71]

Moreover, the current stage of socioeconomic oppression in the form of globalization affects groups of people except for the rich and powerful. In addition, with its inception, there has not been peace, but to the contrary, increasing violence, exploitation and death. The rich of the North continues to sacrifice the wealth of the poor for nothing, but greed through a mechanism of indebtedness. It has been reported that, "in terms of ideology and religion, globalized neo-liberalism is a totalitarian world-view that presents itself as the only true one and, theologically speaking makes money it's God through its total commitment to individual profit and economic efficiency."[72]

The religious, cultural, social, economic and political contexts, within, which Third World countries do Christology clearly exhibit how contextual, ecclesiological and eschatological they are. Postcolonialism can be seen as a strong driving force to this end of ensuring Jesus is found in the daily lives of Third World people by presenting Jesus as the one who went about doing good to the poor and oppressed. Liberation theology therefore, focus on the basic reality that Jesus has taken a preferential option for the poor.

Some Critical Issues and the Criteria for Doing Theology Today

The first challenge that contextual Christologies tend to present is the many Christologies commonly termed "faces of Jesus." The second challenge is what to do with the many faces of the Lord Jesus as some do

---

71. Shiva, "Earth Democracy," 117. Shiva is a philosopher, environmental activist, and eco-feminist. Currently based in Delhi, Shiva has authored more than twenty books and over five hundred papers in leading scientific and technical journals. She was trained as a physicist and received her PhD in particle physics from the University of Western Ontario, Canada, in 1978 with the doctoral dissertation "Hidden Variables and Locality in Quantum Theory."

72. Kruger, "Biblical and Theological Significance," 231.

not want to respond to them perhaps because they are reactionary and fragmentary in outlook or mere sketches making it difficult for a systematic response.[73] What is now suggested is the stronger focus on commonalities and cross-fertilization among the many faces of Jesus in the Third World.[74] It is suggested that contextual theologies ought to reach out from their localities to the world-wide community.[75]

Sugirtharajah confronts numerous critical issues in the Asian theological arena, which has a greater intensity than elsewhere. Some of the critical issues he presents include syncretism, fundamentalism, and theological rivalry, to mention a few. Sugirtharajah deals with the issues in quite a lucid manner as he states that "the anti-syncretic lobby on two ideas. One is that there is pure unalloyed gospel that can be planted in any situation. The second is the notion that culture, especially the receiving one, is a static, finished product that is usually evil and waiting to be purified."[76] He explains as follows: "First, the gospel narratives indicate that the gospel never existed in a pure state and its power is evident only if it is couched in the historical and cultural experience of people. Second, cultures are constantly in a process of radical renewal and enrichment."[77]

Another issue is that christological reflection ought to fully represent the historical accounts namely, incarnation, death, resurrection, ascension, Pentecost, and the eschatological/apocalyptical account in the *Parousia* (Christ event).[78] In deciphering authentic and unauthentic Christologies, Küster suggests the criteria of identity, context, and dialogue.[79] The identity refers to the established traditions of the church that must be followed strictly. The context refers to the religio-cultural and socioeconomic and political relevance of the christological construct. In some sense, if the criteria of Paul Tillich (1886–1965) are employed, there should be an ultimate concern and this ultimate concern ought to be a matter of being and nonbeing for the context.[80] (When a subject

---

73. Küster, *Many Faces of Jesus*, 15–36.
74. Küster, *Many Faces of Jesus*, 159.
75. Migliore, *Faith Seeking Understanding*, 221–22.
76. Sugirtharajah, *Asian Faces of Jesus*, 258–64.
77. Sugirtharajah, *Asian Faces of Jesus*, 260.
78. Bosch, *Transforming Missions*, 512–15.
79. Küster, *Many Faces of Jesus*, 27–28.
80. Tillich, *Systematic Theology*, 1:12.

is becoming a being or nonbeing means when the subject is important/relevant to well-being.)

The excursion to see in glimpses the nature of Christology is complete and it is necessary to evaluate the essential criteria which shall be useful for any contextual Christology for today. The first criterion is realized following the notion of Volker Küster and Paul Tillich regarding the need to have an ultimate concern, contextual, and ecclesiological identity framework as criterion for doing Christology. The second criterion is that contextual theologies ought to be intercultural/ecumenical to wit; there should be a dialogue to promote cross-fertilization for all theological discourse within and without the southern and northern hemispheres. The third criterion is that it should be eschatological. A fourth criterion is that it should be Trinitarian. Finally, a fifth criterion is that it should engage the salvific event or the Christ event.

The criteria herein established is the basis for analyzing and evaluating African Christologies in the preceding chapter. And it is clear that most theologians in Africa while paying attention to contextual issues failed to deal with the other components of the criteria. Of particular interest now concerns ecclesiology and theology, Trinity and theology, ecclesiological identity, and eschatology. The criteria will be the basis for constructing an African Christology of Christ the Potentate, Priest, and King in the *Okpelejen Wulormor*.

Dichotomies of African Christian Theology

The dichotomies of African Christian theology refer to the inherent fragmentations associated with doing theology in Africa. Be they deliberate or not, the lines drawn are distinct. They include the Christology below and Christology above dichotomy, the liberation and inculturation paradigm, and African theology and science for example and many other epistemologies that occupy the African mind.

Christology Below and Christology Above

Just as it was between two major schools as to the measure of weight either the humanity or the divinity of Jesus Christ should carry in the interpretation of Christian faith in both Nicene and Chalcedonian creeds, so it has been with African theologians. Knowingly, or unknowingly, contemporary African theologians seem to have been limited and caught up in the web of the dualism of which emphasis is placed on the humanity or the divinity of Jesus Christ at a given time.

Koo Choon-Seo shows that a Christology that flows from the divinity of Jesus Christ above and through the incarnation represented the Christology from above. Clearly, in this way, the theological insight to be appreciated is bound to reflect the majesty of Jesus Christ in whatever way at the expense of the humanity of Jesus. Today, such an endeavor may not be strictly viewed as erroneous if not heretical as was the case of the Niceno-Constantinopolitan Creed. Yet a careful look reveals the fundamental flaw when in pursuing the divinity of the Lord, the humanity which is equally crucial in the interpretation of the person and work of Jesus Christ is ignored or sidelined.

A typical African Christian faith is prone to associating with the *Christus triumphans* as they rely on that to accept the Christian hope. The resurrected and the ascended Lord Jesus Christ is the symbol of the power that is appropriated to overcome the cosmic forces of evil. And Mbiti is so clear regarding this position which also serves as one basis for African Christianity. For example, though Bishop David Oyedepo may be associated with Charismatic faith preachers, his theological disposition toward the *Christus victor* is natural insofar as he is African.

Oyedepo places the victory which Christ won as the center of his teaching when he affirms the Christian's place in the kingdom of God as "greater than John the Baptist, and if greater than John the Baptist, then greater than the bosom of Abraham." Again, since believers "are reigning with Christ *far above* principalities and powers" there is ample reason for believers to extend that to existence. In this regard, the bishop accentuates Christian victory even in the face of Christian suffering by faith. These are his words when he was reminded about his suffering early days in ministry.

> There is a way you love God that blinds you totally to your needs and circumstances. I met one of our daughters in Canada some time ago, and she tried to cast my mind back to our early days in ministry. She said, "I know how much you suffered when this church was starting." It sounded like news to me, because I did not know that I suffered at all. Me suffer? I couldn't see what I went through as suffering....
>
> However, I couldn't see those contrary circumstances, because there was something driving me on the inside. I would so

> often kneel down and thank God for giving me the privilege of serving as a worker in his vineyard. Until this daughter of mine mentioned it, I didn't know that I went through such "hardness." The Lord told me that it was because of the love I have for Him.
>
> The Love of God in the heart is a bedrock; and it is a gift from the Holy Ghost. The Bible talks about "faith which worketh by love" (Galatians 5:6) This means that whatever you speak, believe or act, without love it is futile; and when faith fails to work, it results in frustration.[81]

J. Kwabena Asamoah-Gyadu attests to the dominion theology of contemporary African Christianity which is arguably represented by the rapidly growing Pentecostal and Charismatic churches. And in particular he cites David Oyedepo as one who "specializes in book titles that directly address issues of dominion, two of the most important being *Possessing your Possessions* and *Walking in Dominion*."[82]

And moreover, Asamoah-Gyadu appeals to Wariboko to buttress the point further that the *Christus victor* theology of Oyedepo is an "excellence model." Again, Asamoah-Gyadu indicates the Africanness of Oyedepo when he extended the essential *Christus victor* to Ghana existentially at the "Maximum Impact Summit" in 2002.[83] He writes that

> the most fascinating part was when Bishop Oyedepo, using a typical African libation prayer form, poured oil on the ground, declaring that by this act the land of Ghana has been anointed to be productive and her people blessed to prosper in all they did from then on.[84]

Wariboko has shown that the greater portion of influence on the ministry of Oyedepo is the latter's background in the AICs and particularly the Aladura Church.[85] Therefore, the point that the African worldview, or particularly the African religious worldview, accentuates the Christian notion of the Divine cannot be overemphasized. However, it should be observed that there is a need to link this position with the humanity or historicity of Jesus Christ in order not to plunge the church

---

81. Oyedepo, *Anointing for Exploits*, 61–63.
82. Asamoah-Gyadu, *"Taking Territories,"* 4–23.
83. Asamoah-Gyadu, *Contemporary Pentecostal Christianity*, 125.
84. Asamoah-Gyadu, *Contemporary Pentecostal Christianity*, 126.
85. Wariboko, *Nigerian Pentecostalism*, 21.

in Africa into a docetic slough. As it was the tendency in the period of the African church fathers, the lessons ought not to elude us.

The link of the AICs and the PCCs on one hand and early African Christianity on the other hand may have to inform and guide today's theology in Africa, and how it influences the churches and their membership. African Christians must endeavor to appreciate the historical nature of the gospel and appreciate its relevance to the contemporary Christian life. One should be quick to state conceivably, that though African theologians have spent more time in dealing with the historical and the human Jesus, it has not yet percolated into the soil of the African church that is also the consciousness or being of African Christians. To date, the activity of dominating the supernatural realm and transposing it into the natural realm of existence remains the preoccupation of many African Christians and churches.

African churches still spend much time on what is popularly known in Ghana as the "PHD" ministry, which is an acronym for the Preaching, Healing, and Deliverance (exorcism). Inasmuch as PHD ministry should be commended, as it affirms strongly the indispensability of the subjective knowledge of the triune God, it is prone to becoming irrational because of distorted understanding. Today, the abuse of subjectivism without an accompanying objectivism has led some African Christians and pastors to be caught up in a web of unethical behaviors and heresy. This worrying and sometimes embarrassing trend in African Christianity continue to be a recurrent media reportage.

So long as African Christianity cannot see the link between natural reason and the supernatural reason as seemingly contradictory, but actually not, the problem of suspending human reason in dealing with the problems of Africa will lead to the latter's retrogression. African Christians ought to know that God is the basis or ground of human reason, though God is above human reason. And that it is sensible and reasonable to have faith in God which is noncontradiction of reason itself. Moreover, insofar as Christianity is not madness but rather promotes the well-being of all human beings, all human abuses arising out of the distorted person of Jesus Christ by overstretching the divine nature at the expense of the human nature is unethical.

Furthermore, with respect to the Christian experience of the victorious Jesus Christ of Africans, there seems to be a correlation of those unethical issues associated with the *Ngangas* with some pastors and bishops of African Christianity. Thus, it is imperative to bring to the fore the human Jesus Christ of Nazareth, who being anointed went about *doing good* and *healing* all manner of diseases. And since the human Jesus who is divine is the basis for all Christian ministry, Jesus the *Nganga* or Healer of African Christian theology should point to Jesus as the perfect (ethical) healer. This ought not to be forgotten in view of the backdrop of pastors who abuse their members in the name of the supernatural healing. Moreover, the perfect healer that Jesus Christ is and was and will be should show that African Christian appropriation of the divine healing of Jesus ought to be based upon the human goodness of Christ. African Christian ministry of PHD, hence, should operate in divine power that is infused with uprightness and the good.

One striking issue is that the overstretching of the divinity of Jesus Christ in Africa has prophetic eschatological implications. The prophetic eschatological implications refer to this-worldly, political and ecclesiastical goals. Fortunately, for Africa and unlike in the United States of America, the prophetic eschatology associated with the PCCs and to some extent AICs is not political. Political goals of an eschatology that is entrenched in apocalypticism leads to distortions of the Christian hope. Some of the distortions include the absolutization of race and nations. The ecclesiastical distortions that may also be related to some fundamentalist interpretation of the apocalypse also leads to the absolutization of some churches. This distorted ecclesiastical ambition of some churches perhaps may be lurking in some PCCs or AICs. All the above forms of distorted view of eschatology are utopianism.

Another thing is sure, which is that prophetic eschatology is this-worldly and it is akin to the promises of God made to the patriarchs. So many churches in Africa, like other places such as the United States, are this-worldly insofar as they lay claim to the very prophetic declarations to the patriarchs. This-worldly eschatological vision itself is God's vision revealed by the Father through the Son in the power of the Holy Spirit in the cosmos. Yet it also tends to be distorted when it becomes the sole end of all creaturely existence. This distortion shows up when the humanity, the suffering and the death of the Lord Jesus Christ is brushed aside and it has no real significance for our suffering and dysfunctional cosmos.

Consequently, the sense of apocalyptic eschatology that works with the coming aeon or the kingdom of heaven and thus otherworldly eschatological paradigm ought to be cosmic and also an embodiment. This ensures correlation of the otherworldly eschatology with this-worldly eschatological paradigm. Moreover, it is in view of maintaining consistency with a theological understanding and celebration of the Jesus Christ who resurrected from the dead and who is the Savior of the cosmos. Christianity needs to pay attention to the fact that to be a true disciple of Jesus means to have a fair share of suffering. African Christians need to be sensitive to missionaries and other workers who are in constant danger and laboring under suffering and death. Such workers who long for the new earth and the new heaven as the early Christian believers who also experienced the victory of Christ over the enemies of death.

A Kpelelogical theology is a cosmic understanding of reality in which the triune God is the ground and the end of all existence. On that score, the issue of Christology from below or Christology from above as a dichotomy or duality or a dialogical position does not arise. A Kpelelogical theology proceeds from both the above and below and more accurately from a cosmic point of view in which the ground of creaturely existence below is reverenced as above all creaturely existence. It is an African worldview that is also fully restored to the reality of the divine as the goal of human existence. In the *Kpelelogical* sense of the Akan, it represents the sense and longing for *Nyame*, since there is nothing that satisfies except *Nyame* itself. *Nyame* could be explained perhaps in a Kpelelogical or philosophical longing as that which satisfies all human desires.

Therefore, theologically, *Nyame* is the symbol of God in cosmic reality that satisfies and brings meaning to human existence. It is both the ground of creaturely existence and the goal of it. Moreover, Kpelelogically it may be described as the religious philosophy of *Gye Nyame*. From a theological perspective or *Kpelelogically*, *Gye Nyame* as a philosophical symbol becomes also the symbol of God that is the *cosmic* ground from which all creatures derive their existence and toward which they move to find their Goal and End of being.

If as revealed to the African Christian in the power of the Holy Spirit by Jesus Christ the Son of God the Father, that God is the only One that brings creaturely estrangement to an end; and that this reality is achieved by grace through faith in the only begotten Son of the Father in the power of the Holy Spirit; then Jesus is *Nyame*. *Kpelelogically*, Jesus Christ is the cosmic ground that cannot be grounded from a parochial view. Hence the call for a dialogue between a fragmented position of the Christology below and Christology above is unfortunate. *Kpelelogical* theology is a paradoxical apprehension of one God in three persons in holistic and cosmic manner. It moves beyond the dialogue and the fragmentation of the one person of Christ who is united in human and divine natures without confusion and without separation.

Now having noted the propensity for African Christianity to be skewed in the direction of triumphalism or Christology on one hand, on the other hand, the theological paradigm is rather skewed in the direction of human suffering in Jesus or Christology below. African Christian theology seen first, in the category of kinship including, Jesus as the *Luaba* of *Mulaba* (Chief), the *Cimankida* (Hero), the Prince, and the Elder Brother shows a Christology from below. Second, another Christology from below is Jesus as the Master of initiation. In this, African theologians discuss the rites of passage in African culture such as birth, puberty, marriage and death in relation to the life of Jesus Christ. Third, liberation Christologies such as African black theology, African liberation theology and African women's theology derive their inspiration from a Christology below. The liberation theologies of Africa look at Jesus more as a human being though the divinity is fully acknowledged. However, the tendency to see Jesus Christ from his suffering and poverty as the hope for the poor and oppressed may be prone to ebionism.

There two main characteristics that point to the nature of the African theologies that look at Jesus Christ from below are ecclesiology and politics. Unlike the triumphalist Christianity in Africa, it is a theology that focuses on the crucified Jesus and reflect on its ethical implications for worship, fellowship, witnessing, preaching, teaching and serving from the church community. Again, it is a theology that focuses on the crucified Jesus and reflect on its ethical implications for society, politics, economics, religion, culture and so on. Therefore, though it is triggered by the context of the church and society it is not materialistic as may be recognized in the Christology from above of most African Christians. A theology from below is important insofar as the faith community as well as the society and the cosmos as a whole is challenged to be ethical.

In other words, a theological perspective from a Christology below enables the church to be purged of distortions that show the lack of agape in the community of faith. Similarly, the human predicament that is often characterized by selfishness and is challenged by the revelation of the crucified Jesus. In fact, the African initiation and kinship Christologies like the liberation Christologies has the capacity to enrich the understanding of ecclesiology eschatologically. And though they may seek a very this-worldly eschatological end, they in the process engender otherworldly eschatological ends. The understanding that initiation and kinship Christologies bring to the table engages the realm of both the present and past. The past according to Mbiti may also be the future that is shared with the living dead in the present and anticipated by the living. While this conception of Mbiti may be deemed the nature of African primal worldview, it has the power to enlighten Christian understanding of eternity and temporality in the present and eternity at the end of history. It may also represent the idea that creatures will finally return to their creator at the end of history (in the future).

However, a challenge associated with a Christology from below is its lack of holistic appreciation of reality. The need to take the two natures of the person of Jesus Christ seriously and not confusing them or separating them is essential. The fragmented approach immediately truncates the holistic divine economy that is weighty in the African worldview or Kpelelogy. Thus, a Christology from below may be prone to becoming a geopolitical ideological tool, which may seem good initially but is ultimately destructive. And even if the destructive element becomes dormant due to other factors, it fails to address other pertinent issues. For example, African Christian theology thrived on the waves of Black theology in South Africa when the struggle against apartheid was on. However, today Black theology is seriously challenged at a time that there is no longer apartheidism and black Africans are in the helm of affairs. Black theology is challenged at a time that the presence of other black Africans is now a threat. These challenges reveal the inadequacies inherent in ideological theologies. But the worst form of this Christology from below that theologians from Africa may have to appreciate is the totalitarian nature of ideology. In the long run, when the conditions are set, a hibernating theology of ideology will rear its ugly head as it manifests its absolutist and oppressive tendencies.

The question is, what becomes of a theology that is conditioned to fight from below when it gets the upper hand from above? Since such a theology is conditioned to fight from below, it has no sense of fighting from above, therefore, when it gets the upper hand from above, it may not know what to do. Thus, the deviation from the tradition of Christian theology, which does not separate and confuse the two natures of Christ leads to crippled theologies that are not capable of expressing the full power of Jesus Christ in the Spirit.

This sense of keeping to the creeds was a key component of the African Christian theological enterprise in the 1950s. It is quite difficult to understand now, why such a position is virtually missing in the major works of contemporary African theologians. And at this point, it may be quite important, to reiterate the importance of respecting and keeping to the teachings of the early African Christian theologians like Origen, Tertullian, and Athanasius, and Cyprian and Augustine among others.[86]

As African theologians, there is the need to know how to better honor our elders, which the best way to honor them is to vigorously and critically engage their instruction and wisdom. It may be right, thus, to assert that any contemporary African theological enterprise that does not listen to or pay attention to what past African theologians have done is un-African itself. And it does not need to be accorded the respect it deserves by the younger generation.

The point being raised here is that failing to acknowledge the works of previous African scholars in theology is tantamount to presenting problems that they might have resolved in the past. This is an attack on Christian faith itself as theological errors deliberately espoused become heretical teachings that impinge on the economy of the triune God. Many of these contemporary theologies have become misleading as long as they have been driven by largely, parochial motives of ideology. As stated earlier these positions of ideology sought to put Africa at the center, instead of the revealed Son of the Father in the Spirit. Hence, though, the African element was critical, it masked the critical function of the Trinity. Theology is about God, and in the principal sense, about the triune God who alone helps every creature to know itself by an initial knowledge of the triune God in revelation. It is not just as we see ourselves in our own eyes, but rather as revealed to us by the Father in the Son in the Spirit. So the question "Who do you Africans say that I am?" ought not to lead African theologians into "christomonisms" and ideologies of utopian nature as is pretty much the case. For the affirmation of the true identity of Jesus himself was only based upon the corroborating work of the Spirit. Jesus was emphatic regarding the knowledge that is revealed by the Spirit as that which reveals and confirms his being.

Thus even though in the AICs, PCCs and even the renewing HMCs the role of the Holy Spirit was paramount, African theologians did not pay attention to who the Spirit of God is. A few theologians such as Mercy Oduyoye engaged the AICs in their works, however, much of the theologies have very little to show how the Holy Spirit enabled African Christians to understand and know God revealed in the Son of the

---

86. Ositela et al., *African Initiatives in Christianity*, 3–25; Gonzales, *Story of Christianity*, 76.

Father. And how it also shows them their true identity as well. This may be elaborated further in the subsequent discussions.

The foregone discussion dovetails into what the knowledge about the triune God reveals and does regarding the destiny of all the creatures of God including Africans. It is here that Africans can tell their true destiny as they discover it in the economy of God the Father, Son, and Holy Spirit for the world. The destiny is not, of course, fatal, whereby it is static and predetermined. Rather, it indicates the plan of God for Africa that is constantly coupled with the freedom of their being, and, which is tied to all other races and creatures of the world. This freedom of Africans that has a destination, is derived from a thorough understanding of the relationality that characterizes the triune God *ad extra* and *ad intra*.

Thus the unreasonable fragmentation of African theological discourse is a false start arising from ideology. And the neglect of the rich African Christian encounter with absolutely universal in concrete reality who is Father, Son, and Holy Spirit is the result of the distortions inherent in contemporary African theology. The famous Christian song which arises from the church in Africa below has been ignored.

1. Take glory, Father; Take glory, Son;
   Take glory, Holy Ghost, I am born again
2. Take glory, Father; Take glory, Son
   Take glory, Holy Ghost; I am victorious[87]

African Christianity is full of expressions of and allusions to the Trinity as in the early church because it is daily encountered. In Africa, the doctrine of the Trinity ought not to be viewed as speculation at all, because it is its lifeblood. Consequently, there is a call for all African Christian theologians to understand and appreciate theology in the terms of the Trinity and as situated in the encounter of Africans in the church.

The Inculturation and Liberation Dichotomy

It should be stated that the chief motif for the espousal of African Christian theology is self-identity. That the struggle for self-identity is clear, and this has been shown in previous discussions. In fact, gleaning from the African Christian definition of John Mbiti shows the stress on who qualifies

---

87 Bible Study and Prayer Fellowship, *Choruses We Love to Sing*; see Omenyo, *Pentecost*, 225.

to be an African Christian theologian. Mbiti is unambiguous as he stated that it surely must be an African theologian who is also a Christian.

The background of Mbiti's definition points to the suspicion that abounded with regards to the negative mindset some missionaries and colonialist had about the African. These suspicions may be that, first, the African is not civilized, and second, the African did not have "proper religion," and thus, third, the African is incapable of managing his own affairs. Thus the African theologian is challenged on many fronts, including, intelligence, leadership, in the areas of culture, religion, social and economic organization and politics. That those things which border on the creative human spirit is far away from the spirit of the African person is thereby challenged by the assertion that African theology should be done by Africans who are theologians and Africans.

This inherent and pervasive conscience of the African mind had developed slowly but steadily until it became a watershed in the mid-1800s and the mid-1920s. Thus the ground was set for reactions in the mid-1900s which resulted in political freedoms of many nations. The ground was ripe as discussed earlier for the African conscience to be fully aware of the dire situation in which their person was impoverished. The struggles and responses from the cultural, religious, intellectual, social, economic, psychological and political aspects of the African people were expressed in various ideologies, art forms, and drama, literary works and music. Therefore, it was imperative for the African theologian to articulate their own understanding of the Christian faith in the African context taking all the sources seriously. It was done as shown already, to demonstrate that the African can manage his own affairs.

Nonetheless, the approach that sought to explicate the Christian faith in the terms of God was actually done in the terms of Africa. African theologians seem to have been carried away by the euphoria associated with the independence struggle as well as the struggle for self-identity. Some theologians seem to have aligned on the ideologies perhaps suspectingly or unsuspectingly on the sides of socioeconomic and political struggle on one hand, and anthropologico-religio-cultural struggle on the other hand. These theological positions, which more or less are ideological, sadly, have been ossified in deep-rooted positions. The ideological positions may be clearer when a closer look is taken at the development of Ghanaian political history.

Therefore, it is not quite surprising when Martey shows that Francophone countries tend to be more socioeconomic and political, while the

Anglophones tend to be more anthropologico-religio-cultural in their approach to doing African Christian theology. Martey together with other theologians have indicated the unrealistic, or better put, the un-African way of fragmenting the two positions above. Although, Ghana through Kwame Nkrumah at the time of independence was tilted in the position of liberation associated with socioeconomic and political struggle, and its idea is pervasive today, its rootedness is questionable. And unlike the liberation paradigm, the inculturation trend on the side of anthropology, religion and culture is deeply rooted in the major or pioneering schools and institutions of the nation Ghana. These major sides also form the backgrounds more or less of the two major political parties in the country.

The call that African Christian theology needs both positions had been raised by contemporary African theologians. Therefore, it is quite baseless and difficult to perceive why theologians today in Africa should be aligned in either of these two entrenched positions. As discussed earlier, a cultura-libero African Christian theology that might have been suggested is also not a true reflection of the Trinitarian God who also resides in Africa. And the Kpelelogical experience with the Trinity certainly brings all things including all the aspirations of the African people be they liberation or inculturation together. The Kpelelogical mindset being holistic rejects the fragmentation of salvation and embraces emancipation as encountered in God as holistic.

Thus the motif of ideology had led to some levels of unhelpful cynicism as well as naivete on both sides. The cynicism is to be found in the antipathy against theological ideas that may not be found in the category of the two positions. And in Ghana, it is pretty clear that many theologians on the side of inculturation are cynical to theological ideas regarding liberation or those of traditional theology from elsewhere. Thus, though the particularity which is so important in African Christian theology is stressed it is done at the extreme. And furthermore, it has led to some kind of isolationism that is not quite healthy if African Christian theology is also about sharing. The theological naivete in contemporary African theology concerns theologians who more or less are not interested either in liberation theology or inculturation theology but may want to theologize.

Obviously, it has also led to serious errors that are a result of not engaging the effectively Christian experience in Africa as well as the theological source of tradition in doing African Christian theology. For example, this fragmentation would not have arisen if the doctrine of the one person and divinity and humanity of Jesus regarding the Nicene and Chalcedonian creeds were taken seriously.

This raises issues regarding how African theologians have actively engaged Christian theological heritage to elucidate the faith in the context of Africa. In the following chapter, the interest will be probed regarding the manner in which Christian theological heritage, including that of the African past, were taken seriously.

5

The Essence of African Christian Theology as Faith in the Absolutely Concrete

Christian Faith and African Christian Theology

THIS CHAPTER CONTINUES THE critical discussion on what African Christian theology stands for and what it has achieved in its contemporary form. This is done to bring into sharp focus the essence of African Christian theology as the absolutely concrete.

First, is African Christian theology an interrogation of faith or is it an academic exercise that does not fancy personal faith and the practical faith of the community of faith? Does it take a look at the current kerygma, practices and actions of the church in light of the cardinal themes of faith that have existed in the church since its inception? Is the theological enterprise in Africa primarily motivated by a sense of elucidating Christian faith in the light of the challenges African Christians face or is it a mere academic exercise? These are pertinent questions that ought to be raised if there is a genuine desire to grasp the true essence of African Christian theology.

Second, it is important to find out to what meaningful ends African Christian theology leads. The connection of African Christian theology to ideological ends is utopia and does not have meaning. Thus, the meaningfulness of African Christian theology lays in its connection of the inherent divine human qualities in Africa to the Divine from where it finds fulfillment. But how has African theologians seen this reality as against its tendency for parochialism?

Third, this part asserts the position that the essence of Christian theology in Africa lays in its comprehension within the global context. It attacks the notion that theology in Africa will be successful only if it operates in the narrow African religio-cultural and socioeconomic and political milieu. Hence, it delves into the thesis that African Christian theology is a manifestation of the absolutely concrete, which is also universal.

African Christian Theology Is Not Mere Intellectual Exercise but an Interrogation of African Christian Faith

Theology in Africa is challenged by many issues that may range from isolationism to credulity regarding theological contexts.[1] It is also important to state that in Africa, there are issues that may be related to methods of doing theology as we have discussed in the previous chapter.[2] Besides, what may be of grave concern with regards to these isolationist and naïve theologies and the nonexistent or inadequate methods are the issues of distorted theologies of identity and utopianism. It ought to be stated also that the underlying factors include the missing axiomatic themes of the Trinity and eschatology in African Christian theology.

The missing axioms of the Trinity and eschatology in the thorny issues of identity and utopianism also arise as a result of, first of all, the failure to start theology from the African Christian encounter with the triune God.

Second, inability to incorporate the African Christian experience of the liberating action of the economic Trinity in the cosmos which is the source of Christian hope distorts the natural identity of Africans. Besides, the inability to involve a proper eschatology in the African's encounter with the triune God has led to utopian perspectives. These utopian perspectives involve African identities of culture and religion on one hand and socioeconomic and political identities on the other hand.

Ultimately, failure to recognize that the traditional sources or themes of Christian faith are living realities of the church in Africa undergirds the ideologies of identity and utopianism.

---

1. Bediako, *Jesus in Africa*, 54–55.
2. Mugambi, "Theological Method," 5.

The Impact of Distorted Christian Theologies in Africa

One perturbing situation that may be associated with contextual theology globally is their inability to find real connection to the faith of ordinary Christians and the church. African Christian theology in general is a thoroughgoing contextual theology, and though it seeks to connect with native Christians, it ironically loses contact with them.[3] The phenomenon of losing touch, significance, or meaning or importance to the thriving churches in Africa had led to a strong hesitation by the Christian community in Africa to engage theology as a whole. The mention of theology seems to suggest abstract, cerebral, and academic speculation that certain classes of Christians enjoy among themselves but which is of no essence for "practical Christianity."

Furthermore, even though it was generally agreed that the AICs were to be the source and a fertile ground for doing theology that was in touch with the African Christian experience,[4] it is doubtful that African Christian theology took the AICs seriously. Today, some ecumenical theologians from other continents prefer dialogues with the AICs directly or may prefer studies with African scholars in African Christianity. Having theological discussion on the themes of the Christian faith in Africa ought to be the prime objective of African theologians and inability on their part means a distortion of the Christian message. This clearly reveals the inadequacies of African Christian theologies in providing theological insights regarding the faith of Christians from the African perspective.

This distortion of Christian theology in Africa has led to the relegation of theology to the background. Theology seems to be unsuccessful in its bid to provide leadership roles insofar as it ceases to be recognized as faith building, faith affirming and faith elucidating in the challenging contexts of Africa and the world. Today, it may be said that theology in religion departments of universities is rapidly losing its place to the study of Christianity in world religions.

Similarly, in the seminaries, theology is no longer becoming central to the training of pastors and lay workers for the community of faith who need strong theological knowledge to advance Christian mission in Africa. This fundamental challenge may be attributed partly to the distorted

---

3. Ross, "Nicene Methodology"; Bediako, *Jesus in Africa*, 77–79; Nyamiti, "African Christologies Today," 11–12.

4. Martey, *African Theology*, 76–78; Oduyoye, *Daughters of Anowa*, 126–27.

contemporary African Christian theologies which do not connect theological ideas to faith building and faith affirmation.

Unlike the theological writings of Paul the apostle and of Origen that continues to inspire and guide Christian faith, contemporary African Christian theology does not provide much inspiration or guide to contemporary African churches. Many pastors have been trained to appreciate African Christian theology, yet in their churches, those theologies hardly find their place as inspiring and guiding. For example, even in the Historic Mission Churches (HMCs) where knowledge in African Christian theology is high, the place of this contemporary theology of Africa is wanting.

When it comes to the fastest growing communities of faith in Africa, and in particular, the Pentecostal and Charismatic Churches (PCCs), the theological positions as in doctrine that defines the faith is largely lacking. Moreover, there is nearly a theological blackout in most of these institutionalized and growing churches. And although, theological education is now being pursued in the Historic Mission Churches (HMCs) seminaries such as the Trinity Theological Seminary in Legon, Ghana, by some members of the PCCs, they focus mostly on practical theology. Thus, there is a clear indication that theology as a matter of understanding the Christian faith in the context of the church in Africa and the world today is not regarded as very important. The unpalatable results of the lack of proper understanding of the Christian faith emerges from the poor explication of Scripture, heretical teaching, and myriad unethical pastoral ministries associated with the PCCs. Also, some of the abuses perpetuated against some members of the Christian community by some pastors may be due to ignorance arising from the lack of sound theology.

Having indicated the lack of contextual relevance to the churches, we should not hesitate to state that, during the struggle against apartheid and colonialism, African Christian theology provided leadership.[5] In elucidating the Christian faith from the context, many African Christians were empowered to engage in the struggle for independence and freedom. Furthermore, concerning issues of gender were also brought on board, which today influence many Christian communities in Africa to empower women both in ministry and society as a whole. At this point, one may have to acknowledge the great contribution of Mercy Amba Oduyoye in

---

5. Martey, *African Theology*, 81–82.

this regard. Her writings and her engagement with the women of the community of faith had gone a very long way in achieving this.[6]

However, there seems to be lacking the creative energy that was in the early contemporary theologians of Africa such as Mercy Oduyoye.[7] Today's postcolonial context of African Christianity has changed from what it used to be. Moreover, it was then that the PCCs were burgeoning and classified as movements. Today, the PCCs are now institutions and the impact of their presence has been felt in all the HMCs. Thus, the context of doing theology in Africa ought to arise out of the issues that these African Christians face. Postcolonial theology of contemporary Africa seems to have lost touch with the experiential realities of African Christianity today. And it is certain, insofar as contemporary African Christian theology has relied simply on the ideology of identity. Besides, it is the simple ideological position of showing that Africans can manage their own affairs.[8]

Today, there are many issues regarding how the Christian faith ought to engage culture, religion, arts, entertainment, politics, ethics and even science and technology among the many other issues that Africans raise. How do we interpret the Christian faith so that Africans, Africans in the diaspora, women and their oppressors are liberated from their estranged predicament in Africa and beyond? And how is Christian theology shaping the Pan-African discourse and development as a whole?

It should be pointed out that today, many Christians at various positions of influence are looking to the church for direction. Christians in various capacities want to know how to keep their faith in the religious pluralistic Pan-African space. They want information regarding law enforcement, peace and security, and sound judgment regarding foreign policy. In other words, the current dispensation demands a faith interpretation that informs the Christian community in general to make

---

6. Oduyoye, *Beads and Strands*.

7. The creative work of Mercy Oduyoye is also preceded by another great Ghanaian in the person of Dr. Kwagyir Aggrey, whose approach to identity was more holistic, in that humanity was placed in the context of the harmony between blackness and whiteness. Their influences mostly were felt in the World Council of Churches and All Africa Conference of Churches. Ward, "African Christianity in the Twentieth Century—Part Two," 357.

8. See Aborigines' Rights Protection elite's contributions in Laryea, *Ephraim Amu*, vii, 17–26; Kraemer, *Christian Message*, 338; Address of Welcome by Nana Ofori Atta II to the Synod of the Presbyterian Church in the Gold Coast, 1954, 4–6, in Parsons, *Churches and Ghana Society, 1918–1955*, 30–31; Martey, *African Theology*, 63–65.

sound judgments that are amenable to the liberating plan of God for all people having Africa born in them and the whole universe.

By so doing also, a new paradigm of liberating, healing and renewing society emerges. This is against the backdrop of the liberating and self-asserting or even the reconstruction paradigm that may be embedded in liberation and inculturation theologies. For example, contemporary black theology needs to be interpreted in the new context of Africa where blacks are in the helm of affairs. This is a theological paradigm that does not only inform, but critiques the Christian community in Africa in the light of God's kingdom that is at hand. Therefore, though it must not lose sight of the old enemy it must also know the new enemy and interpret the faith in the light of these experiences.

African Christian theology ought to provide a guide to the growing church in Africa. Now that there is a high demand for theological understanding as a basis for Christian mission and ministry, African Christian theology needs to provide the theological resources that may be the foundation of the newly institutionalized churches in Africa.

Not an Ideology of Identity but a Trinitarian Theology of the African Christian Experience

The problem of identity surfaces when the motif is to legitimize or authenticate being through religion and culture on one hand and socio-economic and political being on the other hand. African theology is distorted if its motivation is to show the world that God is at home in Africa. The central question of Jesus Christ to the disciples, "'But what about you?' he asked. 'Who do you say I am?'" (Mark 8:29), shows the biblical posture that underlies this ideological motif.[9]

Moreover, this central biblical question has led to a Christomonism that distorts the image of God as Father revealed in the Son of God in the Holy Spirit. Insofar as this ideological motif is prone to becoming an isolationist and an ideological tool, it is antagonistic to other forms of Christian traditional faith expression. Indeed, its ideological posture does not reflect the Christian experience of the African Christian community and thus misleads them. On the contrary, since the African Christian faith

---

9. Martey, *African Theology*, 79.

experience of the Trinity[10] expresses openness to diversity[11] it opposes the Christomonistic ideological tendencies of contemporary African theology. This position is reinforced by contemporary theology. Pannenberg as he works with the objective Christ shows the Trinitarian way by which God is revealed as Father, Son, and Spirit with priority given to the threeness.[12] This is also firmly supported by Moltmann.[13]

The identity of the African Christian in theological exposition ought to show what Africans *ought* to think of themselves in the light of the encounter with God who is revealed in the crucified but risen Lord in the Holy Spirit. It must show not only in linguistic terms, but conceptually, and systematically, who the triune God *ought* to be to them and how they *ought* to see themselves in the light of that experience. For instance, African Christian theology needs to show how African Christians ought to appreciate God as their Creator, Redeemer and Sanctifier both in the subjective and objectives senses in faith. It is in this paradigm that African Christians will understand who they ought to see themselves in the light of their Christian experience of the triune God. Over here too, there is great resonance with John Zizioulas's emphasis on the experience of the triune God as in the subjective sense.[14] John Zizioulas and Karl Barth (and Paul Tillich), who strictly employed both the objective and subjective sense,[15] clearly appreciate the whole theology of how people become Christians in the manner Africans do. As such, works of theologians such as Mowry LaGugna and Ted Peters, which follow Karl Rahner's linking of the immanent Trinity with the economic Trinity,[16] could be essential in doing theology in an African context and vice versa. Thus, the identity of African Christians is located in their communion with the triune God expressed concretely in the African context. One should be quick to caution that this paradigm is so different from showing what African Christianity is, in the light of how they see it of themselves. African theology

---

10. Martey, *African Theology*, 77.

11. Nelson, "For Such a Time as This"; Omenyo, *Pentecost*, 90.

12. Grenz, *Matrix of Christian Theology*, 47–49; Pannenberg, *Systematic Theology*, 1:299, 304; Pannenberg, *Jesus, God and Man*, 181–83, 340.

13. Grenz, *Matrix of Christian Theology*, 47.

14. Grenz, *Matrix of Christian Theology*, 52–53; Zizioulas, *Being in Communion*, 15–17, 39–44; Zizioulas, "Human Capacity," 401–48.

15. Grenz, *Matrix of Christian Theology*, 53.

16. Grenz, *Matrix of Christian Theology*, 54–55; LaGugna, *God for Us*, 13, 209–24; Peters, *God as Trinity*.

has the task of setting the rule of Christian faith in the light of African Christian experience, Scripture, tradition and other sources of theology.

Furthermore, African Christian theology's exclusion of the African Christian experience has led to a Christomonism that does not appreciate the cardinal role the Holy Spirit plays in African Christianity.[17] For it is through "pneumatic Christianity"[18] that African Christians experience the liberating power of the crucified but risen Lord Jesus, as well as the abiding love of God the Father—their maker.

Granted, not all the African theological schemes of identity are Christomonisms, and in particular, Charles Nyamiti advanced a Trinitarian view of African Ancestral Christology, but there is still a cause for concern. Nyamiti's Christology is based on the fatherhood of God (Ancestor) as the Supreme Being and the brotherhood of Christ (Descendant) as the Son of the Father by the power of the Holy Spirit.[19] It tends to set the rule of faith for African Catholic Christianity especially by placing emphasis on the role of the Holy Spirit and Christian fellowship among others. Nonetheless, for Protestants and PCCs it seems to be more tilted in the direction of *trinitatis ad intra*. The *opera trinitatis ad extra* ought to show objectively and subjectively, how contemporary African Christians really experience the economy of God. This Nyamiti tries to do, yet the whole concept of the Ancestor does tilt the Trinitarian explication in the direction of the immanent Trinity. The reason being that these Christians could hardly perceive Jesus as Ancestor. In other words, Nyamiti's work is abstract and more cerebral than could be imbibed as a church doctrine in Protestant and PCC circles. This then shows how the search of a religio-cultural identity could distort Christian faith if not limit it.

Nonetheless, inasmuch as theology ought to expand the horizons of African Christian faith, and the church needs to imbibe some of terminologies like "Trinity," *Nyonmorr*,[20] and "Sacrament," theologians in Africa must be sensitive to categories that may not be helpful.

---

17. Omenyo, *Pentecost*, 227–31.
18. Asamoah-Gyadu, *Contemporary Pentecostal Christianity*, 1–15, 179–83.
19. Nyamiti, "African Christologies Today," 11–12.
20. Adjei, "*Nyonmor*"; Laryea, *Yesu Homowor Nuntsor*, 60–61.

Not Utopianism but a Trinitarian Theology of African Christian Experience and Eschatology

How is African Christian theology leading Christians in Africa to have a reason to live, and a meaningful life toward a goal at the end of cosmic existence? It has been mentioned that African Christian theology reflected the mood during the struggle for independence as well as the struggle against apartheid. And two main views, represented by the religio-cultural view on one hand and the socioeconomic and political view on the other hand, all seemed to be motivated by the goal of proving to the world that Africans can manage their own affairs. The differences arguably may be counted as political inclinations that were equally based on ideology.

African Christian utopianism may be found in the liberation theologies of African theology including Black South African theology. The ideological ideas provoking the struggle against white dominated rule and for independence in Africa is undeniable.[21] This situation of ideological proclivity that shows in the theological faith understanding of the church, may be traced to the New Testament. What it does is that it distorts the faith of believers in racism, classism and supremacist beliefs.[22] Therefore, while African Christian ideology of identity on the basis of religion and culture distorts the Christian faith, so does the Christian ideology of utopianism on the basis of socioeconomic and political liberation.

African Christian theological utopianism is a one sided interpretation of Christian hope. Owing to the heteronomous starting point of this theological paradigm, it associates with Christ to bring the hope of peace, security, and freedom and prosperity in concrete. That means its hope and aspiration is to dwell on achieving a certain fulfillment of socioeconomic and political prosperity in the milieu of absolute self-reliance.

Indeed, this-worldly eschatological interpretation of the African context being ideological in nature is tantamount to becoming a demonic that has its own destructive tendencies. Though the demonic participates and dwells on the power of the new creation which is the cosmic Christ, it denies that very reality as it assumes itself as the end or goal or achievement of existence. African Christian theological utopianism in a this-worldly frame is prone to ignoring the other—worldly understanding of Christian hope. This eschatological hope preached by Jesus Christ that

21. Martey, *African Theology*, 82.
22. Evans, "Eschatology," 346–73.

its "kingdom is at hand," which is that it is *here already* and *not yet* and that it moves beyond this earthly realm is lacking.²³ The one side of *here already* is appropriated at the expense of the other side which is the coming kingdom of God that is not yet.

It also thrives on the material and the physical realities only, instead of embracing the additional reality of the coming Lord Jesus. African Christian theological utopianism errs insofar as it makes only material and physical reality its goal instead of the additional coming Lord, and the coming Lord's kingdom.

Utopian and ideological eschatological understanding of Christian hope misleads the African Christian church so long as it remains potentially totalitarian. And such a totalitarianism shows how this distorted Christian eschatology is so narrow minded and thus failing to see Christian eschatology as not just historical but a cosmic reality that brings all of God's creation into focus. In other words, it is potentially divisive and adversarial to other peoples being and existence as well as the threatening of all other creaturely existence. This ideological stance fails to appreciate even the very worldview of African Christians that God's reign is cosmic or all-encompassing (*Kpelelogical*).²⁴ This is why Archbishop Desmond Tutu's concept of Ubuntu becomes a critique to African Christian theology in general.²⁵ It shows the limitations of the theologies of identity and utopianism as misleading theologies in Africa since they do not represent the relationality that underlies African reality of being; and which so projects the Trinitarian relationality of God in the *oikonomia*.²⁶ The theology of Ubuntu also works as a corrective to Black theology in general, in promoting reconciliation. Throughout this paper, this missing *Kpelelogical* eschatology has been described as the distortions of the ideologies of identity and utopianism.

Furthermore, it misleads inasmuch as its eschatological understanding does not help African Christians to appreciate that Christian hope is not only individualistic but communal, and not only in concrete

---

23. Asamoah-Gyadu, *Contemporary Pentecostal Christianity*, 105–20.

24. The word *Kpelelogical* is a hybrid terminology of the Ga word "*Kpele*" and the Greek word "*Logos*" I use to represent the African Christian mind whereby being grasped by the Divine Presence, it is animated to think holistically. It is related to the *kpelelogical* worldview of the African in their pre-Christian experience. Kilson, *Kpele Lala*, 18.

25. Battle, *Reconciliation*.

26 Bevans, "Inculturation and the Church's Mission," 214–31.

ecclesiastical terms but instead seeing the church as the bearer of the kingdom of God which is here already and not yet. For example, the distorted eschatological vision held by some Pentecostal and Charismatic churches of building "perfect" Christian cities is a utopian view that may lead to the demonic in ecclesiastical terms.

When African Christian theology proceeds from the African Christian experience it cannot fail to ignore the Trinitarian revelation of God in African history as a microcosm of the macrocosm of the overall agenda of God in the *oikonomia*. This is the axiom of Christian faith that through the subjective and objective encounter with the triune God, African Christians do appreciate the Father who is the ground of their being and the embodied New who is the cosmic hope symbol of the resurrection of the crucified Jesus—the Son of God in the power of the absolutely free—the Holy Spirit.[27] This autonomous Christianity is a characteristic feature of all African Christianity. Hence, dwelling on the heteronomous theological scheme creates a yawning gap between itself and the reality of African Christianity. Indeed, autonomous Christianity especially as expressed in Africa ought to be appreciated in heteronomous terms as well.[28] And the failure to move from the autonomous expression of African faith and spirituality to heteronomy leads to a misrepresentation of the context as well as a mere repetition of protestant theology.[29] The starting point ought to be located within the autonomous Trinitarian experience which then connects to heteronomous Trinitarian experience of cosmic existence.

The Distorted Theology in the New Testament

In the early tradition of the New Testament, both apologetic theology and kerygmatic theology feature prominently, especially in the theology of Paul the apostle. The basic function of Christian theology has always been to maintain the traditional knowledge of Christian faith.

---

27. Tillich, *Systematic Theology*, 1:49–50, 194–95; 2:10–12, 86–96.

28. Larbi, *Pentecostalism*, 349; Asamoah-Gyadu, *Taking Territories*; Gifford and Asamoah-Gyadu, "Enlarging Christian Coasts," 8–17; Carpentar, "New Evangelical Universities," 151–86.

29. Sanneh, *West African Christianit*, 180; as noted previously, *autonomous* and *heteronomous* are terminologies of Paul Tillich to describe the Christianity of Protestantism and Roman Catholicism, respectively; Horton, "Tillich's Rôle in Contemporary Theology," 42.

The Jerusalem Council actually shows us how a particular theology was suspected of misleading the church (Gal 2:11–21; Acts 15). Emphatically, the Jerusalem Council showed how the errant theology of some apostles actually distorted the teaching of Jesus Christ, misled, and confused the Christian community; when they discriminated and imposed the Jewish culture on the non-Jewish Christian community.

The failure to lead the wider context of the Christian community that embraced increasing number of non-Jews led Paul to interpret the Christian faith both in the apologetic and the kerygma. Furthermore, the reinterpretation led to the correction of distorted faith knowledge of those early Christians who, in particular, did not belong to the Jewish culture. Does theology not mislead when it assumes ultimate position? Or does it not, when it becomes the isolationist absolute? When theology fails to lead, then it has entered into a phase of an extreme theological cynicism. And it has transited into ideology. It is now a partisan position that does not provide leadership to whole world (Mark 16:15), or to all the nations (Matt 28:19) but only to a sect. It cuts relationship with the one who is *ta panta archiereus*—the Cosmic High Priest (Heb 2:10; 9:11; Eph 1:22–23)[30] and assumes its limited power as the absolute (reveals its demonic utopian character).

In another vein, theology is distorted when it is uncritical and gullible such that it fails to recognize that the central doctrines of the faith are being distorted. Hence, by a pacifist absolutism it fails to recognize and appreciate its own unique situation for which the gospel must be reinterpreted to bring hope and a liberating meaning to the community of faith. Thus Paul's theology as a remedy seeks to call all the non-Jewish Christians to order. Paul the apostle's position is right inasmuch as there is the need for a theological guide to forestall any destructive tendencies occasioned by creativity associated with the human spirit.

Taking cognizance of the Jewish Christian isolationist absolutism upon one hand, it is imperative to note, also, the invasion by politics and religion of the credulous non-Jewish Christian culture upon the other hand. For example, Paul needed to deal with the politics associated with the Greco-Roman world that was infiltrating the church in Corinth (1 Cor 1:10–17; 3:3, 4–23). Pauline theology is thus against any naïve theology.

---

30. Ekem, *Priesthood in Context*, 183.

The Distorted Theology Addressed by the Early African Church

One convincing reality about the early African Christianity was that it was a very proactive as well as a dynamic community. It had a vibrant Christian community that was not only steeped in deep theological work but was also, thoroughly immersed in the Christian experience. Indeed, early African theological formulations did not arise out of the intellectualism of the day but on the contrary, out of the day-to-day faith experiences of the Christians.

Origen (AD 1842–53) was one such, inflamed with fiery zeal to love God and to teach at the catechetical school in Alexandria, Egypt. He, like any African, did not fancy empty speculation about the Divine, instead he reflected upon personal experience, with the Divine. J. N. D. Kelly reveals this Origenist attitude when he compares the Latin and the Greek theologians as follows:

> An extreme example of this difference we need only juxtapose conceptions of theology held by (a) Irenaeus and Tertullian, and (b) Clement and Origen, in the latter half of the second and first half of the third centuries. Deeply suspicious of, even hostile to, philosophy, the former limited the function of theology to expounding the doctrines set out in Holy Scripture; they applauded the simple believers who were content with the rule of faith. The latter, on the other hand, went so far as to distinguish two types of Christianity, with two grades of Christians corresponding to them. The first and lower type was based on "faith," i.e. the literal acceptance of the truths declared in Scripture and the church's teaching, while the second and higher type was described as "gnosis," i.e. and esoteric form of knowledge. This started with the Bible and tradition, indeed was founded on them, but its endeavor was to unravel their deeper meaning, and in the light of it to explore the profounder mysteries of God and his universe and scheme of salvation; it was supposed to culminate in mystical contemplation or ecstasy.[31]

Paul Tillich deepens this position further that

> Origen begins his system with the question of sources. He takes the sources much more seriously than Clement. The sources are the biblical writings and their summary in the ecclesiastical teaching and preaching. The ancient "rule of

---

31. Kelly, *Early Christian Doctrines*, 4–5.

faith" provided the systematic scheme of his thought, but the Scriptures are the basis of its contents. The first step for the true theologian is the acceptance of the biblical message. Nobody can be a theologian who does not belong to the church. A free-soaring philosopher is not a Christian theologian. But more than this is required of the theologian. He must also try to understand things philosophically, and that means for Origen in terms of Neo-Platonic philosophy.

... There are two classes of Christians: (1) The many simple ones, who accept on authority the biblical message and the teachings of the church without understanding them fully. They take the myths literally. As Origen said, they prefer the healing miracles to the story of Jesus going with his three apostles to the mount of transfiguration, which is an allegorical or metaphorical expression for those who go beyond the literal meaning to a transformed interpretation of it. Origen referred to the attitude of the primitive believers as "mere faith." This represents a lower degree of Christian perfection. All Christians begin at this level. (2) There are those to whom, the charisma of gnosis, the grace of knowledge, is given ... For Origen the first step is the acceptance of authority; the second is the autonomous rational understanding of the biblical message. The second step does not do away with the first step, but is possible only on the basis of it.[32]

The impact of this theology was to be felt in the defense of the Christian message against Gnosticism[33] and Celcus.[34] So then apologetic theology and kerygmatic theology become relevant to the wider world and thereby providing meaningful spiritual leadership for the world. Similarly, the defense was a means by which believers were strengthened and saved from being misled.

The process of finding meaning to the Christian faith that is experienced leads to higher forms of reflection. And it is interesting to note this point, insofar as this form of contemplation is a characteristic of the Greek Church, is actually original to Africa. And further, it is important to underscore the point that the notion that contemplative theology is not African is completely false. Rather, it ought to be asserted that contemplative theology is original to Africa and African people. But the contemplative theology that is of African origin is not hypothetical insofar

---

32. Tillich, *History of Christian Thought*, 57, 58–59.
33. Kelly, *Early Christian Doctrines*, 5.
34. Origen, *Contra Celsum*.

as its origin is inspired by the Christian experience or faith that is based upon Scripture and tradition. Thus, the early African theology represented a theological form that represented the African Christian community and the African context as a whole. In fact, debates that were held were done not in academic atmospheres, but rather in church settings. These showed a very strong connection between apologetics and kerygmatic theology to the church.

The position is firmly buttressed by the factual evidence of the Niceno-Constantinopolitan creed as well as the Chalcedonian creed. The end result of those contemplative theological work of the early African Christians like Clement and Origen, I dare say, spawned, traditional Christian theology.

At that point, "the Church was a persecuted body, struggling to adapt itself to its environment and to fight off such foes as Gnosticism. It is to its credit that, in spite of all difficulties, it was able to produce great constructive theologians like . . . Origen."[35] At that period the church once again, provided leadership to the world in terms that could be understood by them. Moreover, at the same time, they provided leadership to the Christian community in terms of enduring doctrines that has lingered on to the present generation. And in doing this, prominence was given to sticking to the traditional faith in its objective and subjective experiences.

These traditional sources are first and foremost crucial to any Christian theological undertaking as we may have appreciated in the Pauline theology as well as early African theology. It always maintains the salvation plan of God, i.e., the *oikonomia* for the cosmos as the Trinity. Again, it ought to be pointed out that sticking to them avoided moving theology into errors like ideologies of identity and utopianism.

In concluding this section, a short discussion on the traditional sources of theology with regards to the ideology of identity and utopianism in African theology will be done. This discussion is a call to engage thoroughly, the theological sources of theology in the African context.

The Call to Engage the Sources of Tradition in the Context of African Christianity

On the face of it, African Christian theology takes seriously, the sources of theology. These sources include "1. the Bible, Christian tradition and

---

35. Kelly, *Early Christian Doctrines*, 5.

theological heritage; 2. African traditional religion, culture and philosophy; 3. African anthropology and other social sciences; and 4. African independent churches."[36] These may be fine-tuned to include simply, the Bible, reason, the African ontological and existential context (sources) through African Christian faith experience (medium) under the norm (symbol of Christ).[37] Unfortunately, a scrutiny of these sources of theology as employed by contemporary African theologians showed inadequacies in the foregone discussion.

The sources within Christian traditional heritage are: the Apostle's Creed, the Nicene Creed and the Chalcedonian Creed that include the Trinity, God and Creation, and the estranged cosmos and the liberating person and works of Jesus Christ, and the Holy Spirit's renewal of the cosmos and the church, and the end of the present cosmos and the coming of the kingdom of God at the eschaton. These sources of tradition also form the basis of the criteria for doing theology in general. One of the criticisms leveled against African Christian theology is the inability to adequately incorporate the criteria of doing theology.[38]

More so, the criteria of doing theology include ecclesiological relevance, the Trinity, and salvific event, and eschatological relevance, and contextual relevance, and the ability to dialogue or relate to other theologies consistently.[39] Granted, the focus of African Christian theology has been founded upon a contextual relevance. This is actually one criterion that African Christian theology is thoroughgoing. In fact, the late Professor Kwame Bediako asserted that the whole theological enterprise of Africa is an identity issue.[40] He goes on to develop his method of identity that seeks to locate the identity of the African Christian in the concrete context by looking at the continuities and discontinuities of the Christian message in the African milieu.[41] Moreover, context in African Christian theology has been broken into the religion and culture as one part and socio-politico-economic context as the other part.[42]

36. Martey, *African Theology*, 70.
37. Tillich, *Systematic Theology*, 1:64.
38. Schreiter, *New Catholicity*, 81–83.
39. Schreiter, *Constructing Local Theologies*, 117–21; also Schrieter, *New Catholicity*, 81–83; Migliore, *Faith Seeking Understanding*, 187, 221–22; Küster, *Many Faces of Jesus*, 15–36.
40. Bediako, *Christianity in Africa*, 5–6; Bediako, *Theology and Identity*.
41. Bediako, *Jesus in Africa*, 63.
42. Nyamiti, "African Christologies Today," 17; see also Martey, *African Theology*, 81.

Therefore, it is pretty much clear to understand the angle from which African Christian faith understanding is viewed. The arguments for the strict contextual relevance is very deep, to the point that it is revealing its inherent ambiguities and destructive tendencies. The context is a criterion for theological reflection yet it should never attempt to be the sole object of Christian reflection. The point here is that the object of Christian reflection is One God, the Father, revealed by the Son Jesus Christ in the Holy Spirit. And it is on the basis of this sole object of Christian faith, i.e., the Trinity, that the context becomes important. Effectively, the above discussion should lead us to the criteria of the *ultimate concern* as a matter of being and not being to the theologian.[43] Thus, the ultimate concern of African Christian theology is not identity but rather the hope engendered by faith in the love of God the Father revealed in the resurrection of the crucified Son in the Holy Spirit to Africans. And certainly, it is the triune God who is the matter of being and not being for African Christians not necessarily identity.

The significance is that African Christian reflection on the faith ought to be focused on the Trinity, whose mission in the whole of the cosmos, including Africa, is to liberate and renew until the eschaton. Hence, there is a need to reflect on the missing axioms of the Trinity, ecclesiology and eschatology, which seem to have been barred from African Christian theological reflection of faith.

Having said this, one may wish to add that the manifestation of the economic Trinity in Africa cannot be reflected upon without an appreciation of the encounter of the Trinity by African Christians. The faith of African Christians cannot be reflected upon without an understanding of the liberating power of God the Father, Son and Holy Spirit. Africans do not merely experience the Holy Trinity doxologically, they experience the Trinity as they experience the love of the Father as expressed in the liberating resurrection of the crucified Jesus Christ in the power of the Holy Spirit.[44] This experience of God is the basis of African Christian faith expressed in the contextual distinctiveness of African Christianity. Therefore, the theological source of Christian experience which has not featured in theological discussions of African Christian theology is also the source of the distortions in the theology that in turn misleads the church in Africa.

---

43. Tillich, *Systematic Theology*, 1:11–15.
44. Oyedepo, *Anointing for Exploits*, 61–64.

Meaningfulness Is Based upon the Connection of *Logos* and *Logoi*

The Kpelelogical theology that African Christian theology is, requires a consistent holistic approach to its theology in toto. Hence in the discussion here, I intend to focus on the issues that present African Christian theology as parochial and for that matter does not seem to edify the large majority of Africans and other Christians in the world as a whole.

It will be based on the discussion that human understanding is a by-product of the connection between two realities. Therefore, it will indicate the need to have a sense of openness in discussions regarding African Christian theology. Meaningfulness is only the result of the interaction of "thought language" that has the potential or capability of relating all realities one to another. Thought language thus is a reality that enables comprehension in general. Though it is particular and is shaped by the reality of the particular, because it has a universal appeal it allows for the comprehension of the particular in the context of the universal.

This is the reason why it important to underscore the point that meaningfulness sought after in African Christian theology is operates with and under both a universal and a particular regime. This "thought language" also known as logic is in the human self-awareness as well as the whole of reality and it is the connection between the two that promotes relatedness and relationship. It is the same reality that promotes knowledge of self or self-awareness or self-centeredness in all of humanity.

Moreover, the self-awareness is only possible insofar as it dwells on a reality beyond itself. For the ability to look at oneself while projecting from beyond oneself shows there is an element of the human person beyond the self. It is this transcendent element that gives the power to understand oneself in relation to other realities that actually shapes all human understanding as well.

Thus the human self-understanding that cannot be divorced from the transcendent element has implication for African Christian theological reflection. Besides, it leads us to diagnose the parochial problem of African Christian theology. The parochial problem of African Christian theological reflection is that, first, it debars strong analytical reflection and second, it stymies efforts at using other "thought languages" apart from its own thought patterns.

Consequently, African Christian theological parochialism as I term it has relegated theology to a certain ideological identity such as in language with such a stark narrow-mindedness. It fails to recognize the fundamental duty of theology which is to interpret the Christian faith to contemporary Africans not only in language they understand, but also interpreting the faith to address the myriad issues that affect them. This is particularly crucial if Christianity is to thrive in Africa, because I dare say that the many young people in African who are Christians do not read their Bibles from the local languages. So that when all the attention is narrowed on only one area of the myriad human endeavors, theology becomes irrelevant to the people.

Christian theology is there to tackle contemporary issues as well as emerging issues and to aid the training of pastors and other church workers to be most effective. It is not only the role of theology to aid in the translation of the gospel into the local languages which area, is even more on linguistics and biblical studies. Theology is there to shed light on issues that continue to challenge the faith of African Christians. If theology is narrowed to only language and meaning and ethnography as may be the case in some jurisdiction in Africa, how could the church navigate times of Covid-19 where issues of science and faith, politics and faith, and ethics and faith arise? Theology especially in West Africa and other parts of Africa needs to take a new look of itself and the way forward.

The issues arising out of the African Christian theological parochialism are obvious insofar as analytical frameworks remain a mere colonial attachment. The analytical mode of reflection that restricts the mind to data collection and ensuring that the data is kept in its natural state as much as possible without or with limited scientific interpretation is one serious problem that ought to be looked at. The reasons are that, first of all, though such forms of analysis is part and parcel of African worldview, it *betrays* the African thought pattern because the African thought pattern is holistic and not fragmented.

Positivism, a direct colonial vestige when adopted in any theological institution as the only theological tool for reflection obviates theology itself. Consequently, theologians in Africa following this pattern of thought do not only betray Africans, they also betray Christianity in Africa by failing to do proper theological reflections. Traditionally, Africans do not report events without stating, first, their own sense of meaning or nuance; second, their own symbolism of it; and third, the medium of presentation. That animated sense of transmission may be found in folklore, tales and songs, and dance, and meals, and carvings, and sculptures and so forth. These African mode of reflections acknowledge the element of empirical science by ensuring that the event being reported on, has a historical core message in it. These fall under the dimension of human sense of *self-creativity*[45] that may include language, the technical, the cognitive and the aesthetic.

Also, they employ other thought forms which include the *self-transcendent*[46] element because without it, there will be no proper sense of meaning. This kind of reflection beyond the realms of existence are encapsulated in symbols and transmitted in tales, songs and dances and so forth. The art forms in symbols of painting, music, dance and folklore are all part and parcel of the African holistic thought pattern we call the Kpelelogical mind.

Again, the African person has a deep sense of *self-integration*,[47] which brings to them the element of morality and all that pertains to their inner being and psychology. Thus the embodiment of all the above three elements that define their being is brought to bear in a Kpelelogical manner. It behooves African theologians to be aware of the perennial fragmentation of African thought pattern that is perpetuated by attaching financial baits to it. Furthermore, they need to wake up to realize that they are acquiescing to the notion that serious analytical reflections cannot be done by Africans. And further, that African theological work should remain in the realms of simple African storytelling and not the complicated African storytelling that involves the whole of the creative senses. The senses that involve the Divine in religion, the self and morality, and the sense of holistic creativity in culture.

Theological reflections are reflections on the Christian faith experience and that has to be interpreted in the light of the present context as in apologetic kerygma. And the goal of theology is to bring light to the Christian faith in a forceful and persistent manner. Therefore, reducing theology to ethnophilosophy, ethnography (some parts of West Africa) and development (Southern part of Africa) is neither here nor there. African Christian theology is relevant insofar as it employs the tools of ethnophilosophy, ethnography and contemporary developmental issues to bring light to the gospel and the goal of the gospel which is Jesus Christ. Thus neither development nor ethnicity becomes the goal of the gospel but rather Christ who fulfills all things. The gospel is not to be used as a

---

45. Tillich, *Systematic Theology*, 3:50–86.
46. Tillich, *Systematic Theology*, 3:86–106.
47. Tillich, *Systematic Theology*, 3:32–49.

tool for utopianism, ethnocentrism, racism and apartheidism and totalitarianism among others. Consequently, the gospel, then cannot be used as a tool for development as an end in itself but instead, that faith in the gospel of Jesus Christ as the ultimate, will bear its fruits in the world of estrangement, while anticipating the coming reign of God.

The Christian message therefore, offers hope to the world of its dent that reveals the ambiguity of existence. This does not lie in any form of parochialism or fragmentation but instead, it is an expression of God's mission to the whole of the universe where all things including all humanity share each other in love and in everlasting bliss. It is not parochialism, it is a sharing that resonates with the African Ubuntu that actualizes the Kpelelogical worldview of African Christianity as love for all.

In the same vein, the sharing of Christian experiences with other friends elsewhere in creative theological works like was done by the African Christian ancestors of Origen, Tertullian and Augustine ought to continue unabated. That ecumenical relationship of giving and taking can only be a manifestation of the power of the revealed God the Father in Christ the Son. Hence, it is crucial to bring on board thoughts of Europeans, Arabs, Jews, Latinos, and Asians to bear on African Christian theology as far as sharing of both old and new Christian heritage only serve to *enrich* and *authenticate* the Christian message.

Additionally, it is crucial to note that since two wrongs do not make a right, African Christian theology insofar as it remains contextual, should not repeat the problem of orthodoxy which *ostracized* the Third World. Thus reflection of the African Christian faith experience should right the wrongs of the past as it engages other Christian theological orthodoxy of the past and present as a Christian heritage. African theology should also reflect on the heritage of Christians in the whole of the Third World. And this discussion brings us to the conclusion that there is meaningfulness in sharing the Jesus Christ as Savior and Lord we have experienced with others and theirs with us. It also involves the courage to be open in inviting all others to critically engage with us regarding the knowledge we all have in the Lord Jesus Christ in the present.

This call that may be viewed as radical, may be rightly so when African theologians start to engage orthodoxy in both a critical and realistic way. On the one hand, this is indeed a radical position because it departs from a Christian theology that seeks to become a new product which new product then undercuts the basis of Christian truth claims of Jesus Christ over the years. Thus, in its quest to interpret the Christian faith in the context of Africa, African Christian theology need to be realistic. On the other hand, it is also radical because it is a bold stance whereby the static notion of the Christian heritage is critically reviewed to bring about a better appreciation of the faith today. The position or posture is a daring one that critically engages theology in any context and seeks to bring fresh meaning and power to the faith. It confidently dares wrestling with anyone in any given context and time to sincerely bring transformation to the faith for the benefit of all who are Christians in the world.

This radicalism may be found when African theologians shift from a new theological product tendency involving current radical shift from a perceived static Christian orthodoxy to a transformative view. This view of critical realism may lead African theologians to be more open to other theological works of orthodoxy as well as other contextual theologies in any part of the world. This ecumenical spirit which is realistic but also very critical engagement over long periods certainly is more true to Christian theology than any other. As it has been stated earlier on, theology in Africa may be better of when it follows the very ecumenical but critical mood in Africa that helped to develop the Nicene and Chalcedonian Creeds of the church over thousand years ago.

This implies that African Christian theologians should have an even space or a holistic view for theology. Theological studies should aim at a round-learning approach that seeks an interpretation from the context of the theological student or researcher. And the resources for being well-rounded should be made available. In other words, a transformative theological paradigm requires a very comprehensive theological enterprise. As it may be noted, comprehensiveness is a hallmark of a Kpelelogical theology which Christian theology is.

Consequently, involving native theologians as well as theologians of other continents in a comprehensive manner as one engages them realistically but critically is the transformative view which African theologians may have to adopt. Theological works of the past and present in all places may have to be meaningfully engaged in a transformative sense for today. And this leads us on to think about how theological transformation may be realized in the dynamic relationship between the absolutely universal and the absolutely concrete.

Meaningfulness without the Absolutely Universal or Absolutely Concrete?

Knowing that the Christian message has a universal appeal should instruct us to understand that Christianity in all its manifestation in human history has a particular and universal reality to it. Certainly this idea is hinged on the revelation of God the Father in Jesus and in the Holy Spirit regarding the cosmic dimension of God's reality. John the apostle as well as Justin Martyr have demonstrated that the essence and the power of Jesus Christ is his universal appeal. Thus for them, Jesus Christ is Lord not only to the Jew or to the Hellenist but to every being. The claim of the Lordship of Jesus Christ ought not to be presented as a tribal deity rivaling other tribal *Jemanworjii* (deities). This position alluding to absolutizing our particular understanding of Jesus Christ as may be realized, has been repeated over and again because it cannot be overemphasized. The contextual nature of theology is a given, nonetheless, it must constantly be aware of the inherent dangers. And African Christian theology needs to pay attention to it as well.

Hence, apologetic kerygmatic theology even if presented with the particular context in mind ought to connect the universality of the message to it. That will open up the minds of the hearers of the Gospels to embrace other people and indeed the whole creation of God as part of God's plan. Today, the church is faced with the reality and quagmire of many "Christianities" because of parochialism. "What is Christianity?" is now the question bordering scholars in the subject of religion. But there is a core message and a core Christianity proclaimed, lived and defended by the apostles, early fathers and the church fathers. Theology must understand that its key role is to reinterpret the core message according to the prevailing context in a manner that is true and meaningful. And connecting the particular to the universal is inevitable in faithfully executing this task.

Therefore, the meaning of the Christian message cannot be fully grasped when its universal reality is not brought to bear or appreciated. There is a great beauty in holding the dynamic relationship between particular theologies to the universal which implies theology ought to be a product of critical engagement with other views.

Now what is the difference between the universal and particular on one hand, and the absolutely concrete on the other hand? First, the universal and particular, at least from the Christian point of view, is the general revelation of God in the cosmos that finds its varying expressions in different locations and experiences in the world if not in the entire universe. And second, the concrete expression of the absoluteness of God who is universal refers to the Christian revelation of God as the Father in Jesus Christ as the Son and in the Holy Spirit in history. It means that God has appeared to the whole of the cosmos in materiality from spirituality in the person of Jesus Christ the Son of God and in the power of the Holy Spirit by the love of God the Father. This is the objective presentation of God to the cosmos. Thus Christian knowledge of God is no longer a fabrication but a historical record.

Now the extension of this historical and objective presentation of God in history as the special or unique claim of Christianity is also objectively evidenced by the presence of the church. And no church can claim any authenticity without accepting the objective presentation of God in Christ in the Holy Spirit as absoluteness presented or revealed in history. Thus, the meaningfulness can only be derived from Christianity when the particular church understands that its being or emergence is hinged on the universal absoluteness in the person and works of Jesus Christ.

Moreover, the particular expression of African Christianity is the manifestation of both the particular and the concrete which are hinged on an encounter with both the universal as well as absoluteness. Therefore, meaningfulness of faith should always be interpreted from both the particular and the concrete experience. Nonetheless they will fall short of great meaningfulness and fulfillment when their universality and absoluteness are excluded. Lessons for African Christian theology are that, first, it ought not to rely only on the concrete subjective experience of the triune God but also on the concrete objective experience in history. This is important in guiding pneumatic Christianity and preventing it from plunging into Docetism. Second, it ought not to focus on the concrete objective experience and its relationship with the particular experience only, but additionally, it ought to bring on board the concrete subjective experience and the universal experience as well. It is extremely important to note the above lesson as a measure in guarding against ideological tendencies such as totalitarianism that undermine the Christian message. And insofar as the concrete subjective experience is hinged on the concrete objective as absoluteness which in Christ is universal, African Christian theology is bound by universal claims expressed in particular ways.

Thus in the following discussion, the challenge associated with the quarantining of personal faith, the sciences (*wissenschaften*), and religion and culture, and social justice is reexamined. With regards to the sciences, only postmodernism, secular humanism and science and technology, and including a few pertinent others are mentioned.

The Challenge of Quarantining Personal Faith against Religion and Culture, and Social Justice, and Ecology, and Science and Technology in African Christian Theology

As it has been pointed out above, it is clear that the ideologies of general culture distort the true articulation of the Christian faith in Africa. And it is noted that there is a need to dwell on the core issues in the Christian message which finds its concrete expression in African Christianity. At the same time African Christian theology cannot fail to neglect the Christian heritage bequeathed to it although it needs not repeat them nor make them a new product. What African Christian theology needs is a transformation of the Christian faith within their present context through the medium of African Christian experience.

Thus while it is good to see the elements of faith experience on one side and on the other side, social, economic, political, and ecological justice or issues of religion and culture in African Christianity, they have no connection to one another. African Christian theology is made up of a faith which is very devotional but seldom deployed into the religio-cultural, socioeconomic and political and ecological, and science and technological spaces. As many scholars in African Christianity may have stressed on its pneumatic nature, it is also observed as a danger when its docetic character rears its ugly head. The fact that African Christianity has a problem with docetic tendencies is evidence by the little or no attention that Christians and churches give to societal ills.

The issues of poverty, the issues of discrimination against people with respect to gender, age, and tribe, and caste, and class and the environment seem not to be issues that concern African Christians insofar as there is a disconnect with regards to their personal faith. Personal faith issues in African Christianity remain a life-and-death issue because devotion to God with regards to worship, ministry, fellowship, teaching and the preaching of God's Word is accorded the greatest honor. The time spent in a day, time spent in a week, month and a year both privately and corporately in worship is so huge. And most African Christians devote a substantial amount of resources to their churches and its programs.

It could be asserted that almost all churches in Africa are devoted to contributing resources to their churches in building infrastructure for worship and other services.

Unfortunately, the kind of passion which goes into individual devotion to God and to the church cannot be found outside the church. Churches get involved in coming out with social intervention programs. Yet the members do not feel or think they are directly responsible for ensuring that their societies are working so well because God has called them to do so. In other words, there is no sense that social justice is their act of devotion to God and by which the salvation of God becomes a living witness to the world. Thus the increasing numbers of Christians who do not pay attention to social justice bear a false witness against the gospel and of God alone who is the Father, Son, and Holy Spirit.

And the sense of complete lawlessness and anarchism in different parts of world Christianity which Africa is part bespeaks of the lack of a holistic understanding of the Christian faith. The theology that pays close attention to the absolutely concrete reality of God in a particular history through Jesus Christ the Son in the power of the Holy Spirit cannot turn a blind eye to the universal reality that it represents. A Kpelelogical theological exposition is thus the *sine qua non* of theology itself and African Christian theology must not deviate from it.

The impact of COVID-19 bears witness to the fact that theology can no longer remain a tribalistic venture rivaling another tribalistic venture. Today we are learning that, although we are particular people in history, whatever goes on in our particular part of history may have a lot of consequences on other parts of the world. And that there are issues in the world relating to health, economics, and the environment and even of culture that has repercussions worldwide. This lesson is not an assertion to promote irrelevant theological issues that are not particular, but rather, it is to state that the particular can in one way or the other be influenced by or influence the universal. Theological parochialism itself is so dangerous in view of a certain demonic element it possess. This disposition of a church or group of persons indoctrinated by such parochialism is so destructive that it bears a false witnesses to the gospel of Jesus.

The world has already experienced how theological parochialism such as was in Germany and South Africa destroyed many lives. Its propensity to foist on others a lower caste[48] and stand upon that to denigrate

---

48. I prefer using the terminology of caste instead of race in order to clarify what other Christians do to other Christians. The issue of racism has been misinterpreted

and oppress them is replete in human history. African Christians and for that matter African theologians should not also forget how theological parochialism energized slavery, colonialism and in today's oppression of Black people worldwide. Theological parochialism seeks abundant life for one at the detriment of the other. Such theologies in the end are no Christian theologies at all inasmuch as skin color, caste and nation and political party and patriarchy become preeminent in their consciousness than the God they profess they know. How can God be God and Christ be real when such earthly things become the foremost. Thus theological parochialism is tantamount to idolatry because it fails to see the good creation of God. It is very self-centered in nature and does not want to see the other person or creature in the light of the fact that they are all the beloved of God. And because it does not fully appreciate the universal nature of God's redemptive plan and the compassion and love with which it is manifested in Jesus Christ in the power of the Holy Spirit, it is crucial to blatantly state that it is antichrist.

It further implies that African Christian theology cannot fall victim to an idolatrous theology where its theology pays attention to the discrimination against poor people on the continent but turns a blind eye to the discrimination against poor people in the world as a human catastrophe. Similarly, it should not be a theology that seeks the well-being of women in Africa and yet is less concerned about the suffering of women in other parts of the world. Certainly, it cannot find solace in deriving fresh meaning and transformation of its faith for the benefit of the present generation from its religio-cultural viewpoint alone without engaging the theological views conditioned by the culture and religion of the other. This is the theology enmeshed in the empathy and compassion and love of the triune God at the outset. Thus theological discourse cannot be taken as if it is an ideological pursuit. It should be taken by African theologians as a reality that is conditioned by a divine initiative that is meditative, and that recognizes the theological enterprise as a spiritual enterprise.

Thus the spirituality and the holiness that ought to be associated with theology in Africa stems from the fact that theology is not a work of a human being. Furthermore, that theology is the doing of God in history which without the grasping of the mind and heart of the theologian by

---

because there is only one human race and the reality of racism itself is rather a designation of black people to the lowest castes and all other people of lighter skin color above, with whites on top of it. This is the true nature of "racism" in the world, particularly in both the West and the East; see Wilkerson, *Caste*.

the power of the Holy Spirit concerning the love of the Father as revealed by the Son, there can be no true doctrine. And hence, there is a need to criticize the African Christian theology which made no sense to the ordinary African Christian because it was largely detached from the personal and ecclesiastical foundations of the Christian faith.

Consequently, foremost among the tasks for African theologians today is how theology could emerge out of the theological medium of the African experience of God in Christ and in the Spirit when it has embraced the sources of theology. Enough lessons ought to be learned regarding the inherent problems associated with the liberal theology of the social gospel which characterized modern theology. The lessons ought to be learned because it presented a distorted gospel that had no implication for personal faith and salvation. It lost out the main issue regarding the person and works of Jesus as both objective and subjective, which prominently Karl Barth and Paul Tillich sought to call attention to. That Christian faith and its actions cannot be based upon mere intellectual appeal as was the case of Schleiermacher and Ritschl but that which is based upon the knowledge revealed in the historical Jesus and further, about that which is based upon personal (subjective) encounter with that objective Truth by the person who becomes a Christian.

As a result, it is crucial for African Christian theology to embrace both elements of personal faith and social justice. Here, the method of theology as already discussed above is crucial. The method needs to realistically look at the questions of all human anxiety including the fear of nonbeing and all its forms of manifestations in human finiteness. At the same time, a good theological answer from the Christian message is needed which a Kpelelogical mind endeavors to do as shown in the foregone.

Having noted the above, there is a need to go back to the issue of Covid-19 that has a global impact. Bluntly stated, it is incomprehensible for some African theologians in their sense of theological parochialism to assume that global thought patterns or systems have minimal impact on African societies. It is sad to say that on many occasions, and especially as shown in the works of theologians of the continent, there is no or little space for engaging Western thought critically. Two acknowledgments ought to be made notwithstanding the above that, first, there has been the use of Marxian analysis in liberation theology. And second, there is a constant use of postmodernist thought as may be seen in postcolonial interpretation of the Bible and the use of hermeneutics of suspicion. While acknowledging the use of these ideas in African theology and in biblical studies, it should be noted that sadly, their acceptance is highly limited to African women's theology and black theology.

The pithy part of the apathy in employing Western thought is the presumption that thought can be so localized that it never has any universal dimension. Thus, there is no attention paid to the reality that universal thought pattern particularly in postmodernism and secularism could ever be an issue to Africans and African Christianity. To the contrary, there is so much evidence to show that although much of African societies remain religious, secularism is gaining space. The issues of postmodernist ideals certainly cannot be reduced to philosophical issues resident only in Europe and America. On the contrary, they ought to be seen as the thought driving the free market and the free market policy, and political institutions and educational institutions which shape culture, religion and socioeconomic and political issues in Africa.

Consequently, it is naïve to assume that Africans are immune and forever will be immune from the onslaught of Western thought naturally without any deliberate attempt to address the issues they present. Addressing the issues cannot also remain in the realms of ethnophilosophy, ethnography and biography and political history and history of civilization and anthropology and philology alone, but rather opening up the issues of agnosticism, naturalism and secular humanism and deconstruction and relativism and pluralism. The roles that these issues of thought in the world have on African culture, religion and socioeconomic and political structure ought to be recognized and directly tackled in African Christian theology. If indeed African Christian theology ought to present a holistic theology, it should not ignore issues that directly and daily disrupt and shape African destiny whether they are local or imported.

Furthermore, one cannot pretend to be doing a theology on the soil of Africa and with the soil of Africa without paying attention to the storms that come from far away and threaten the very survival of the structures that has been built. This actually exposes the weakness of theological parochialism as so inward looking that they fail to see the dangers, which threaten the very survival of African Christian theology. A hypothetical example is when all attention is used to research and teach students to discover and imbibe the nature of African religion and culture without self critique, and in terms of understanding its strengths and weaknesses in both local and global contexts. Still on this example, specifically, when the meaning of a word in the local language is unearthed with the assumption that the discovery alone could improve translation of the Christian message without paying an equal attention to how secularism, and say postmodernism may suppress the meaning, it certainly may have no relevance at all.

Emphatically, African Christian theology, and for that matter the whole of Christian theology, needs to pay attention to issues of science and its impact on world Christianity. It needs to find a space for delving into the conversation on science and theology from the African theological perspective. Fundamental questions of how science should relate to Christian theology in general and in the African soil can no longer be viewed as alien to Africa. These should also contribute to how science could be handled by geopolitics as well as national politics in the midst of a world that is inundated in religion including Christianity. African Christian theology should guide the path of science in Africa by promoting its role and ensuring it stays within its limits.

Similarly, the role of naturalism, scientism and secular humanism should be addressed in African Christian theology if indeed African Christian theology is to answer the question "What does the Christian faith mean today?" It should deal with the issues above insofar as they question the essence of faith in general and in particular African Christian faith. Critical questions raised by these issues are not only stacked in the Western world but through science and technology they are present in Africa. Their role ought to be researched thoroughly to see the extent of the impact they make on African societies and the churches in particular. The church ought to understand that most African nations operate with secular systems although they are very religious and to assume that these secular institutions do not undermine faith is to be naïve. To think that secular humanism is not present in Africa and that it has no propensity to undermine African religiosity in general and Christian faith in particular is a failure of Christian theology.

This failure is serious as long as African Christian theology cannot define its context and diagnose its problems. And the problem is worsened when African theologians fail to think in holistic terms but splinter theology into bits such that it loses its sense of urgency and relevance to church and society. Theological works in Africa cannot survive anymore when they fail to acknowledge the presence of other confessions and other faiths. More especially, Africans need a more ecumenical approach at bringing meaning to Christian faith in the face of religious pluralism.

Theology in Africa should seek to explain or interpret the faith of African Christians in a way that seeks to promote faith in all the confessions and denominations generally. Diversity in every confession and denomination should be welcome, yet the theological enterprise for African faith should be so inspirational that all confessions and denominations could refer to it for clarity or for creativity.

Furthermore, African Christian theology cannot ignore the presence of other religions, particularly that of Islam. Theology in Africa needs to be sensitive to the needs of Islam and yet it needs to be aware of the dangers it may pose to Christian faith in Africa in general. In the past, Christianity and Islam together with ATR got along without crises of conflicts. And the European missionaries towed the line by cautioning their African evangelists and pastors to stay away from the territories in which Muslims lived.[49] And further, there remain considerable traditions in Africa where Christians and Muslims of the same family, ethnicity and country and perhaps same continent as Africa could live in harmony. In particular John Azumah had shared his personal experiences and used it to inspire both Christians and Muslims to live in harmony worldwide.[50]

He pioneered the Interfaith Centre of the Presbyterian Church of Ghana which exists to foster Christian—Muslim relations and to present a platform for dialogue and exchange of ideas that seeks to promote peace and security in Ghanaian society. And so has Lamin Sanneh in showing that West African Islam is very peaceful and had coexisted with other religions for many centuries.[51] Nowadays, however, although it may not be pervasive, the tension in some communities in Africa have seen conflict between Christians and Muslims. The situation has now become a security issue for all as Christians, Muslims and Traditionalists need peace and security in order to go about their normal duties. Johnson Mbilla we must note especially has taken the Christian—Muslim relationship from academia and church into the media by educating the public and in particular Christians about the need to foster peace with people of other faith which Islam is part.[52]

In view of the situation above, Christian theology in Africa may now have to draw a lot of inspiration from the life of Jesus as the Son of God in the Spirit. These should also go a long way in informing ministerial formation in Africa. What role has theology in comforting and

49. Clarke, *West Africa and Christianity*, 216–24.
50. Azumah, *Legacy of Arab-Islam in Africa*; Azumah, *My Neighbor's Faith*; Azumah and Sanneh, *African Christian and Islam*.
51. Sanneh, *Beyond Jihad*.
52. Mbilla, "Let's Stop Politicizing Religion"; Mbilla, "Religious Leaders Cautioned."

strengthening the faith of Christians living in conflict prone areas? Moreover, how should this inform mission and evangelism studies among others in Africa? Moreover, the role of African Christian theology in promoting the faith of African Christians as one that is desirable in the societies in which they are, cannot be ignored. Issues of Christian witness of the Truth ought to be expressed in missions and evangelism, it has to be enshrined in Christian behavior and character.

Kpelelogically speaking, the role that Islam plays is a *partial* complement of Christian ethics especially in areas of godliness and also with regards to the fight against the profanization of our communities as Africans. This is in view of the understanding that acceptable values though initially rejected could be transformed and used to promote the well-being of African society and which ultimately glorifies God. And Islam like ATR could be connected to Christianity in terms of shared values. This is firmly based upon the reasoning that kpelelogical conscience even though it has not been transformed into a Kpelelogical mind still possesses the mind structure that is amenable to the well-being of all Africans. African Christian theology may have to humble itself in accepting Islam and other religions as partners especially with the understanding of Islam being a source that could criticize Christianity even on the basis of its own faith proclamations.

Additionally, it may have shed light on the Christian faith as it serves as a *preparatio evangelica* or means of transmitting Christian truth. Again, it should be understood rightly, that Islamic teaching itself is not absolute whereby it is not God; and that it could be made whole by God through Jesus Christ in the Spirit. This cause of action or understanding of course demands humility and as well as the courage needed at the same time to stand by the Truth revealed by God, which the Holy Spirit testifies about in Jesus Christ, the Son of God. Admittedly, this poetic stance needs further interrogation and Africa may have to understand how Christian-Muslim relations or Christian-Islam relations are experienced elsewhere in the world like in some Asian countries. The point is, theology in Africa cannot ignore anymore the presence of Islam as a vital part of its experience. And this means that Christian theology needs to be theological on the basis of realizing all realities as a whole so as to clarify the faith and help Christian to meaningfully live with Muslims.

Furthermore, regarding the subject of religion, the phenomenon of New Religious Movements (NRM) in Africa and the roles they play in African Christianity ought to be brought into the issue of African Christian theology. In Ghana for instance, there is Rastafarianism, Etherean Mission, Zetahel, and Afrikania Mission. The question is, what do these religions serve to provide and why do African politicians in particular and African Christians in general gravitate so much to these religions? What is it about the Christian understanding and of the African person that promote these NRMs? These are theological questions insofar as African Christians who flock to these places cannot or do not find answers to questions of faith in African churches. And these questions above and more ought to be answered by African Christian theology.

Again, the presence of world religions in Africa ought to be brought to bear like all the other religions referred to above. Particularly, the religions of the East need some degree of attention as African Christianity finds convergencies and divergencies. African Christian theology should be able to deal with the issues of African Christian relationship with Asian religion and culture. This ought to be anticipated with regards to missionary activities in Asia and Africa coupled with African interaction with Asians in Africa and elsewhere. The presence of Harikrishna, Saibaba and Hinduism and Buddhism in African societies ought to be brought into sharp focus together with African Traditional Religion in African Christian theology. The questions of both faith and existence they raise ought to be taken seriously as a Kpelelogical answer is given.

In the Kpelelogical theology below, the revelation of God in Christ which is also the faith experience of the church in Africa becomes the medium within which it is understood. In other words, unlike the approach in which the theology of the triune God starts the theology, over here, the person and works of Christ as the person through whom the knowledge of the triune God is revealed starts. Indeed that is the order of the subjective medium and the objective source of the Word of God proclaimed from the Scriptures as the Christian message. Yet that reality it is acknowledged, is not without the triunity of the Godhead but it only comes alive in looking at Jesus and the work he accomplished once and for all. And it is through the encountered Jesus Christ that African Christian theology comprehends the Trinity and the whole plan of God in creation.

Thus it is in the fully human and fully divine nature of Jesus Christ that we acknowledge the triune God: creation and eschatology; and the triune God: church and cosmos. So the Kpelelogical theology will be started with the person of Jesus Christ in this introductory volume. And it is about the comprehension of Jesus Christ as the revealer of the cosmic ground of all reality and meaning and concretization of same as the *Okpelejen Wulormor*. Thus Jesus Christ himself is all-encompassing which in the Ga context is known as *Okpelejen*. And because in the Ga context, Jesus the *Wulormor* presides over the *Kpele* religious institution as *a more than a priest, prophet and king*, a Kpelelogical reflection is done.

Conclusion

Chapter 3 critically engaged the schools of thought associated with African Christian theology. These schools of thought involve inculturation (emphasis on religio-cultural sources) or liberation (emphasis on socio-economic and political sources).

The critical questions raised border on how these theologies in Africa were done while paying close attention to the elements of eschatology, salvific event and the Trinity. Unfortunately, most of them did not show the interconnections that exist within their theologies with the Trinity, eschatology and the salvific events. Thus leaving out these axioms of doing theology makes it very difficult to appreciate their theologies in the light of the contemporary Christianity of Africa.

Furthermore, as to why these christological ideas were not in mainstream Christianity in Africa was the lack of ecclesiological relevance. Additionally, the un-ecumenical approach, which reflected in the lack of dialogue with the Western theological heritage, led to a parochialism that limited African Christian theology in general.

Another important element identified was the *cultura-libero* theology. A *cultura-libero* theology fused elements of inculturation and liberation. Examples could be seen in the works of Samuel Waje Kunihyiop, Diane Stinton and Philip Laryea. Of particular interest was Philip Laryea's *Yesu Homowor Nuntsor* that used the Ga concept of *Kpele* in the celebration of the *Homowor* festival.

However, the discussion showed that fusing inculturation elements with liberation elements per se, does not really do justice to the subject of African Christian theology. The reason is that the African reality at least from the Kpelelogical point of view is an all-encompassing reality. And that it is this all-encompassing Kpelelogical reflection that actually represents the African "logos-Logos" structure of the mind. This *cultura-libero* theology with its self-limitation to the realms of culture, religion, socio-economy and politics ignores other realms of thought such as science and

The Essence of African Christian Theology as Faith in the Absolutely Concrete 167

technology. Hence, theology derived from African Christianity cannot be ethnography with its limitations but, rather, Kpelelogical.

Yet, it was discovered that African Christian theology cannot be done without ethnophilosophy or ethnography. It is a crucial source upon which the Kpelelogical ontology is founded in existence, life and history of the African Christianity. Nonetheless, African Christian theology depends upon other important sources as the Bible and Christian tradition itself.

In chapter 4, the question of method, criteria, and objective and subjective faith were discussed as very crucial is dealing with African Christian theology. In this work, the Kpelelogical method was advanced as a replacement for theological methods of identity/continuity and discontinuity and the method of praxis. Thus significantly, it dealt with the method of identity that "technically" did not allow the African religious and cultural history to relevantly inform the Christian message because the method is committed to the fulfillment paradigm.

Again, it dealt with the challenge associated with the method of praxis on the basis of not paying adequate attention to the subjective reality of African Christianity that landed African Christian theology into the liberalism of modernism.

Moreover, the confusion associated with different categorizations of the method of doing African Christian theology is also resolved in the Kpelelogical method. And it forms the basis of African theology of culture and sciences in general.

Assigning criteria for doing African Christian theology ought to be on the basis of the best theological practice that was gleaned from the early church, the church fathers, and the medieval period and the reformation, and the modern period and finally the contemporary postcolonial criteria. The challenge of the context in doing theology is resolved by understanding that most theological works were shaped by the realities of their time. Moreover, another good lesson was that some of the theological works were actually born out of the ecclesiastical as well as ecumenical settings. And in most of these cases, the salvific event of Jesus Christ has been central in relation to the Trinity.

There is also a strong critique for the inherent dichotomization associated with African Christian theology today. Thus, the fragmentation of Christology from below and Christology from above from the Kpelelogical perspective is deemed un-African. The Kpelelogical understanding is an ecclesiastical position of African Christianity whereby in a holistic fashion, the African Christian sees Jesus Christ instantly as the Lord who died. This paradox of faith[53] is normal for the African Christian who is grasped by the Spirit of the Father in the Son. And this ought to be seen as an extension of the reasoning behind the Chalcedonian fully divine and fully human natures of the person of Jesus Christ.

Furthermore, in that same vein, this Kpelelogical theology is an amalgamation of inculturation and liberation and beyond. African Christian theology by expressing itself from the viewpoint of African Christianity dwells on the faith that is grasped beyond the realms of dichotomies as they become irrelevant. And this in the person of Jesus Christ and in his death on the cross and resurrection has been firmly grounded.

Chapter 5 delved deeply into why African Christian theology missed when it forgot to begin its reflections on the subjective as well as the objective redemptive work of Christ. This is associated to the lacking Trinitarian explication of the theology as well as the lacking axiomatic eschatology. Thus African Christian theology from Kpelelogy alleviates this theological poverty and as it recognizes the Trinity as inherent in African Christian experience and in the salvific work of Jesus Christ. At the same time, it recognizes the Lord who is, was and is to come as Jesus Christ the Son of God the Father in the power of the Holy Spirit. Thus in Kpelelogy, eschatological hope is what has being experienced in conversion and upon which it understands what is revealed in the past (world history including African history) and also, regarding the longing of the new at the end of all history.

Thus meaningfulness of Christian theology in Africa is based upon the absolutely universal and the absolutely concrete. That means, it draws a lot from the ontology of the African who is a make of the African experience in history and also salvation history. It then looks at African experience in history as part of salvation history based upon the present experience of the Divine and hopes for the renewal of being and existence in the future. And thus, engaging the particular experience of Africa ought to be seen as part of what God is doing in the life of the world. In that way, the particular will then find fulfillment in the universal as manifested as the absolute concrete.

Unfortunately, since the focal point of African Christian theology has been identity of the particular, it missed the focus and center of theology, who is the Trinitarian God revealed in the Son in the power of the

---

53. Amarkwei, *Christian Life*, 73–75.

Holy Spirit. And this led to the ideological problem that came up in the New Testament as well as in the times of the church fathers. Furthermore it led to the problem of utopianism in African Christian theology. And now, Kpelelogical theology advocates for a theological paradigm that ensures that personal faith engages religions and cultures, and social justice and ecology, and science and technology.

Part 3

A Kpelelogical Theology

Kpele and the Kpelelogical Theology of the *Okpelejen Wulormor*

HAVING LAID A FOUNDATION for doing theology in Africa, I now seek to engage the understanding of it to express our sense of being theological. This is achieved, first, in chapter 6, by accentuating the questions existing among Ga Christians regarding their faithfulness as Christians and their being. These form the antecedents which actually lead to the location of the cosmic Jesus Christ in Ga history and holistic existence as expressed in their annual *Kpele* celebration of the *Homowor* festival. Thus, the cosmic Jesus Christ is identified as the *Okpelejen Wulormor* in his *munus triplex*.

Second, I seek to achieve a Kpelelogical reflection in chapter 7 that indeed the cosmic Jesus Christ is *Okpelejen Wulormor*, by engaging John Calvin, Karl Barth, and Douglas Waruta and John Ekem regarding their understanding of the *munus triplex* (threefold office of Jesus Christ) using the *Okpelejen Wulormor*.

So in this part of the book, we engage a Kpelelogical theology as a reflection on the revelation of God in Jesus Christ in the Spirit from the Ga people's context in Ghana. This particular Kpelelogical theology stems from the objective and subjective encounter of the saving power of God the Father through the Son in the Holy Spirit. It is the proclamation of the Word of God from Scripture as the historical work of God and also the experience of this reality indeed.

This Trinitarian acknowledgment of God is also seen as a cosmic reality in the light of the Kpelelogical import of the African Christian mind.

And this cosmic understanding of God's plan in the whole of creation leads to an open or comprehensive or a transformative theological end from an African position.

Jesus the *Okpelejen Wulormor* is thus a reflection on the Christian message, which is based upon the death and resurrection of Jesus Christ as God's love and which answers the question of creation's predicament in the Spirit and in the Kpelelogical sense. It takes its sources from Scripture, Christian history and the history of religions and culture in general and in particular context of Africa.

6

The Concept of *Okpelejen Wulormor* in the *Kpele* Traditional and Religious Institution of the Ga People of Southern Ghana

An Antecedent of Jesus Christ the *Okpelejen Wulormor*

THERE ARE TWO MAIN antecedents to this christological work. First of all, it is important to establish the fact that the work, *Yesu Homowor Nuntsor* of Philip Tetteh Laryea is a bold step in theology using Ga categories. This teaching is from a gentleman whose work really created boldness among Ga Christians at home and abroad regarding their identity. His work was revolutionary because prior to it, there was a violent debate regarding the celebration of the *Homowor* by other religious groups, including Christianity, civil society groups and the government.

This issue happened in the wake of the reaction which ensued after the violation of the Ga traditional ban on drumming and noise-making. The Ga traditional ban on drumming is part of the religious activities undertaken every year during the *Homowor* festival. The Ga Traditional Council announced its decision to enforce this ban and warned churches, night clubs, and bar operators to cooperate with the custom of the Ga people. However, the contravention of the ban resulted in some violence and the vandalization and confiscation of some church properties by operators of the Ga traditional authorities. Consequently, it led to a series of dialogues among key stakeholders. The end result was that the churches, night clubs and bar operators should comply with the annual ban on drumming and noise making custom.

Thereafter, many questions were raised including whether the Ga Christian can become an active participant of the *Homowor* or not? While some Ga Christians condemned the celebrations of the *Homowor* as unchristian, there were others who found nothing wrong with it because, it was their heritage and they could not be detached from it. It was out of this background that Laryea came out with *Yesu Homowor Nuntsor* to inform and to critically engage the minds of the Ga Christians in the year 2004.[1] This interpretation was that the *Homowor* is fulfilled only in Jesus as Laryea dialogued with the Ga Kpele traditional and religious institution. This theology was written by and large for Ga Christians, but also for other interested people, such as theologians and scholars of religion and philosophy. Most importantly, it should be mentioned that his work has made many Ga Christians in the old established churches like the Catholic, Presbyterian, Methodist and Anglican traditions to feel that it is fine to participate in the festival. Moreover, it removed the uneasiness in the enjoyment the festival as a heritage and a blessing from God, which is fulfilled only in Jesus Christ.

Another item that made Laryea's work so radical was the use of the Ga language. *Yesu Homowor Nuntsor* was published at a time that many Ga people home and abroad were alarmed about the destruction of the Ga customs and particularly the Ga language. Therefore, as a mother tongue theologian at the Akrofi-Christaller Institute of Theology, Mission and Culture (ACIMC), at Akropong, Ghana, it was both impelling and natural to theologize using the Ga language. This feat is revolutionary because it came at a time that the teaching of the Ga language in the Ga society was in distress. Many Ga people could not speak Ga properly and many Ga scholars were the bane on the development of the Ga language because they seldom used it. And so, Laryea's work was a radical challenge to all scholars, while at the same time giving hope to the traditional Ga people and also providing an opportunity to propagate the gospel within the Ga religion and culture.

Nevertheless, the main concern is that Laryea opens up a theological discussion which ought to be explored further. Indeed, Jesus is the Lord of *Homowor*, which may be defined as a revolutionary action of God to deliver God's people from hunger, thirst and famine. It was liberation, a

---

1. Laryea, *Yesu Homowor Nuntsor*.

redemptive act of God, which led the Ga people to a land flowing with milk and honey. It was a liberation which indicated a political, social, and economic struggle within the religio-cultural setting of the Ga people. God is the One and Only God who the Ga knew, that in spite of their numerous *Jemanworjii*, God is the one who ultimately supplies their needs. No Ga, including the *Wulormor*, i.e., "Traditional Priest" of the Ga, may challenge the view that it is *Ataa Naa Nyonmor* (God) who *ultimately* provides abundant water and food for the Ga people. God is certainly the Lord of the *Homowor;* however, the question which exists is how Jesus fits into the shoes of God as the Lord of *Homowor*?

And it is at this point that one particularly identifies a gap between the *Homowor and* Jesus as Lord of the *Homowor*. What category within the Ga conceptual scheme could be employed to fill in the gap? For example, we know that for the *Homowor* celebration to begin and end, there is an Overseer who ensures that there is total celebration and commemoration of the *Homowor*. The overseer or president (*Wulormor*) of the Ga *Homowor* festival is the stepping stone upon which we could clearly see how Jesus becomes the Lord of the *Homowor*.

Jesus is the One who was incarnated among the creation of God and thus the old idea of a transcendent God who was also the immanent God comes to the fore. The Ga conceptual scheme perceives *Naa Nyonmor* as immanent and yet transcendent,[2] thus the provision of the *Jemanworjii*. This idea reveals the gap, which was filled by the incarnation as a solution to the problem of transcendence. How does one deal with the same problem without repeating a transcendence of Jesus? What should be the imagination of Ga Christians regarding the work of *Yesu Homowor Nuntsor* is that Jesus makes concrete the transcendent God they knew. Thus, it is vital to locate Jesus within the *Homowor* celebrations and the entire life of the Ga people. And this is where I locate the role of the *Wulormor* as the "presiding priest" of the entire *Homowor*. The question is, how *and* why could Jesus not fill that gap? Jesus the *Okpelejen Wulormor* therefore seeks to concretize the fact that Jesus is Lord of the *Homowor* and to authenticate that Christology as a revisionist African theology.

The second antecedent to the use of Jesus Christ the *Okpelejen Wulormor* is the African Christian reality of appropriating Jesus as the ultimate problem solver, a position every *Wulormor* occupies.[3] In the African

2. Henderson-Quartey, *Ga of Ghana*, 57; see also Osabu-Kle, "The Ga People and the Homowo Festival."

3. Field, *Religion and Medicine*, 7, 6–8.

church, as could be gleaned from the works of Cephas Omenyo[4] and J. Kwabena Asamoah-Gyadu,[5] the emphasis on the prophecy, miracles and divine healing and power for success shows clearly the imagery of who Christ is to the ordinary Christian. The fact that these Christians see Jesus as their prophet, priest and king, who becomes everything to them, is the conviction that the *Okpelejen Wulormor* is an authentic christological title which represents the needs and aspirations of the Ga Christians if not the needs of African Christians. It has to be quickly stated that, in this particular exposition of Christian doctrine, it is hoped, would be found significantly meaningful by theologians in other contexts in the world as they relate this theology to their situation.

In Ghana today, as may be the case elsewhere in Africa, the Charismatic and Pentecostal nature of Christianity has become pervasive. This fact is because emphasis is placed on spiritual matters as well as the material concerns. The Preaching, Healing, and Deliverance (PHD) ministry is characteristic of every church. Thus all, including Roman Catholic, Anglican and Methodist and Presbyterian, and certainly all the Charismatic and Pentecostal churches, have this ministry. Therefore, it may be right to posit that the preaching, healing and exorcism and prophetic ministry is a unique nature of African Christianity where the power of God is not abstract and absent but concrete and present to all as a testimony of what God is doing. This ministry is surely found in a Christology of a liberating Christ who sacrifices for the people with his blood, and by his power raises them in holiness to a life of concrete blessedness and whose liberation is manifested by the works of the Holy Spirit in the church and the individual alike. Therefore, Ghanaian Christianity represents a practical demonstration of the triune God's activity in the world.

Kpele Religious Thought in Ga Life

The Ga people are organized according to the Kpele religious institution organized by the *Wulormor*. For example, the annual celebration of *Homowor* (hooting at hunger) which occurs at the beginning of the New Year (May-August) of the Ga calendar is presided over by the *Wulormor*

---

4. Omenyo, "Charismatic Churches in Ghana," 250–77; see also Omenyo, *Pentecost*. See Larbi, *Pentecostalism*.

5. Asamoah-Gyadu, "Pulling Down Strongholds," 305–17; also Asamoah-Gyadu, *African Charismatics*.

who is the custodian of the Kpele religion.⁶ In the Ga setup, there may be different *Wulormei* who have been placed in charge of different aspects of the Ga life. A priest, i.e., *Dantu Wulormor*, is specifically designated for calculating the time for the Ga Mashi people and initiating the planting season.⁷ This shows how the *Kpele* religious institution organizes everyone in the community to ensure peace, security, and development in every area of life. Thus, the multidimensional nature of the *Kpele* religion could be located in the celebration of the *Homowor*. Moreover, it is the same system of community living that ensures there is a strong connection among members of the Ga society.

The Ga people are those whose borders are the Akwapim range in the north, the sea to the south, the Owutus and Fantes to the west and the Adangme's to the east.⁸ The *Gamei*, as they call themselves, speak the Ga language while their Adangme counterparts speak Dangme. These two people group are of the same stock because of the similarity in the language, sociopolitical structure, circumcision, naming, and patrilineal inheritance as few sociocultural examples.⁹ The Ga language has been classified among the *Kwa* group of languages in the Niger-Congo area.

The Ga people are made up of six groups which comprise the Ga-Mashi, Osu, La, Teshie, Nungua and Tema.¹⁰ All groups have their own territories with their own systems, which run autonomously. However within these groups are further divisions known as the *Akutsei* or quarters, comprised of *Wei*, or patrilineal houses, which is further divided into *Shiai*—the individual houses, making up the *We*.¹¹ The Ga are named according to *We* names, gender, the rank among other siblings, circumstances of birth, and the day of birth, with the latter being borrowed from the Akans.¹² This shows the order and arrangement for everyone in the traditional Ga society. The kpelelogical mind therefore beholds reality in the holistic terms while paying attention to details of individuals who are properly linked up to the whole. The individual owes allegiance to the Father and the head of the house (*Shia*). The Father is accountable to the

---

6. Asamoah-Gyadu, "Pulling Down Strongholds," 305–17; also Asamoah-Gyadu, *African Charismatics*.

7. See Field, *Religion and Medicine*, 89; see also Kilson, *Kpele Lala*, 20–180.

8. Odotei, "External Influences," 61.

9. Odotei, "Ga and Their Neighbours."

10. Odotei, "Ga and Their Neighbours."

11. Odotei, "Ga and Their Neighbours."

12. Odotei, "What Is in a Name?"

head of the *Weku* (patrilinear head of individual houses belonging to a group identifiable by name). And the head of the *Weku* owes allegiance to the head of an *akutso* (quarter) which comprise of various *Wekui*. Finally, the head of *akutsei* (plural *akutso*) is the *Mankralo*, who works in the absence of and on behalf of the *Mantse* (king) installed by the *Wulormor*.

The origin of the Ga people has many hypotheses according to Odotei.[13] The *Nai Wulormor* (the Ga Mashi principal *Wulormor*) assert that the Ga people came from the sea, which meant that they migrated from the east either by canoes or along the beach.[14]

Although Odotei prefers to suggest a migration from a lower Volta basin,[15] by reason of the Ladoku excavations,[16] currently there seems to be more weight placed upon the suggestion that the Ga had migrated from the east and particularly from Benin in Nigeria.[17]

Under the *Kpele* institution spearheaded by the *Wulormor*, the Ga people were organized agriculturists, salt miners and craftsmen and women, and hunters and fisherfolk.[18] They farmed various crops such as millet, corn, yams, cassava, tomatoes, and peppers and other crops. There were livestock rearing, including cattle, goats, and sheep, and fowls.[19] They mined salt from their lagoons, which is scattered along the towns in which they resided, but particularly from the *Sakumor*, *Kpeshi*, *Sango*, and *Mokue*.[20] They were also engaged in hunting of all types of game including antelopes, bush pigs, leopards and even elephants.[21] The Ga people were also engaged in blacksmithing and goldsmithing.[22] And as said earlier, most of these activities were organized around the *Kpele Jemaworjii* (deities) and their *wulormei* that define a group and their profession as well as the location of their work such as the sea and lagoon. Indeed, in the *Asere* quarter of the Ga Mashi, there is a *Jemanwon* (deity)

---

13. Odotei, "Ga and Their Neighbours."
14. See also Reindorf, *History of the Gold Coast*, 5–6, 3.
15. Odotei, "Ga and Their Neighbours."
16. Ozanne, "Ladoku," 6; Odotei, "Ga and Their Neighbours."
17. See Ward, *Short History*, 16–19; Reindorf, *History*, 21; Romer, *Reliable Account*; Field, *Religion and Medicine*, 2–3; Laryea, *Yesu Homowor Nuntsor*, 22.
18. Odotei, "Precolonial Economic Activities of the Ga."
19. Odotei, "Precolonial Economic Activities of the Ga."
20. Odotei, "Precolonial Economic Activities of the Ga."
21. Odotei, "Precolonial Economic Activities of the Ga."
22. Odotei, "Precolonial Economic Activities of the Ga."

"Gua" associated with thunder and blacksmithing who may be in charge of farming tools, weapons, jewelry, and war.²³

The *Wulormor* of the *Kpele* Institution

Prof. Odotei explains further that

> the Ga organized themselves into independent groups which were comprised of major and minor lineages. Within the groups, each lineage has its own god [*Jemanwon*], and there was furthermore a senior [*Jemanwon*] for the whole group. The priests of the supreme [*Jemaworjii*] were the leaders of the groups. For example, the Las were under the leadership of the *Lakpa Wulormor*.²⁴

Each of the groups of the Ga people scattered along the coast have their own principal *Jemanwon*, who for them is very important for their day-to-day life and activities. These *Jemaworjii* acted to provide protection and solutions to their very pressing needs. A faith in God is not that which allowed them to trust God for everything. To the best of their knowledge, God is very good and very near, but very far away from humanity because of evil or sin. So the *Jemaworjii* serve the people because they need constant and immediate spiritual protection. In doing so, they required the commitment of the people within their various jurisdictions. And perhaps it is the interest in the *Jemaworjii* that tended to shift their focus away from God.²⁵

The principal *Jemaworjii* of the various Ga groups exists to provide security, peace and prosperity for the people.²⁶ The security is important for the promotion of socioeconomic and political prosperity of the Ga

23. Field, *Religion and Medicine*, 86.

24. Odotei, "Ga and Their Neighbours"; see also Field, *Religion and Medicine*; Kilson, *Kpele Lala*.

25. Henderson-Quartey, *Ga of Ghana*, 57; Osabu-Kle, "Ga People and Homowo Festival."

26. See Field, *Religion and Medicine*, 4–5, and then 28–29, where Field describes it in detail: "The drum *Tele*, in which the first Borketey Larweh brought *Gbobu's dibo* from Tetetutu is treated as a god [*Jemanwon*]-the only example I know of a fetish in *kpele* worship. It is beaten so that its voice may call upon *Gbobu* when rain, better crops, or more fish are needed. *Gbobu* himself, like the head god [*Jemanwon*] of every town, is the giver of all good things. His name is said to mean 'the one whose wings are spread over us all.' He has various descriptive titles in *Fon* and *Obutu*, among which are, 'the one who can fly,' and 'the one whom everybody needs.'"

people. The arm, which ensures that the socioeconomic and political prosperity of the Ga people is taken care of, is the religio-cultural aspect. This worldview has been woven together to the extent that like a typical African community, it is difficult to differentiate between the secular and the religious. The individuals who lead the people to achieve "holistic prosperity" were initially the principal leaders who double as priests and prophets of the people. These theocratic leaders ruled their groups and towns till they relinquished their political leadership in order to concentrate on the religio-cultural aspect of the life of the communities within which they resided. Abraham Akrong writes concerning the theocratic governance of the high priests of the Ga people, saying,

> The Ga priestly theocracy that preceded chieftaincy was a highly developed governance structure based on the political philosophy of what could be described as graduated authority, as opposed to the centralized authority of the Akan chieftaincy model. The philosophy of graduated authority is based on the idea that the real ruler is the deity, who rules through the *Wulormor* (priest), the primary and direct representative of the deity. The status of the priest as the representative of the deity defines the primacy of priestly authority in the Ga theocracy. It is out of this primary authority that different grades of authority are delegated to different offices in the theocracy governance system. This implies that the authority of all office holders in the theocratic governance system derived their authority from the deity through the priest and hence all political authority is essentially derivative and delegated. However, the borrowed institution of chieftaincy came with a different ideology of political authority.[27]

Carl Christian Reindorf shows us that the Ga form of government was a theocracy, whereby the leader was called *Lomo*—the title of a king.[28] He showed the progression from "prophet-priest-king,"[29] who was elected by the *Jemanwon* (deity in-charge) of the community. He adds that the person could be elected "from any tribe whatever, and not by hereditary right or popular election."[30] This stance is the first and original state of Ga governance. What happened next? According to Reindorf, the *Lomo*s forfeited their position, which was given to the officiating priests

27. Akrong, "Pre-monarchial Political Leadership," 141–42.
28. Reindorf, *History of the Gold Coast*, 106.
29. Reindorf, *History of the Gold Coast*, 106.
30. Reindorf, *History of the Gold Coast*, 106.

of the highest deity in charge of the particular community or nation, and due to the "extravagant use of that power." These officiating priests were called *Wulormor* which he interpreted as *fetish-man* or *fetish-servant*.[31] Reindorf continues,

> This class of people became the ruling family, instead of the former, from which a priest was elected, who was acknowledged as king or chief in every town, and had to serve in the fetish yard, keep the place clean, administer the holy water for the worshippers to wash with on fetish-days. He also instructed the people in the fetish laws, ruled over them according to the instructions of the fetish, offered sacrifices on their behalf, and prayed for them. But such priest-kings were ruled by the advice of foretelling priests, who were considered as mouth-pieces and representatives of the fetishes, by whom the whole constitution was framed. The government was therefore a fetish monarchy. It sometimes happened that the priest-king was also one of the foretellers.[32]

This is the second stage of the theocratic governance system of the Ga. Following this second stage, was the third stage of the priest relinquishing the kingship of the *Wulormor*. According to historians, this happened at different times and under similar, but different circumstances. For instance, what necessitated both Ga-Mashi and La *Wulormei* to relinquish their kinship was the pressure, which was probably caused by the brisk business activities with both the Akans and the Europeans.[33] The Osu people possessed this change when the *Wulormor* was changed and the younger brother was brought into the office. The elder brother later came and ruled as a king.[34] But one could agree with Akrong that it was because of the civil and secular activities by which the *Wulormor* was limited which prompted the final change. The original roles of the *Wulormor* such as priest, king and prophet in the context of the *Kpele* religion are discussed below.[35]

---

31. Reindorf, *History of the Gold Coast*, 106.
32. Reindorf, *History of the Gold Coast*, 106.
33. See Kilson, *African Urban Kinsmen*, 5; Quacoopone, *Impact of Urbanization*, 33; see also Odotei, "Ga and Their Neighbours"; Akrong, "Pre-monarchial Political Leadership," 138–39.
34. Akrong, "Pre-monarchial Political Leadership," 144.
35. Akrong, "Pre-monarchial Political Leadership," 137.

The *Wulormor* as Priest

It is important to reiterate the work of the *Wulormor* which includes managing the shrine of the *jemawon* and the environs. This means that the *Wulormor* as a priest should ensure that the place is well weeded, cleaned, and beautified. He ensures that the thatch roof is in good condition and water and stool are provided for the *Jemanwon* at all times. There should also be water, which Carl Reindorf calls "holy water" for the cleansing and healing purposes of worshippers.[36]

Rituals to pacify the deity, such as sacrifices, which are needed for the blessing of the deity for the people, are carried out by the priest. They also teach the laws of the deity to the people and further see to the implementation and enforcement of all the laws of the deity. They perform rituals also to cleanse the people from curses and transgressions.[37] They say prayers for the people and at various functions, such as festivals. This role may therefore be related to prayers of intercession for the people within the community for the deity to bring peace, security and prosperity. When there is a calamity, the priest intervenes by carrying out the necessary rituals to pacify the deity. Apart from teaching, the priest also serves as counselors within the community. In most instances they may be drawn into arbitrations of all sorts, which work also falls in the purview of the king and the prophet.[38]

The shrine is called a *Gbatsu* and within it is kept sundry insignia, such as brooms and pots of holy water for ceremonial cleansing and a stool for the *Jemanwon*. The priest is required to sleep in the *gbatsu* and maintain it as aforementioned.[39] Magaret Field reveals that

> all trouble is caused by wrong doing. If the priest himself were immoral, partial, or guilty of personal envies and spites his prayers will be ineffective. Furthermore, if he sinned or connived at sin his [*Jemanwon*] will kill him. The white calico vestments which he wears are the symbol of his purity.[40]

She continues to show that the Ga priest is supposed to be morally upright together with his wife. The *Wulormor* is supposed to observe

---

36. Reindorf, *History of Gold Coast*, 106.
37. Reindorf, *History of Gold Coast*, 106.
38. Field, *Religion and Medicine*, 7.
39. Field, *Religion and Medicine*, 5–7.
40. Field, *Religion and Medicine*, 7.

certain sacred rules (taboos), such as not seeing dead bodies, the prohibition of dead material from the shrine, and the prohibition of uncircumcised men and women in their menses.[41] In addition, the *Wulormor* must not eat fermented food and also refrain from sexual intercourse on certain days and before performing important rites. He is not allowed to own property, but all his needs shall be provided.[42]

This type of religious observance and activity of the *Wulormor* could be related to the theocracy in Jewish history (Lev 10:1–5; 21:1–4; 7–9). Consequently, it is enough to apply ideas as expressed in the New Testament, particularly in Hebrew 6–9.[43] A note with interest is also how Reindorf described the position of the *Wulormor*, when he observed that the position of the *Wulormor* is "fetish-man" or "fetish-servant."[44] This understanding of Carl Reindorf clearly shows his attempt to reflect on the person of Jesus Christ in his Ga context. Significantly, it identifies Carl Reindorf as the earliest native theologian in the Gold Coast (Ghana). Interestingly it reveals the *admirabile commercium* (wonderful exchange) theological imagination in Carl Reindorf shown in theology of John Calvin. And it is very much consistent to the "Yes" of Christ, and with the "No" of humanity in Barthian soteriology.[45]

This concept allows the Ga to appreciate that Christ is the one who shares in the sufferings of the people far more than what the *Wulormor* could offer. This analogy enables one to look at the possibilities of the *Wulormor* dying for the sake of the people. There is a general belief that the *Wulormor* had not reached the level of dying for the sake of the community or nation he serves.[46] However, it may be discovered otherwise when the dynamics of the original Ga polity is studied. Carl Reindorf reveals that the priest, called Apagbe of the Adangme people, had upon enabling the people to cross a river on the back of a crocodile, sat on the back of the crocodile and together dived into the water, never to be seen again.[47] This action requires an enormous sacrifice which demanded the life of the leader, who was also the prophet and priest.

41. Field, *Religion and Medicine*, 7–8.
42. Field, *Religion and Medicine*, 8.
43. Ekem, *Priesthood in Context*.
44. Reindorf, *History of the Gold Coast*, 106.
45. See Barth, *Church Dogmatics*, IV.1, §13.58.
46. Ekem, *Priesthood in Context*, 196.
47. Reindorf, *History of the Gold Coast*, 48.

Further, the story is told of how Numo Borketey Larweh, *Wulormor* of the Nungua people, fought for the people of Nungua to the peril of his life and then entered the sea, and never to be seen again as follows:

> The Ningowas, who had been long established near the Coast at *Wodoku*, were owners of the land from thence to Teiashi near Christianborg, and the Labades were obliged to ask Afote Okre to grant them a piece of land to build on. Adshei Onano was then their king, and Numo Ngmashi his great chief; the number of the king's army was 8,000 and his great chief 7,000 men. The priest of the Ningowas, Borkete Lawe, objected to the king's allowing the Labades to live near them; but his opinion was overruled. The Ningowas being very powerful, the Labades never dreamt of making war with them, so they lived at peace a long time.
>
> The Ningowas sacrificed a human being annually to their *Angmu*, the Black Rock. Victims for that purpose were kidnapped from any town by the Ningowas. When the custom was performed, the people went to the shore where the *Angmu* is situated, and after singing and dancing, the priest Borkete Lawer was said to pray till the sea was divided and access gained to the foot of the rock, where they all spent the day in making sacrifices. When all the others returned to the shore, the poor victim was left behind, and the priest prayed that the water should flow back and drown the victim.
>
> Odole, daughter of the king of Labade, was one day missed; and after fruitless search for her, it was said she had been sacrificed to *Angmu*. The Ningowas were accused of the girl's murder; they denied it, and war was declared against them: Borkete Lawer was the most powerful archer among his people, as Sowa, the priest of Lakpa, was the famous hunter and sharpshooter among the Labades.
>
> The war lasted for months, so that the Ningowas could not remove their salt from Kpeshi. The Labades carried off all the salt and threw it into every water hole and pool belonging to the enemy. This brought on a terrible scarcity of fresh water in all the towns of Ningowa and in addition, ambushcades were arranged by the Labades at any place where water might be obtained. Thus the Ningowas were reduced to awful distress.
>
> In this condition of things, the Labades cunningly proposed to the Ningowas that the hands of both priests, Lawe and Sowa, should be cut off, to bring peace again, because they were the chief cause of war between them. They tied up their own priest, and brought him to the Ningowas. The deluded people of Ningowa readily consented to the proposal, when they saw

Sowa with his hands pinioned behind him. Lawe was called upon and required to consent to have only one hand cut off to preserve the people from death by thirst.

The priest addressed the whole assembly: "Children, do you mean to cut off my hand, the hand that draws the bow to save you? Do you mean to ruin yourselves by cutting off my hand which defends you children?"

Without delay the Labades who had made the proposal and therefore ought to have cut off their huntsman's hands first, overpowered the old man, and his hand was cut off in presence of the whole assembly. After this he assembled the whole of his family and relatives at *Bobowe*, gave them a song, and marched to the sea at their head, where, tradition says, he prayed, and the sea divided, and he and all his followers entered and disappeared.[48]

Thus, the fact remains that in the time past it may have become necessary for priests who were the governors of the Ga people, to surrender their lives for the sake of their people. This sacrifice may be a shadow of Christ, who lived among his people, did mighty works, and died for them so that they might live. One also has to be cautious in thinking about the end of Apagbe and Borkete Lawer as ordinary deaths. This caution is necessary because there is a lingering belief that these priests are alive, but perhaps in a different state of being, which may be a possible physical and spiritual life.[49] Although they have not arisen from the waters they entered, it is believed they are continuing life.

The difference is that although these *Wulormei* may have died or entered the sea for their people, it ended there; it did not generate any

---

48. Reindorf, *History of the Gold Coast*, 43–44. I have quoted extensively to ensure that the original text to the story which is very dear to the towns involved is not misrepresented.

49. Reindorf, *History of the Gold Coast*, 48; before he disappeared with the crocodile, Apagbe the *Wulormor* in reference to crocodile fetish commanded the successors thus: "Crocodile, leopard and hyena are sacred animals which must never be killed; gold and ivory must not be touched, neither should they have anything to do with human and animal blood." During Nungua *Kplejoo* festival, and the *gbermlilaa*, the priests, together with other functionaries like the *woryei*, *worhii*, and *agbaafoi*, solemnly process through Borkete Lawer Street. This path is followed in commemoration of *Borkete Larwer*'s movement into the sea. It is also done as a ritual or ceremony to create a path for the *Jemanworjii* and *Borkete Lawer* to visit the Nungua people. A path is created for him at *Tertsonaa* grove, where it is believed drops of blood from his maimed hand fell. The whole ceremony is like the preparation Christians make in anticipation of the coming of Jesus Christ.

power[50] or bring transformation as to what Christ did, which suggests that Christ is the authentic *Wulormor* who does not curse his people when he is rejected. Christ's resurrection and exaltation is proven in the life of all believers and even as in the life of the church; this cannot be said of the Ga *Wulormei*. When they die, they are gone and forgotten and offer no significance to the people again. It is only in Nungua or possibly Adangme that it could be surmised that the ritual at the beach, where a symbolic way is paved for Borkete Larweh to return together with the *Jemaworjii* may provide an indication for an eschatological hope.[51] The priest is also limited to the communities in which they reside but unlike Christ do not possess a certain sense of universality. The importance of the *Okpelejen* title is to serve as *ta panta* (all things) for the *archierius*, i.e., *Wulormor* and the absolutely concrete of the Lord Jesus Christ.

The *Wulormor* as a King

Akrong gives a very good analysis of the original Ga polity. He shows that the *Wulormor* is the political leader and that this authority is conferred on him by the principal or highest *Jemanwon* of the people. This governance system is based upon a decentralized administration where people are appointed into various offices to steer the affairs of the nation. He elaborates by writing that

> under the priestly theocracy the centre of secular political power resided in the *Akwaashon*, from which different types of delegated authorities were given for specific political functions. The administrative authority of the priestly theocracy was expressed in the rule of the *Akwaashontse* who handled day to day political matters on behalf of the priest, and the *Asafoatsemei* who commanded the clan militias in times of war.
>
> One feature of the priestly theocracy is that authority was not centralized in one person but rather was dispersed and shared by various categories of leaders. The graduated authority structure of the priestly theocracy allows for diffusion of authority, which prevents the development of centralized authority.

50. Although the lives of Apagbe and Borkete Lawer may trigger an eschatological hope in the people, it has to be recognized that Borkete Lawer cursed the Nungua people due to their betrayal, unlike Christ who prophesied doom for Jerusalem but forgiveness on the cross. And in Nungua there has not been any revolutionary impact like the death and resurrection accomplished in Jesus Christ.

51. See notes above on the eschatological hope of the people of Nungua.

This means that political authority is mediated from the deity through the priestly governance to the various political offices. This feature of Ga political philosophy has cultivated the culture of criticism of delegated political authority as a permanent feature of Ga political life. Some features of this culture of protest and dissent can be found in the *kpaashimor* aspect of *Homowor* at La and Teshie.[52]

So in short, the priestly theocracy of the Ga people is a highly advanced governance system which is highly democratic, but yet done with control and decorum. This governance system is to ensure that power is truly in the hands of the people and at *Homowor*, a protest is made against all known misdeeds of persons or group of persons in the society. Osabu-Kle elaborates on this liberating phenomenon known as *kpaashimor* during the *Homowor* Festival:

> *Kpaashimor* is of two types. The more gentle type is in the form of traditional songs and dancing and it is called *Amlakui-Akpaa* meaning the *Kpaa* dance of the nobility. The *sese* carrying group engages always in this type. The other type is very democratic and aims at exposing the wrongs committed by the nobility and commoners alike during the past year with the view of making them change their behavior for the better. The *kpa* groups from the seven quarters [of Teshie] of the town engage in this type. After *sesefaa*, the *kpaa* groups break into their separate groups and begin to expose the wrongdoings of the nobility beginning with those of the *Mantse*. The wrongdoings of the head of State of Ghana and his Ministers may also be exposed. They then proceed to expose the wrongdoings of individuals. Any person whose wrongdoings are exposed is expected by tradition to provide some gift usually money to express his or her appreciation. This goes on from Sunday to Friday while the *sese* carrying group continues to engage in *Amlakui-Akpaa*.[53]

This tradition also endorses, in many ways, the authority of the *Wulormor* as a king. One may evaluate this point when we look at *Homowor*. In the Christology of Barth, one sees the servant-God in a below upwards movement in which the suffering servant is lifted up together with the suffering people. This belief is what he calls sanctification and an upliftment. Therefore, Christ in the *Okpelejen Wulormor* sides with

---

52. Akrong, "Pre-monarchial Political Leadership," 143–44.
53. Osabu-Kle, "The Ga People and the Homowo Festival."

the masses in their suffering, their oppressed state and their humiliation and shares his power with them. This stands as a pure liberation of Christ in the life of the suffering masses. He empowers them by giving them a moral authority to challenge the status quo by giving them a prophetic voice. Here, even the weakest among all people is given a chance to tell the political king whatsoever he or she feels. Traditionally this event was done within the Ga community and all persons, including foreigners, whose conduct leaves much to be desired, are all confronted squarely. The payment of an "appreciation" is simply a polite way of saying a fine for the offences committed by said individuals. Therefore, this authority of Christ is the authority of the church and the individual.

Another issue which is striking is the kingship of Jesus as it relates to the kingship of the *Wulormor*. Jesus obviously had a kingship, but the kingship is not of this world, and Calvin says it is a kind of spiritual kingship (John 18:33–37). The Jewish kingship was relinquished within the priestly theocracy (1 Sam 8 and 9) of the nation, but Christ is the one to fulfill all. Jesus Christ did not assume the former position of kingship as it were in the Jewish priestly theocratic context, but in another form, which could be described as spiritual.

In the same manner, the Ga priestly theocracy relinquished its kingship but it still persists in installing the king and also giving much power to the people through the *Homowor* celebrations. It should be noted that it is not the political king who controls the *Homowor*, but the *Wulormor* and this position displays his governing power, but quite differently from the king. Moreover, if there be a war for which the various *Asafo* may wage war, even under the command of the *Mantse* (king), the groups may not proceed unless assured by the *Wulormor* of the protection of the national deity.[54] So even in the Ga tradition, like that of Christ, there exist a kind of kingship within the *Wulormor* and Christ, which is different from the secular kingship. The Jesus and *Wulormor* kingship empowers the powerless and the subjugated. This category of kingship is surely at variance with the worldly power, which is characterized by greed, oppression and the dehumanization of people. This kind of kingship ensures that power is by the people, belongs to the people and for the people.

---

54. Field, *Religion and Medicine*, 4; Reindorf, *History of the Gold Coast*, 209; Compare Mark 16:17–18; Luke 10:17; Acts 1:8; 2:4; 5:16; The enormous power Jesus has made available to the saints is abundantly richer and beyond ethnicity, race, chronological age, sex and socioeconomic status.

The worldly kingship breeds hatred and strife among people as well as wars. Some Ga kings in contemporary Ghana have abused their power by amassing for themselves wealth through the indiscriminate sale of Ga lands as the Ga people become poorer and poorer. Their leadership is not the kind of kingship, which the *Wulormor* stands for. In fact, as Akrong had revealed, it is diametrically opposed to it. Similarly, the power, which Christ wielded as he stood before Pilate, was not the political power, which for the sake of selfish ambition, does injustice by killing innocent people who are hated and persecuted for righteousness sake.

The *Wulormor* as Prophet

As already realized, the prophetic work of the *Wulormor* is based on foretelling and revealing hidden challenges of the people. It also requires giving appropriate instruction to the people to live in accordance with the will of the deity. Originally, the position was all vested in the *Lomo* and was delegated to the priest who was also the king. According to Carl Reindorf, the abuse of the use of this position resulted in the delegation of the prophetic role to other people like the *woryei* and *worhii*, who are mediums of the *Jemanworjii*.[55] However, the prophet did not lose all prophesying abilities, in that occasionally he may do so.[56] The *Wulormor* works with the *woryeii* and *worhii* of the highest deity of the land.[57] Therefore, this prophetic office is administered by the deity who uses the mediums in foretelling or forth-telling.[58]

One could find the delegation of the prophetic office to the people. The outpouring of the Holy Spirit in Acts 2 illustrates how the Holy Spirit was released to all the believers. It is a fulfillment of Joel 2:28–29

---

55. Reindorf, *History of the Gold Coast*, 106.

56. Field, *Religion and Medicine*, 50. This is narrated as follows: "During the night which follows this busy Tuesday, seven chosen *amlakui* carry out a secret ceremony called *Lebo*. As in Nungua and Temma the townspeople are forbidden to leave their houses or show a light. The seven *amlakui* go first to the *La Kpa* priest, who sprinkles them with holy water but does not join them. They go round the town to every *otutu* mound and perform their secret rites over it. In the morning there is no trace of these doings on the mound except 'something like ashes.' . . . A story is told of a Christian catechist who was caught spying and taken to the *La Kpa* priest to have his blood drawn. The priest was not angry, but said casually, 'You will not live to see another Homowor.' The offender died within a week."

57 Reindorf, *History of the Gold Coast*, 106; Field, *Religion and Medicine*, 100–109.

58. Field, *Religion and Medicine*, 46–109.

and this experience provided the church and the believers the authority to acknowledge the work of Christ in their lives. The Holy Spirit is the Truth witnessing about the humiliation and exaltation of Jesus Christ, and confirms it by the lives of the believers. In the prophetic ministry of the *Wulormor*, the power of the deity is released upon the mediums and the ordinary people of the land as true witnesses of the act of the deity.

As seen earlier in our discussion, the prophetic role of the *Wulormor* was relegated to allow others to reveal the minds of the *Jemanworjii* to the people to avoid abuse and also to authenticate the messages of the *Jemanworjii*. The manifestation of the cult of *Wulormor*, with the mediums of *woryei* and *worhii* and the ordinary people of the land, is the seal of the deity of the land. This arrangement is a witness of the truthfulness of the acts of the deity. Therefore, anybody could be possessed by the deity at anytime as witness to the truth of the acts of the deity.

This *Kpele concept* is very striking because it engages women. The *woryei* and *agbaafoi* are very important in the prophetic ministry of the *Wulormor* and, when they are possessed by the *Jemanworjii*, they are said to be married to the *Jemanworjii*. Within the body of Christ, one could definitely see the role of women in the day-to-day activities of the church. Therefore, it could be surmised that the apostolic ministry was probably filled with women, but due to patriarchy it was difficult for them to be noticed. Perhaps this issue of the *woryei* is featured prominently in the AICs where many women are founders as well as prophets and priests. Fiorenza had particularly handled that issue regarding the contribution of women in the church's history in her book, *In Memory of Her*.[59] The point is that the Ga prophetic ministry as found in the office of the *Wulormor* is released to all, including foreigners. This principle concurs very well with the traditional teaching of the church.[60]

Another aspect of the prophetic office of the *Wulormor* could be identified in the *kpaashimor* during the celebration of *Homowor* festival. In addition, it is worthy of note that such a categorization, could also be linked to the kingship of the *Wulormor*. The composition of the lyrics and songs in the *kpaashimor* is mainly inspired by the *Jemanworjii*.[61] It is done as a demonstration of the prophetic role of exposing the wrongs of everyone during the year under review. The power to sing and to go

---

59. Fiorenza, *In Memory of Her*.
60. Barth, *Church Dogmatics*, IV.1, §13.58.4.
61. Field, *Religion and Medicine*, 45–46.

round in a typical *kpaashimor* is not a jamboree; it is a religious activity involving the *Jemanworjii*. It is a demonstration of the power of the *Jemanworjii* through the people.[62] Similarly, the African church worship is vibrant and full of the presence and manifestation of the Holy Spirit with accompanying songs and dancing. What may be lacking though is the appropriation of the power of the Holy Spirit in living a conscious life of liberation in every sphere of life. The church in Africa must be more vocal and more visible as the body of Christ and through the individual Christians. Corruption, which is the bane of African development, could be dealt with if individuals become true witnesses of the work of Christ in their lives.

Homowor Festival

The *Homowor* is a festival that ensures that the Ga is organized to be productive throughout the year. And it is very special because it exposes the role of *Kpele* religion in the Ga life. The *Homowor* (hooting at hunger) is a special celebration, which commemorates the struggle to end the Ga suffering from hunger and famine. It is about a time that the Ga people suffered much drought, resulting in famine and subsequently, hunger. The hunger ended with the provision of enough rain followed by planting which brought about abundant food.

The people were overjoyed and celebrated the occasion for what *Ataa Naa Nyonmorr, Jemanworjii, wojii,* and *sisai* have done for them. It is crucial to follow the account as offered by Margaret Field in all the major Ga towns. However, since there are variances, we have merged the customs based upon the similarities and also the relevance of rites to the total philosophy of the *Homowor* celebrations. The customs and rites of the holistic nature of the *Homowor* or *Kplelejoo* festival include *Bloiahejuu, Manjuramo, Dudonnuwoo, Nmaadumo/Nmafaa, Gbermlilaa/Odadao,* and *Awitsermor*/Secret rites. Also, they include the *Nmaakpamor/Loohee, Obeneshimorr/Kpashimo/Oshi, Koyeli,* and *Kpeleshwermo*. As stated earlier, the main purpose of the *Homowor* is to hoot at hunger; and thus, it involves all physical and spiritual activities amenable to it. The sequential arrangement above, may offer insight into this philosophy of *Homowor*.

---

62. Field, *Religion and Medicine*, 45–46; see *Amlakui Akpashimo* at BRCDesign, "Gbemlilaa" (YouTube video, 1:45).

Bloiahejuu

This rite is performed as the preceding rite for all other rites and it is the first of its kind. The Tema and La perform this ritual, which is the cleansing or washing and whitewashing of the brooms, stools and other sundry insignia, including staff, hats, horns, hoes, and pots of the *Wulormor*.[63] The washing is done with lagoon water (the lagoon is *jemawon*) and the *Wulormor* is in charge of this activity. Sick children are bathed and blessed and all who need the blessing of the *Wulormor* are smeared three times with myrrh (*krobo*) around their necks.[64] The striking issue here is the significance located in the cleansing of the brooms rite which is the release of the power of the *jemawon*. The Ga people believe that holiness is paramount for securing the blessings of the *Jemanworjii*. So at the time of washing, the sick are brought to be healed by the fresh power of the deity through the *Wulormor*.

This is comparable to the Jewish priestly preparation for the Jewish worship. It is believed that inadequate preparation of the *Wulormor* will incur the wrath of the *Jemaworjii*, with consequences of death. In addition, improper preparation may negatively affect the whole celebrations with many repercussions such as strange diseases and deaths on the people. As this whole ceremony is comparable to the Jewish priestly ceremonies, it is interesting to connect to the Hebrews' Christology. The reason is because, these rituals are not in themselves efficacious as they ought to be repeated every year.

Furthermore, the rituals performed at this stage of the festival are done with the weakness of the human conscience (Num 19:7; Heb 7:16; 9:6–10). Moreover, the material objects, like the water of the lagoon, even if they are acceptable, is to the *jemawon* who is limited and not to *Ataa Naa Nyonmor*, who is beyond all existence. However, one could take the role of the *Wulormor* to be clearly that of the high priest, which in Hebrews is Christ, the only true High Priest. It is based upon this point that John Ekem appropriated the *Wulormor* in his interpretation and commentary on the Hebrews as an authentic christological theme. Also, one basis is the holiness code of the *Wulormor* as the high priest of the Ga people.[65] These are delved into in the final chapter of this book.

---

63. See Field, *Religion and Medicine*, 14; see also Laryea, *Yesu Homowor Nuntsor*, 27.

64. Field, *Religion and Medicine*, 14.

65. Ekem, *Priesthood in Context*, 154–58; 194–96.

Manjuramo

The *Manjuramo* is the purification rite for the Nungua Township to cleanse the town of any death and other pollution. The *Jemaworjii* abhors corpses and such manner of situations and before their visitation of the town, the town must be cleared of all such impurities.[66] In this rite, a "priest" known as the *Owufu Wulormor* kills a young goat,[67] which must be young enough to have the navel-string still attached, cut into pieces and placed in a special earthen vessel called a *Lalaka*, and then the *Gborbu Wulormor*, the high priest, distributes to all the gods of the town and the places of worship and then finally, the head presented to the *Gborbu* who is the principal *Jemanwon* in the *Gborbukon*, i.e., *Gborbu Jemanwon* forest or grove. Prayers are said at the places of worship for all the *Jemaworjii* with rum by the *Gborbu Wulormor*.[68]

According to Laryea, the *bloiahejuu* rite is similar and they carry the same significance. To a very large extent, they are similar in significance, but not the same, in the rites themselves. In the *bloiahejuu*, there is the use of lagoon water to purify the instruments of worship for the *Wulormor* and not necessarily the purification of the township and the pacification of all the *Jemaworjii* in the town. The second point is that in one there is the use of water and the other flesh and blood. The third point is that it is crystal clear that a sacrifice that is made in the *manjuramo* is not present in the *bloiahejuu*. This is where the true significance of the *manjuramo* appears.

The ritual in the *manjuramo* may have some semblance with the Jewish purification and atonement ceremonies in which lambs are used as sacrifices and especially for the Passover (Gen 22:8; Exod 12:1ff.; 5; 30:10; Num 28:3; Ezek 45:15 Heb 9:6–10). The *Gborbu Wulormor* performs this ritual as the high priest of the Nungua people to purify the people and to atone for all of their evil deeds.[69] This christological matter is handled in Heb 9:11–12[70] to mean that due to the imperfection of such

---

66. Field, *Religion and Medicine*, 29–30; Laryea, *Yesu Homowor Nuntsor*, 27.

67. Field, *Religion and Medicine*, 29; however, Laryea indicates that it is a calf in Laryea, *Yesu Homowor Nuntsor*, 27.

68. Field, *Religion and Medicine*, 29–30.

69. Field, *Religion and Medicine*, 29–30 (emphasis mine). To me, the whole act is atonement for *Esha* (sin) which in the Ga means anything which is rotten, spoiled, corrupted, or gone bad. In this sense the act of the *Wulormor* is to remove *Esha* which also comprise all sins, corpses, curses, and others which are not in consonance with the "purity" and "holiness" of the *Jemanworjii*.

70. See Ekem, *Priesthood in Context*, 157–59; 195–200.

rites, Christ the eternal High Priest appeared to offer once and for all the true sacrifice. This sacrifice is the sacrifice of himself as the Lamb acceptable to God (Dan 9:24; John 1:29–36; Eph 1: 7; Col 1:14; Rev 5:6).

Another point worthy of acknowledgment is the manner the kid is cut into pieces and placed in the earthenware called *Lalaka* and further distributed. This is truly reminiscent of the work of Jesus Christ in the Last Supper whose antecedent is the Passover. Jesus the High Priest takes the unleavened bread and the wine and talks about his flesh and blood while distributing to the disciples and commands that it should be kept as a memorial (Matt 26–28; Mark 14:22–24; Luke 22:19–20; 1 Cor 11:23–26). Perhaps the *Lalaka* is a shadow of the cup of the New Covenant which contains his flesh and blood. It is from the cup that the elements of his flesh and blood are shared for all people. Thus, the activity of the *Gborbu Wulormor*, to distribute the flesh and blood to the *Jemaworjii*, is comparable to Jesus Christ presenting his flesh and blood to the Father. The difference is that unlike the Jews and the disciples of Jesus, who partook of the lamb and meal of the bread and wine, the Nungua people do not partake of the meal in the *Lalaka*. The reason is because it is only for the *Jemaworjii*. However, the yearly ritual performance of the *Gborbu Wulormor* the high priest is surely a shadow of the work of Christ's Self-sacrifice to atone for all creation.

Dudonnuwoo

This event is a religious rite performed by the high priest of Tema *Sakumor Wulormor* in conjunction with the *Na Yo Wulormei* and representatives of the *akutsei* (major quarters) of Tema. They process solemnly to the *Sakumor* Lagoon with the men carrying hoes on their shoulders while six of ten women carry pots of water on their heads. As they process, the *Sakumor Wulormor* beats a drum while only the men sing without turning back. The water is poured into the fourteen pots in the *gbatsu*. The *Sakumor Wulormor* high priest of Tema then prays asking for safety, peace, rain, crops, and human births. After some time he says a closing prayer and they recess into the town.[71] The purpose for this ceremony is to pray for the *Sakumor Jemanwon* to provide for all their needs in abundance.[72]

---

71. See Field, *Religion and Medicine*, 20.

72. Field, *Religion and Medicine*, 20.

Jesus Christ is the one who satisfies with all that we need in abundance. At the wedding in Cana, Jesus demonstrates that he can do far more than one could think or imagine, but even that he required the filling of the jars present with water (John 2:6–11). Furthermore, Jesus and the woman at the well signifies for us the one who knows us and knows our needs and provides us far more than we could contain, even as everlasting water (John 4:1–23). Thus, Jesus is *Wala Nubu*[73]—fountain of Life. Jesus testified that he came that all might have life in abundance (John 10:10).[74] Similarly, Jesus Christ is the High Priest who intercedes for all, so that there is life in abundance. This life is fulfilled in God in every way (i.e., religio-culturally, socioeconomically, and politically) and according to God's original intention.

Nmaadumor/Nmaashwamor & Nmaafaa

This rite is performed among all the towns of the Ga people of Ghana which includes Ga-Mashi, Osu and La and Teshie and Nungua, and Tema and Prampram. This is a continuation of the fertility rites of the Ga, which involves ceremonial planting of corn or millet. *Nmaa* (millet) is planted in Tema on special places designated by the *Wulormei*.[75] The *Wulormei* of all the towns ensure that this is done by the designated priests, as in the case of *Dantu Wulormor* for the Ga Mashi—the first priest to sow.[76] However, in the other towns, the high priest sows the corn together with the other *Wulormei*, *Woyei*, *Wontsemei*, and *Jranoyeii*. This sowing is done amid the singing of *Kpele* songs.[77] The Nungua call this rite *Nmaashwamor* because the *Gborbu Wulormor* does not sow the corn or millet but instead broadcasts them throughout the town.[78]

The Ga people have what they call *Nmaafaa*, which is transplanting the seedlings into specified plots after sowing the millet. This activity is general to all the Ga people and should be a part of the general *Nmaadumor* rite of the Ga people.[79] This ceremony is significant to the *Homowor*

73. Laryea, *Yesu Homowor Nuntsor*, 93–98.
74. Laryea, *Yesu Homowor Nuntsor*, 28–29.
75. Field, *Religion and Medicine*, 89.
76. Field, *Religion and Medicine*, 89.
77. Field, *Religion and Medicine*, 21–22.
78. Field, *Religion and Medicine*, 31.
79. Field, *Religion and Medicine*, 43.

philosophy; it is a religious custom that seeks for abundant food, it also demonstrates that it is necessary for the inhabitants to sow in order for the *Jemaworjii* to bless them. The ethic of hard work through farming is intertwined with the blessing of the *Jemaworjii*. Therefore, it is a liberating act, which seeks to empower the people to drive out hunger and poverty through the principle of hard work. Let us note that these rites are a demonstration of the work of the people in the area. In the outskirts of these major towns are farmlands in which are planted all types of crops, including pepper, tomatoes, corn, cassava, and the rearing of farm animals, including cattle.[80]

Furthermore, if Jesus is the High Priest and King, will he not ensure the growth of their crops, if it is with great compassion that he fed the five thousand people with just five loaves and two fishes (Luke 9:13–17)? Therefore, as the people present to him their needs of agricultural increase, he speedily will multiply their farm produce and cause abundance. And so, like the *Wulormei*, who symbolically plant corn with the sure hope that *Ataa Naa Nyonmor* and the *Jemanworjii* will multiply for the people abundant food produce; Jesus the Christ, the High Priest and King, will present the little farms of seed sown to the Almighty, just as he presented the two fishes and five loaves for God to give the increase.

The symbolic presentation of the seed sowing to the *Jemaworjii* by *Wulormei* in the *Nmaadumor* ritual is analogical to the blessing of the two fishes and five loaves by Jesus. Therefore, Jesus Christ is the Lord of the Sowing (*NmaadumorNuntsor*) because he actually is the embodiment of sowing in his suffering, crucifixion and death and burial. And in the power of the Spirit and by the will of the Father, there is newness of life and first fruits of the resurrection in him.

---

80. The writer acknowledges this particularly when as a boy in Abokobi engaged in farming and witnessed the *Homowor* by moving from Abokobi to Osu for the celebrations. The family carries among other things corn, palm nuts, and other farm products. The other villages like Sesemi, Kweiman, Teiman, Akpoman, Boi, Pantan, and Oyarifa are all surrounding communities in which farming is undertaken vigorously. Each of these communities is mainly for the major towns. For example Abokobi is inhabited mainly by the people from Osu, Teshi, and Nunua while Oyarifa and Pantan are inhabited mainly by La people.

Gbermlilaa/Odadao

This is the period that a ban is placed on drumming and noise-making. The religious interpretation to this is that now that the corn and the millet are in the soil there should be no more noise or drumming because the *Jemaworjii* have been invoked to come and live with the people and bless them. In La, the people are encouraged to confess their sins, so that blessings are received on condition of righteous living.[81] The blessing is found in the increase in the agricultural yield and other forms of blessing.

Having noted the above meaning, it is important to underscore the point that the *gbermlilaa* or *odadao* may have direct implications for the socioeconomic life of the people. When it is planting time, there should be limited play and merry making.[82] It signifies that the war against hunger requires sweat and hard work, which demands a lot of concentration and focus. At this time, people are expected to move to the outskirts and join family relations in the farming activities. It is a real time for work and all other activities, which negate it, are barred.

This very act of solemnity found in the lives of the *Wulormei* for God's intervention is noteworthy of Jesus the High Priest. The commencement of Jesus' ministry was initiated by a solitude period of forty days of fasting and prayers (Matt 4:1–11). Jesus often prayed early in the morning and had a lot of quiet time (Mark 1:35; Luke 4:42). These periods of solitary waiting are for engaging God's power in the ministry of Jesus to the people in which all manner of needs were met. And so, the period of silence for the *Wulormei* and the *Jemaworjii* has implications for understanding both depth of the *Kpele* institution as well as issues of ethics and spirituality in Christianity. Therefore, Jesus Christ is the true High Priest of intercession for the people's blessing from God the Father.

Now remembering how Jesus made Peter and his friends catch a boat-sinking load of fish even under distress shows that Jesus empowers people under dire circumstances to work extra hard for great accomplishments (Luke 5:1–8; John 21:1–8). So like the *Wulormei*, Jesus also, even at the time of human tiredness, expects his people to locate their blessing in the work of their hands by going the extra mile in faith. And both in the *Kpele* institution and in the priestly office of Jesus, there is the call to be ethical, spiritually faithful and hardworking.

---

81. See Field, *Religion and Medicine*, 43–44; 31–33; 89.
82. See Kilson, *Kpele Lala*, 221–22.

Odadao is celebrated to mark the end of the ban on drumming and dancing. It is celebrated after three weeks of the silence in Ga Mashi.[83]

Awitsermor / *Lebo* / Secret Rituals

Following the *Gbermlilaa* in Nungua is the *Awitsermor*, which is a secret ritual, but which involves invoking of a *Jemanwon*. In Nungua, this ritual is performed by the *Mankralo*, the *Mantse*, *Owufu*, *Tsawe*, and *Osabu Wulormei* and then the *Labia* all with knives. The *Mankralo* shouts and then a voice, not human, is heard from the *Gborbukon* (*Gborbu* shrine / sacred grove). This is followed by the king and the rest of the team in succession. Then, they move toward the grassland between the town and the sea, and as they move, they are accompanied by the *Owufu Jemanwon* (*Owufu* deity) as he walks by the *Mankralo;* then, they circle a patch of grass. The others are beckoned to form a circle around the patch with the *Owufu Jemanwon* standing outside panting. They then pull a handful of long grass three individual times and then return to the *Gborbukon* with *Owufu* leading. These grasses are then plaited and placed on the *Owufu gbatsu* (*Owufu* shrine). Meanwhile, everyone is expected to be locked inside their rooms with all lights out.[84] Anyone who breaks this rule is not expected to live. These secret rites also take place in Tema and La (*Lebo*), but with different rite details and different dates.[85]

Perhaps, the import of these secret rites is the renewal of the covenant with the principal *Jemanworjii* of the town. During such occasions, it is clear that the voices of the gods, i.e., *Jemaworjii*, are heard and they appear to the people involved in the performance of the rites. These secret rites are just like the veil and mystery which surround the Old Covenant of the Jews. This is because it was only the high priest who could enter the Holies of holies to offer sacrifices. That veil is the secret in which the Ga people live to date, which is the secret of their *Jemanworjii* because it is hidden from them. Similarly, like the Jewish religion, all the sacrifices and the rituals made by the high priest were in secret. This certainly is the weakness of these covenants in that it is not possible to have direct fellowship with God or the *Jemanwon* the people worship. What Jesus

---

83. Field, *Religion and Medicine*, 89. See Kilson, *Kpele Lala*, 23; says it is the "welcoming gods from field."

84. Field, *Religion and Medicine*, 34–35.

85. Field, *Religion and Medicine*, 19–50.

had done is that he has torn the veil and has given all who believe in his name free access to the throne room of God. Thus, Jesus Christ is the Savior indeed of the world. He has confirmed this by the free gift of the Holy Spirit which is the seal on the children of God (Exod 26:31, 33; 40:3, 21; Heb 6:19; 9:1ff.; Eph 1:13).

Nmaakpamor/Nshorbulemor

The *Nmaakpamor* event is preceded by the imposition of a ban on fishing for two days. Thereafter, the sea is opened for the catching of Tsile, a large red sea bream (*Nshorbulemor*). It is practiced by all Ga towns and this happens mainly in August, coinciding with the harvesting of corn, with the exception of Nungua, which ends the festival ahead of all the other Ga groups.[86] The general principle is to present items to the shrines of the *Jemaworjii* through their representatives, such as the *Wulormei* and the *woryei*. Indeed, at the end of a good catch, all of them are given their share of the first catch of the *Tsile*. It is a type of thanksgiving and appreciation to the *Jemaworjii*. In Tema, the *Sakumor* is presented with corn.[87]

This event explains that the liberation movement of the Ga people is holistic, in that it relates not solely for their human well-being, but a conscientious relationship with nature. There is the rule for the sustainable utilization of the ocean and ensuring there is abundance through a rational and judicious use of resources, which laws are enforced by the *Jemanworjii* or *Jemanwon* through the *Wulormor*. It is comparable to the Old Covenant provision of fallowing for the regeneration of fauna and flora. It is best fulfilled in Jesus Christ, the High Priest, who comes to redeem the whole universe from the bondage of corruption. Jesus is the mediator, not only for humanity, but for the whole universe (Rom 8:19–23).

Obeneshimor/Kpaashimor/Oshi

These events are undertaken by Nungua, La/Teshie, and Ga Mashi, respectively. They normally are held before the day of *Koyeli*, which is the *Homowor* day proper. The *Obeneshimor* is preceded by some rites in the

---

86. Field, *Religion and Medicine*, 89, 22–89.
87. Field, *Religion and Medicine*, 23.

Gborbukon, which is *Wo Obene*, "lifting up" of *Kplele* drums.[88] It may be argued that the *Obeneshimor* is a commemoration that signifies the movement of the Nungua from Benin in Nigeria. As the nine officials of the land come out of the *Gborbukon* they are met with people clad in white attire, turbans, and faces whitewashed, holding *haatso* (touches), singing songs with the *Obene* dance. They do this throughout the night until day break.[89]

The La and Teshie have the *amlakui akpaashimor*, which is made of *Wulormei*, the king, elders, and their entourage and thus, a smaller one.[90] The bigger *Kpaashimor* is one executed by the entire people of the town.[91]

The *Oshi* is performed by the Ga Mashi with clowning and ridiculous dancing.[92] As elaborated on the threefold office of Christ, it is a highly liberating tool demonstrated by the power of the Holy Spirit. This religious activity is a display of a common history of the Ga people. It is a ceremony which tells the history of the people in the past years. One may safely surmise that the songs, like *Kpele* songs, are indicative of what has happened in the past.[93] Therefore, it is most probable the *Obeneshimor* may be more original in that it has maintained the original songs, which hardly make sense to the singers and hearers alike. Yet, a closer investigation reveals the history of the people as to how they arrived in their present abode.

The other towns, particularly the La and Teshie people, have insisted on the relevance of their *Kpaashimor* to the present situation. So in their songs, they reveal the issues, which came up recently, which is a sort of a narration of a recent history of the people. These events obviously have evolved into dealing with moral issues, which affected the people in the past year that has a heavy dose of scurrilous songs. This should be similar to the Ga-Mashi *Oshi*. It is paramount now to realize that the activity has a pure religious origin of recounting what the *Jemaworjii* had done in the lives of the people and other issues. It is also to renounce evil in the society, to shame all who perpetuated crimes, and to discourage others from doing the same.

---

88. Field, *Religion and Medicine*, 35–36.
89. Field, *Religion and Medicine*, 36.
90. Field, *Religion and Medicine*, 46.
91. Field, *Religion and Medicine*, 47.
92. Field, *Religion and Medicine*, 89.
93. Kilson, *Kpele Lala*, 18, 19.

The celebrations of the Hosanna in our churches, signifying the entering of the temple, to violently deal with the corruption in the temple, is a clear demonstration of the priest-kingship-prophetic ministry of Jesus (Matt 21:1–16). Today, such an action may be illegal. Yet notwithstanding, Jesus showed his radical and revolutionary nature by the demonstration mounted by the masses of people, even the women and the young people and the children. For how on earth could one sitting on a "baby" donkey trigger such uproar in Jerusalem with such a massive crowd with palm fronds? It will only take the Anointed One, the Messiah, the only one anointed for the office of the *munus triplex* to do so.

Jesus displayed his kingship; however, not of this earth as he rode upon the "baby" donkey with the people shouting Hosanna. Jesus is the Glorious King (*Anunyam Mantse*)[94] as revealed by Laryea. How dare Jesus, if he were no prophet and a priest, to enter the temple to ransack the place and charge and rebuke the people? This is the Jesus who is present in the True Witness, even the Holy Spirit, which urges the church on to be the witness of the works of the triune God in Jesus. The *Kpaashimor* is a pointer to what Jesus the High Priest and his followers did. Jesus' act was a demonstration of the reign of God, which is the kingdom of God to come when Christ appears. Thus, interpreting the *Kpaashimor* with Jesus in mind, points to an eschatological activity, which looks forward to the Parousia of the ascended Lord with whose power the believers work together to prepare for his coming kingdom.

Koyeli/Homowor

This event is the occasion for eating the special food used in hooting at hunger. This food is made of dry dough, which is effectively steamed and cooked. It is unfermented dough because it is a food both for the ancestors and the *Jemaworjii*. These spirits hate anything which has gone bad or is fermented (*nii ni esha*). This food is mixed very well with some other ingredients, but chiefly palm oil to give it taste and yellow-orange-red coloring; however, no pepper or salt is added to those which shall be sprinkled to the *Jemaworjii* and the ancestors. The king and the *mankralo* also go around the town and sprinkle *kpokpoi* to the *Jemanworjii* and the ancestors. This food is eaten with palmnut soup with the *Tsilei*. Before anyone tastes the food, it is first sprinkled by the elder in the house to the

---

94. Laryea, *Yesu Homowor Nuntsor*, 74–81.

otutu mounds (mounds of household deities), and then to the ancestors before it is dished out to people.[95] Field reveals as follows:

> When the ancestors have been fed, the living eat always at their father's house, the men round one dish in the centre of the yard, the women outside the cooking-hut. Incredible masses of food are consumed. The corn eaten is the old-year's corn, and the idea is that none of this old corn must be left over into the New Year.[96]

Also, it may be suggested here that the food and the celebrations point to that of the Passover, in which there is unleavened bread and wine. According to Jesus, it is his blood shed for humanity and for the remission of sins. What some Ga Christians say is that the *Kpokpoi* is also unleavened and it complements the red palmnut soup. Therefore, contextually, the unleavened bread, which is now a wafer, is *kpokpoi* and the wine—the palmnut soup. Moreover, it is argued that since in the Lord's Supper, the Christian community both earthly and heavenly, meet together for the feast on Christ's flesh and blood; so does the sharing of the *kpokpoi* with the ancestors.

In all this, it is the *Wulormor* who presides over all these functions. The eating of *kpokpoi* is, however, decentralized to the family heads that ensure the due rites are done.[97] As Jesus said to the disciples pertaining to their ancestors who ate manna and died and Jesus revealed himself as the food of life, so it is believed that the Ga *kpokpoi* is a cursor of the real food who is Jesus Christ. Therefore Jesus is known as the (*Anokwa*) *Wala Nmaa*,[98] i.e., the True Bread of Life.

The following day is what is called the *Ngoorwala* (day of giving and receiving life), which is a ceremony to wish life to all and sundry. It is expected that during *Homowor*, all qualms between people and family relations should all be settled. There should be peace and unity at the end of the festival.[99] Thus, the greeting *Ngoorwala* is reminiscent of the life, which Christ promises to all who believe in him. After commemorating the death of Christ in the communion, there is liberation, life and hope. This is exactly what the Ga wishes for themselves that it is well, life and prosperity is theirs until another year. Jesus, the Priest, by giving his life,

95. Field, *Religion and Medicine*, 49.
96. Field, *Religion and Medicine*, 49.
97. Field, *Religion and Medicine*, 89.
98. Laryea, *Yesu Homowor Nuntsor*, 86–98.
99. Field, *Religion and Medicine*, 51.

is the life giver and this is mirrored by the *Ngoorwala*. Moreover, when Jesus resurrected, he greeted the disciples with the peace and this is concurred by the *Ngoorwala* greetings after *Homowor*.

Kpele Dancing

This event is the last of the *Homowor* Festival. It can go on for a very long time. *Kpele* is the ceremony for the *Wulormei* and their respective *woryei*, *jranoyei*, and *agbaafoi*. These people engage in this religious singing and dancing in praise to their *Jemaworjii*. It is their side of the *Homowor* festival. These *woryei* and *wontsemei* are clad in their respective white apparel and dance to the tune of the *agbaafoi*.

They also determine the beats and rhythm by the songs they are inspired to sing. And they dance to and fro and occasionally some of them are possessed by their *Jemaworjii*. According to Kilson, the *Kpele* songs tell the whole story of the Ga people and it is believed that it is handed over by the *Jemaworjii*. It also provides information about the philosophy of the Ga people, pertaining to the creation of the world and their world view. It is about the universe and how it exists. In the following discussion, my intension is to show the nature of the Kpele religion[100] and the role of the *Wulormor*. And in doing so, I intend to show that Jesus Christ is the *Okpelejen Wulormor*. Therefore, dancing in honor of the deities is a pointer to the glorious dancing in the African churches during worship as fulfillment of the kpelelogical life. Again the Kpele dance points to the victory dance associated with the new life in the *Okpelejen Wulormor*.

The *Okpelejen Wulormor*

In the history of Ga traditional worship, there are four different but main religious institutions, which include *me* from *Adangme*, *otu*, and *akon*; all from Akan areas and then *Kpele*, the indigenous Ga religious system. So, *Kpele* is the main religious institution of the Ga people.[101] The *Kpele* institution exists in all the major Ga communities, i.e., Ga-Mashi, Osu, La, Teshie, Nungua, and Tema.[102] According to Kilson, in Ga-Mashi, there exist numerous cults, with each devoted to an individual *Jemanwon*.

100. Kilson, *Kpele Lala*, 3–5; 18–19.
101. Kilson, *Kpele Lala*, 20.
102. Field, *Religion and Medicine*, 99.

Thus, the six *Jemaworjii*—*Nai*, the principal and "god" of the sea; *Sakumor*, the warrior defender of the Ga; *Naa Koole*, the "goddess" of peace and holder of the Ga lands; *Naa Ede Oyeadu*, "goddess" of childbirth; *Dantu*, the time-keeping "god"; and *Gua*, the blacksmith "god"—are the *Kpele Jemaworjii*.

There are lesser *Jemaworjii*, which are referred to as the sons and daughters of the six main *Jemaworjii*. These *Jemaworjii* are located within the true Ga-Mashi native (*Ga la krong*) groups of Ga-Mashi, which are *Asere*, *Gbese*, and *Sempe* and thus rites are performed on behalf of the entire Ga community. It is a calendrical worship with that aims at having harmonious relationships with the *Jemaworjii*. The *Kpele* "ritual is built on a number of dramatic forms, including song, dance, music, prayer and sacrifice."[103] Kilson writes concerning the nature of *Kpele* music as follows:[104]

> Probably *Kpele* music form most clearly differentiates *Kpele* ritual from that of other cults. The style of instrumentation and vocalization is distinctive and readily apprehended even by untutored Western ears. *Kpele* songs integrate a distinctive musical form with textual elements. The content of *Kpele* songs develops a wide range of themes, which includes cosmogony, relations between gods and men, the attributes of natural phenomena and moral beings, the performance of ritual, the nature of Ga society, and events in Ga history.[105]

Another very central issue pertaining to the analysis of the *Kpele* cosmology (and cosmogony) is the notion of the Supreme Being.[106] Kilson further states that the primary analytical value of *Kpele* songs lies in their richness as sources of information about Ga conceptualizations of the universe.[107] The meaning of *Kpele*, according to Kilson, which is "all encompassing," is propped up by the idea of the community of believers (both the living and ancestors) and a total worldview.[108]

As much as one may agree with Kilson on the above, it is also important to raise the critical issue on the Ga understanding of who *Ataa Naa Nyonmor* is. The Ga understanding of *Ataa Naa Nyonmor* in itself

---

103. Kilson, *Kpele Lala*, 24.
104. Kilson, *Kpele Lala*, 20–24.
105. Kilson, *Kpele Lala*, 24–25.
106. Kilson, *Kpele Lala*, 7.
107. Kilson, *Kpele Lala*, 3.
108. Kilson, *Kpele Lala*, 18.

is all-encompassing and beyond all. Thus God is both transcendent and immanent, which in the Ga is rendered *Okpelejen*. God, *Ataa Naa Nyonmor*, is therefore known in Ga language as the *Okpelejen videlicet*, the all-encompassing One. Thus, *Kpele* song is a revelation of the acts of God in the world or universe and other acts in the history of the Ga people. Moreover, understand that central to the *Kpele* cosmology is *Kpetenkple*, i.e., God who is all-encompassing and is beyond.[109]

It is God, the Creator of all things and the One who created it so well for humanity to live in it;[110] and one may infer that this is the genesis of the Ga religious thought of *Kpele*. All the known Ga *Wulormei* are *Kpele Wulormei* (priests who accept the all-encompassing God), but they focus more attention on the other acts such as the acceptance and worship of the *Jemaworjii*, to ensure that the history and development of Ga is sustained. Though in time past, they mentioned *Nyonmor* in their prayers, *Nyonmor* was not given the preeminent position in the prayers.[111] Recently, however, it may be observed that *Ataa Naa Nyonmor* is the first to be mentioned in most prayers of the *Wulormei*, which is telling of the current preeminent position it enjoys among the host of *Jemaworjii*. Furthermore, in today's *Kpele* worship, *Ataa Naa Nyonmor* is the *Okpelejen* (God) and the *Jemaworjii* are *Ataa Naa Nyonmorr's* children[112] who execute judgment on God's behalf.

If it is true that the *Wulormei* cannot work with *Ataa Naa Nyonmor* directly, and for that reason they worship the *Jemaworjii* as mediators,[113] then the office of the Ga *Wulormor* is inadequate and very limited. And so, how can the Ga people have direct access to God, who is the *Ataa Naa Nyonmor*? This is where, once again, Jesus Christ's position of the *munus triplex* (work) and his (person) divine-human deals with the challenge associated with the Ga *Kpele* worshipper. It is because the mediation should be done by a human person because of the people he represents. Second, the mediation should be done by someone beyond the level of

---

109. Kilson, *Kpele Lala*, 7.

110. Kilson, *Kpele Lala*, 114.

111. Field, *Religion and Medicine*, 34,61–62; the position is however clarified by Kilson in the *kpele* songs which acknowledge *Ataa Naa Nyonmor* as the Supreme Being in Ga cosmogony. See Kilson, *Kpele Lala*, 114–23; see also Adjei, "Nyonmor."

112. Kilson, *Kpele Lala*, 192; see also Laryea, *Yesu Homowor Nuntsor*, 46–52; 62–63; I think Ga tradition holds that the *Jemanworjii* are the children of *Ataa Naa Nyonmor*.

113. Osabu-Kle, "The Ga People and Homowo Festival," 6.

the *Jemaworjii*. Third, this person should be able to atone for the sins of the people, which no other blood but the blood of an unblemished being must be offered.

Fourth, this person should be able to draw the people to God through an authority which is above all else. The fifth point is that the person should be able to communicate this reality to the people, such that they know beyond any reasonable doubt that their desired contact with God is a reality. Sixth, such a person would necessarily be an all-encompassing personality—namely, such a person should be incarnated to the people (immanent) and also be beyond the people (transcendent) to atone and unite them with *Ataa Naa Nyonmor* God. Seventh, this person ought therefore to be a *Wulormor*, who is immanent and also beyond all being, including the *Jemaworjii*. This *Wulormor*, who is all-encompassing, is *Okpelejen*, and it is Jesus. Therefore, Jesus Christ of Nazareth is the *Okpelejen Wulormor*.

Having discovered the *Okpelejen Wulormor*, the next chapter will seek to critically engage the *munus triplex* and the other African perspectives of the threefold office of Jesus the Christ. Hence, John Calvin, Karl Barth, Douglas Waruta, and John Ekem shall be engaged to draw useful lessons from the nature and work of the *Okpelejen Wulormor*. Again, the chapter will explain that the *Okpelejen Wulormor* concept, though amenable to Christian tradition, also adds to its meaning and interpretation.

7

The *Munus Triplex* and the Theology of the *Okpelejen Wulormor*

The *Munus Triplex*

AT THE BEGINNING OF looking at this paradigm in his work, Waruta hinted at the fact that the *munus triplex* has existed within the church for a very long time as he cites Eusebius of Caesarea in the fourth century.[1]

And though Douglas Waruta would sound as though the idea did not exist in the accounts of the evangelists of the Gospels, it is evident that the motifs existed. Jesus did not accept titles ascribed to him such as royal messiah, royal priest, teacher, and prophet because he is far beyond those ascriptions. Jesus thus is that eschatological agent, who is also cosmic and exerts his beyondness of being. Rightly understood, the motif of the *munus triplex* is no less a category that resonates in both the Old Testament and the New Testament. Jesus' proclamation of his humanity he insists must not and shall not be without his divinity. This is where the *Okpelejen Wulormor* as the all-encompassing and cosmic symbol of Jesus Christ sheds light on the *munus triplex* and vice versa in its concretization in the African context.

Wolfhart Pannenberg also indicates that the paradigm occasionally existed in the patristic church. Furthermore, it achieved no significance in systematic Christology, not only for the patristic church, but also for

---

1. Waruta, "Prophet, Priest, Potentate," 53.

the medieval church,² even though Thomas Aquinas made mention of it in his *Summa Theologica*.³

Martin Luther (1483–1546) is noted only to have used the kingship and priesthood paradigm without using the prophetic.⁴ According to Pannenberg, it was Andreas Osiander (1498–1552) who presented an argument to the paradigm in 1530 based on his argument on Matt 23:8–12; Luke 1:32–33; and Ps 110:4 for the prophet, king, and priest, respectively.⁵ Osiander's foundation was based on the "Anointing," which he felt authenticated the threefold office in 1530. In fact, one may surmise that Hegesippus (AD 110–180), Lactantius (AD 40–320), Gregory of Nyssa, and John Chrysostom (AD 347–407) followed the belief in the anointment of the threefold office.⁶

However, it was John Calvin who popularized the belief as found in all the versions of the *Institutes of the Christian Religion*. In fact, Pannenberg adds that Calvin used it in the 1535 Geneva Confession and then it was taken up by Lutheran orthodoxy.⁷ Question 23 of the Shorter Catechism of the Westminster Confession reveals how the threefold office known as the *munus triplex*, together with the humiliation and exaltation of Jesus Christ has percolated into the church.⁸ Many theologians, including Emil Brunner and Karl Barth,⁹ worked with and developed the *munus triplex* in a more comprehensive scheme. Therefore it is crucial to look at the *munus triplex* in view of the work of John Calvin and Karl Barth, who works it in the two natures and also in the Trinity.¹⁰

---

2. Pannenberg, *Jesus, God and Man*, 212–13.

3. Aquinas, *Summa Theologica* III.xxii.2; Calvin, *Institutes*, 2.15.1.

4. Pannenberg, *Jesus, God and Man*, 213.

5. Pannenberg, *Jesus, God and Man*, 213.

6. Pannenberg, *Jesus, God and Man*, 213.

7. Pannenberg, *Jesus, God and Man*, 213.

8. Question 23 of the Shorter Catechism of the Westminster Confession is stated as follows: Q. "What Offices does Christ execute as our Redeemer?" A. "Christ as our Redeemer executeth the offices of a Prophet, of a Priest and of a King both in his estate of humiliation and exultation."

9. Brunner, *Christian Doctrine*, 271–315. Barth, *Church Dogmatics* IV.1, §13.58.3–4.

10. Pannenberg, *Jesus, God and Man*, 122–54; see Migliore, *Faith Seeking Understanding*, 186; see also Lowe, "Christ and Salvation," 243.

The *Munus Triplex* of John Calvin

The title of the chapter where Calvin delves into the *munus triplex* officially serves to suggest the main aim of the subject. The title is stated thus: "To know the purpose for which Christ was sent by the Father, and what He conferred upon us, we must look above all at three things in Him: The Prophetic Office, Kingship and Priesthood."[11] Herein lays the soteriology of John Calvin.

Deriving from the concept of the Messiah, which means the Anointed One, Calvin suggests that although the chief meaning of the anointment is Jesus' kingship, the other offices have their places, too.[12] By citing Isa 61:1–2; Luke 4:18, he grounds his idea of Jesus' prophetic office.[13] The anointment of Jesus' body is for teaching as the herald of God's grace and for the church also (Matt 17:5; 3:17; and Joel 2:28).[14] Furthermore, to Calvin, Jesus is the embodiment of all knowing and thus, the sure guarantee of his prophetic office, for Christ was given to the redeemed as wisdom (1 Cor 1:30) and "in Him are hidden all treasures of knowledge and understanding" (Col 2:3).[15]

Regarding the kingship of Christ, Calvin immediately warns that the kingship of Jesus is spiritual and eternal.[16] Citing Dan 2:44 and Luke 1:33, the kingship of Christ relates first to the church and then second to the individual member.[17] The kingship of Christ is after the order of King David, albeit eternal (Ps 89:35–37).[18] Calvin underscores the fact that Jesus is at the right hand of God (Ps 110:1), signifying his kingship and reign with the Father.

There is no enemy who can prevail against the church whatsoever.[19] Concerning the individual member, he exhorts that Christ's kinship is spiritual and eternal (John 18:36) and hence the need to focus on the spiritual kingdom and strive toward it.[20] The kingship of Jesus is a great

---

11. Calvin, *Institutes*, 2.15.
12. Calvin, *Institutes*, 2.15.1–2.
13. Calvin, *Institutes*, 2.15.2.
14. Calvin, *Institutes*, 2.15.2.
15. Calvin, *Institutes*, 2.15.2.
16. Calvin, *Institutes*, 2.15.3.
17. Calvin, *Institutes*, 2.15.3.
18. Calvin, *Institutes*, 2.15.3.
19. Calvin, *Institutes*, 2.15.4.
20. Calvin, *Institutes*, 2.15.4.

avenue for spiritual blessings. Calvin is cautious not to sound worldly and thus indicates that the blessings promised about the kingdom is somehow restricted to spiritual blessings, which eventually is equipment to triumph over the world and the devil.[21]

Lastly, the kingship of Jesus is seen within the ambit of a *perichoresis*, where there is a transfer of the Father's sovereignty to the Son by the power of the Holy Spirit.[22] According to Calvin, Christ is the seat of the Holy Spirit from whom all the heavenly riches flow to the redeemed. Therefore, through the Son, the Father executes his reign of the universe and this is evident in Phil 2:9–11.[23] Serving as a king, Jesus also derives authority to govern the church and to present the church to the Father. This governance includes judgment, which Calvin relates to his context, but which he insists is eschatological.[24]

The priestly office of Christ is seen as a reconciliation and intercession role. In this, Christ the mediator, by his holiness, reconciles the world to God.[25] Here, too, Calvin draws attention to the weakness in the Old Covenant by the need of expiation for propitiation (Lev 16:2–3). And so, Jesus fulfills as the writer of Hebrews indicates. Christ died as a sacrifice to blot out guilt and satisfaction for sins (Heb 9:22).[26] The high priesthood of Jesus is also stated after the order of Melchizedek (Ps 110:4; Heb 5:6; 7:15).[27]

These passages obviously lead us in understanding the role Jesus as the intercessor because he does not only propitiate, but also opens the doors of heaven for others as "companions" through his intercession to the Father (Rev 1:6).[28] One needs to consider that at the point of writing this *munus triplex*, Calvin was incensed with the Roman betrayal of Jesus Christ. This fact may imply the papist recognition of other mediums of intercession, priesthood, kingship, and prophecy. Therefore, to Calvin, Christ is sufficient for all we need in the *munus triplex*.[29]

---

21. Calvin, *Institutes*, 2.15.4–5.
22. Calvin, *Institutes*, 2.15.5.
23. Calvin, *Institutes*, 2.15.5.
24. Calvin, *Institutes*, 2.15.5.
25. Calvin, *Institutes*, 2.15.6.
26. Calvin, *Institutes*, 2.15.6.
27. Calvin, *Institutes*, 2.15.6.
28. Calvin, *Institutes*, 2.15.6.
29. Calvin, *Institutes*, 2.15.1, 6; one notices with interest why Calvin begins his *munus triplex* in this way: "For he was given to be a prophet, king, and priest. Yet it would

Karl Barth's Trinitarian Approach to the *Munus Triplex*

The *munus triplex videlicet munus sacerdotale, munus regium* and *munus propheticum* of Karl Barth are summarized in his own words:

> But in the light of the Christology there have to be these developments: the three great expositions of the fact and the extent to which the reconciliation of the world with God is actual in Him—in his servitude for us, in the humiliation of God for man which took place in Him—in his lordship over us, in the exaltation of man to God's glory which took place in Him, and all this as truth which He Himself has guaranteed and pledged.[30]

Here, one would realize that Barth did not follow the order of John Calvin, which is a *munus propheticum, munus regium and munus sacerdotale*. Also, it should be stated here that Calvin did not state his reasons for arranging them in such a manner. Could it be an unconscious Christology below of Calvin altered by Barth in a Christology above? Or it may be simply the manner in which they were arranged within the context of his writings. As Barth indicates, however, the reason may be due to Christology from above, moving downwards and below, pushing upwards or an ascending Christology, which gives emphasis to the work of Christ in first, his humiliation, and second, his exaltation of humanity.[31]

Barth initially explains that there is a problem with the Christ event which is identified as sin. He proceeds now to deal with the issue of sin, which is a negation or No of humanity. Therefore, Jesus thus is the positive or Yes of God.[32] Simply, in order to deal with the problem of human sin, God in Jesus Christ condescends to humanity by humbling himself, becoming a servant to take to himself and away from humanity guilt and sickness. And as it were, saying, Yes against the No of humanity. Jesus, the Priest, acts to exert his Yes by his sacrifice (humiliation) against the No and negation of humanity which is pride and defiance.[33]

---

be of little value to know these names without understanding their purpose and use." Now for further appreciation of the Roman teaching on the *munus triplex*, see Aquinas, *Summa Theologica* III.xxii.2: "Wherefore, as to others, one is a lawgiver, another is a priest, another is a king; but all these concur in Christ as the count of all grace."

30. Barth, *Church Dogmatics*, IV.1, §13.58.4.
31. Barth, *Church Dogmatics*, IV.1, §13.58.4.
32. Barth, *Church Dogmatics*, IV.1, §13.58.4.
33. Barth, *Church Dogmatics*, IV.1, §13.58.4.

Barth states in relation to the second negation (sin), which is the willfulness of humanity to fall or sloth as against what God did in Jesus Christ, the servant who became Lord through the work of the Father the King, to exalt humanity in his kingship conferred upon Christ by the Father—not to deity, but to his own right hand in a fellowship of life with himself. Barth relates this to the world of sin, the church and the individual Christians. Therefore, the Lordship of Christ is to redeem humanity to be God's children by making the way and exalting humanity.[34]

The third negation (sin), which is falsehood and God in Jesus Christ, is made the Guarantor of the reality (Truth) of what God had done in Jesus from above downwards and below upwards. The fact that believers know their new position confirms the redemption from ignorance, which is freedom. Knowing and being assured of the freedom coming from the work of Jesus is what finally completes Jesus' work. "This is the grace of God in its third form: 'God does not act above our heads, He does not ignore us, but He addresses us and calls us. He tells us what He does and tells us as He does it.' Jesus as the prophet is revealed in this act of God in Him."[35]

Strikingly, we note that Barth deals with the above also in relation to the justification and sanctification and then the call to witness (vocation). By Christ's self-humiliation, humanity is justified and by his exaltation, humanity the redeemed are sanctified. And then, by the reality of that Truth they witness. One could safely suggest that, according to Barth, by Jesus Christ's priesthood there is justification, by his kingship there is sanctification, and finally by his prophetic office, the call to be witnesses of his gracious and glorious act of redemption. Jesus Christ is the One who justifies, sanctifies, and calls. He is the High Priest, King, and Prophet.[36]

Further one should observe that Barth draws from the above the work of the Spirit of Christ, also the Holy Spirit, and places emphasis on him as *conceptus de Spiritus sancto*.[37] This is well grounded also in the work of Christ, which is justification, sanctification, and vocation. The body of Christ may therefore be said to be birthed from the Holy Spirit, who is the awakening power of the Word spoken by the Lord who became

---

34. Barth, *Church Dogmatics*, IV.1, §13.58.4.
35. Barth, *Church Dogmatics*, IV.1, §13.58.4.
36. Barth, *Church Dogmatics*, IV.1, §13.58.4.
37. Barth, *Church Dogmatics*, IV.1, §13.58.4.

a servant and who judges and justifies sinful humanity.[38] The Holy Spirit is also the power of the servant, who became the Lord in Jesus, in which power in his Word is life supplying.[39] Lastly, the Holy Spirit is the power in the Word of Jesus Christ, the Guarantor, with the power to summon humanity to Godself.[40]

An Examination of the Critique of the *Munus Triplex* by John F. Jansen, Albert Ritschl and Wolfhart Pannenberg

It may be suggested that the three main theologians opposed to the idea of *munus triplex* are Jansen, Ritschl, and Pannenberg. This part will look at the objections raised and evaluate them based upon contemporary thought in theology, internal consistencies of original works, and the contemporary African christological milieu.

Jansen's work is mainly based upon the conservative American Presbyterian position of rationality against spirituality, in which there is a fear that if spirituality is enhanced, it may yield high levels of sycophancy and fundamental Christianity. This fundamentalism is a major cause for worry for Jansen and even an embarrassment. Therefore, he states that the threefold office was not necessary and that Calvin used it as a basis to effectively carry out his doctrine of the church offices.[41] The objection that could be raised against his critique is based upon the reasoning of John Calvin regarding the issue of *munus triplex*. As would be realized earlier on in this work, there were other writers who worked on the threefold office, e.g., Aquinas and Osiander and so one wonders why Calvin will make his theology of church office on the basis of the *munus triplex* alone.

Rather what one gathers from the work of Calvin suggests clearly that he wrote it to explain the purpose or the work of Jesus Christ (soteriology), which is a continuation of the work he did on the person of Christ.[42] Moreover, we note with interest his argument against the Roman Church at the beginning and the end of his work on the *munus triplex*. There was no mention of an application of the *munus triplex* on

---

38. Barth, *Church Dogmatics*, IV.1, §13.58.4.
39. Barth, *Church Dogmatics*, IV.1, §13.58.4.
40. Barth, *Church Dogmatics*, IV.1, §13.58.4.
41. See Jansen, *Calvin's Doctrine*; Stroup, "Relevance of the *Munus Triplex*," 22–23.
42. Calvin, *Institutes*, 2.15.

the church offices of teaching elders and ruling elders anywhere by Calvin himself in the *Institutes of the Christian Religion*.⁴³ Jansen's accusation is hereby unfounded and without basis.

For those in Africa, the prophetic office of Christ is most relevant to us in every way. And its full potential has not been utilized, and thus, a *munus triplex* is a *sine qua non*. For Jansen to suggest that the prophetic office be dropped from the *munus triplex* provides the African church one clue to some of the challenges the liberal American church is faced with today. This is so because to Africans, the church ceases to be without the prophetic office of Christ. Also, a careful study of Barth's work on the prophetic office of Christ and the reason for giving much space to it shows his fear that the church may relegate that office.⁴⁴ And lo, his fear for the prophetic writing has come true in some Western churches. For any church, which stays away from the mother who gave birth to it cannot be nurtured to grow and the "mother of the church" (body of Christ) is the Holy Spirit—*Conceptus de Spiritus Sancto*, the Teacher and the Comforter.

Albert Ritschl's main christological emphasis is the person of Jesus Christ. For him, Jesus' main task was about the kingdom of God. Jesus therefore requires no *munus triplex* to function, since he is the King.⁴⁵ It must be said that although the chief function of Christ seems to be his kingship as Calvin admits, the others are equally important. Therefore, Barth delves more deeply on the prophetic office, which did not receive much attention in Calvin's work so as to ensure that the *munus triplex* is not jeopardized in future.

Furthermore, if one employs contemporary theological analysis to Ritschl's suggestion, it may be faulted in many ways. For example, in the face of feminist and liberation hermeneutics, and even the criteria established in this work pertaining to Christology, e.g., Trinitarian relevance, it may be faulted. The idea that the *munus triplex* is not relevant may, not hold in contemporary times. Contemporary Christology is in dying need of a dying savior, a savior who is a voice for the voiceless and a savior who executes judgment by fighting to rescue the oppressed.

Pannenberg also raises extensively many issues regarding the *munus triplex*. The use and appropriation of the anointing for the *Messiah*

---

43. Calvin, *Institutes*, 2.15.1, 6.

44. Barth, *Church Dogmatics*, IV.1, §13.58.4.

45. Ritschl, *Christian Doctrine*, 417–35, 428; McCulloh, *Christ's Person*; see also Stroup, "Relevance of *Munus Triplex*," 24–25.

or *Christus* to him is not acceptable based upon his biblical analysis. He raises an objection to the anointing of Christ as it pertains to his priesthood and kingship.[46] However, the question one raises is whether Jesus needs three different anointing to make him Christ who is the Prophet, King, and Priest? Moreover, for his priestly anointing, one may also question the anointment of Melchizedek, for if it could be proven from Scriptures that Melchizedek was anointed, we may as well require it for Jesus. Does the anointment or non anointment of Jesus debar him from operating in the threefold office? Furthermore, for Jesus' priestly office, which from Hebrews is his death, he confirms his anointment by Mary's anointment (John 12:7). Apart from the priestly anointment, which Pannenberg claims is nowhere in the New Testament the other two offices he grants.

There is also the notion raised by Pannenberg that Jesus' priesthood and kingship only began after his death and resurrection.[47] The question is, what then does the birth and life work of Jesus stand for? Are those works not useful? Was Jesus not a mediator and intercessor when he moved about doing good and preaching (Acts 10:38)? Was he not the king of those who believed in his message? Who was he to those who shouted *Hosanna* and why did he insist that it should be done? What was his response to Pilate about his kingship (Mark 15:2; Luke 23:2, 3; John 18:29, 37)? What does it mean when Christ says "I am" and "I will be" the way, the truth, the life, the light, the bread of life, and so on? Where those things not efficacious before his death? Let us not forget that in dealing with Christology we are also dealing with the activity of the triune God in the affairs of humanity and the world. The Trinitarian approach to Christology surely deals with the issues raised by Pannenberg.

The above issue sought to present the threefold office of Jesus Christ in church tradition. The criticisms have also been reviewed and found largely to be unsustainable. The *Okpelejen Wulormor* fits perfectly within the *munus triplex* and may take the *munus triplex* as its traditional foundation.

Nonetheless, since the work of Calvin may be described as a partial replacement regarding the theology of religions, it differs from the position of Jesus the *Okpelejen Wulormor*, which holds in tension the fulfillment and the mutual types of theology of religions.[48] This stance is important

---

46. Pannenberg, *Jesus, God and Man*, 212–13.

47. Pannenberg, *Jesus, God and Man*, 212–24.

48. See Knitter, *Introducing Theologies of Religion*; see also Migliore, *Faith Seeking Understanding*, 308–13.

because it opens up the discussion about the person and work of Jesus Christ as that which has the ability to incarnate in any place any day.

Another problem with the *munus triplex* lies with its strict sense of Christology from above as realized in earlier discussion. This restriction makes the Christology ineffective in the proclamation of the social gospel, which is equally important. Though it has strong influence on the personal spiritual development of the individual unto salvation and is particularly important in the nurture of believers who have been called to share in the holiness of Jesus Christ, their redeemer fails to deal adequately with the social, economic, political, cultural, and religious issues of today. The *Wulormor* has direct contact with the people and ensures that all that pertains to their well-being is mediated by him as discussed previously. Therefore, the *Okpelejen Wulormor* effectively deals with this serious weakness and presents a truer picture of the Lord Jesus.

The role of the Holy Spirit is emphasized looking at the *Wulormor* in that by the *Kpele* institution, the *Jemaworjii* are able to possess ordinary people and speak through them. The *Okpelejen Wulormor*, who is therefore Jesus the Christ, does better in the Pentecost. Also, the special roles played by women can be found in the *Kpele* arena. Thus, the *Okpelejen Wulormor* is one who establishes all his royal priests without distinguishing between a male or female, Greek or Jew, slave or free, and black or white. This point is buttressed by the prominent role women play in the life of the church in Africa.

In addition, to the above the *Okpelejen Wulormor* seeks to redeem the *munus triplex* from its critics as it presents itself not as an abstraction (i.e., *the munus triplex*), but a concrete witness of how Jesus the Christ functions in his person. Hence, the next discussion will focus on the African contribution to the threefold office of Christ, particularly as it regards the balance for a Christology from below.

The Priest/Prophetic/Potentate African Theological Paradigm

Although Douglas Waruta acknowledges the works of church tradition in the three offices of Christ, he eventually finds them to be inadequate. Waruta locates the foundations of the priest/prophet/potentate paradigm within the Bible. He begins with the office of the prophet and ends with the king, in that particular order. The prophetic consciousness of the disciples (people) confirms the fact that Jesus was at least recognized as a prophet. The answer to the question "Who do people say that I am?" brought up answers, which includes Elijah or one of the prophets. Jesus' own testimony attested to the fact that "a prophet is not accepted in his own town" (Matt 13:57; Luke 4:24; John 4:44). Douglas Waruta also looks at the comparison of Moses to the prophets in the New Testament.[49]

In the priesthood of Christ, Waruta sees Christ basically as the suffering servant (Isa 53:11–12) among others. The priestly office of Jesus Christ, which is the central theme of Hebrews 1–7 and the First Epistle of Peter, show the relationship his priestly office has with his office as king (Heb 2:8–18) and as the leader of his people (Heb 2:10–13) and as a high priest (Heb 2:14–18). Jesus, however, offers a better priesthood (Heb 8–10) because he leads his people into the City of God (Heb 11–13).[50]

For Douglas Waruta, Jesus the Potentate refers to the Son of David, the eschatological Son of Man who is seated at the right hand of the Almighty and coming in the clouds of heaven (Mark 14:62).[51] Note should be taken here that Waruta's Christology is from below. He then relates the categories in the African context. He refers to the prophets in the African context as the diviners, seers, etc who have the capacity to speak authoritatively and thus possess the inclination of leading the people particularly during crises.[52] The priests are those who help religious activities which border on mediation. Furthermore, the priest and the prophet in the African context seem to be closely twined together and are sometimes difficult to separate. The priests engage mostly in the rites and rituals on behalf of the people in the community to the divinities and ancestors.[53] The king in the African context may also be known as the ruler or chief elder, who principally serves as a defense of the community. They may also act as priests.[54]

This idea expressed by Douglas Waruta that strikes a chord in all three offices, which he separates, is that they are found in the *Wulormor* without separation. The work of Douglas Waruta thus helps to make the work of Jesus the Christ a Christology from below. What the *Okpelejen*

49. Waruta, "Prophet, Priest, Potentate," 54.
50. Waruta, "Prophet, Priest, Potentate," 55.
51. Waruta, "Prophet, Priest, Potentate," 55–56.
52. Waruta, "Prophet, Priest, Potentate," 57–59.
53. Waruta, "Prophet, Priest, Potentate," 59–60.
54. Waruta, "Prophet, Priest, Potentate," 60–61.

does is to make the *munus triplex* presented by Calvin, Barth, and Waruta both a Christology from below and above. This is due to the nature of the work of the *Wulormor* among the Ga people. The *Wulormor* is really a special person and in the discussion below Ekem states it quite succinctly. This shall be done by reviewing the biblical authenticity of the *Wulormor* within the Ghanaian context as a foundation for seeking Jesus, the *Okpelejen Wulormor*.

Is Jesus *Okpelejen Wulormor* or *Osorfonukpa*?

Another great biblical scholar who devotes special attention to the priesthood of Jesus as christological theme in Africa is John D. K. Ekem. He has in no doubt succeeded in presenting an Akan Christology based on the Ghanaian priesthood context, generally, but particularly, the Ga concept of priesthood. His goal was to look at the priesthood and see its relevance for mother-tongue biblical interpretation. Thus, his work as a biblical scholar unveils for us the strong biblical foundations for presenting Jesus as the priest in the Ghanaian context, including the Ga people.[55] Taking his exegesis from Hebrews, he examines the dialogue situation between the text and the context.

Indeed, he asserts that the earlier translators of the Akan Bible were convinced based upon their experience of priesthood in the Akan context that Christ's work of shedding his own blood and living as the glorified high priest is a true reflection of Akan Christianity. He then looks at the mediating role of the *Okomfo* (Akan priest) and then examines the continuities and discontinuities regarding the mediatory priestly role of Christ.[56] The continuities, include fellowship and reconciliation with the divine world; having loyal followers; the use of symbols for rituals such as the blood and the sanctity of the *Okomfo*.[57] The discontinuities may include the mortality of the *Okomfo*; restriction of the *Okomfo* to a particular ethnic group or group of people; and the fact that they do not offer themselves as sacrifices.[58]

---

55. Ekem, *Priesthood in Context*.
56. Waruta, "Prophet, Priest, Potentate," 177–82.
57. Waruta, "Prophet, Priest, Potentate," 179–80.
58. Waruta, "Prophet, Priest, Potentate," 181–83.

Looking at the difficulties associated with the limitedness of African Christologies, particularly as revealed in the work of Diane Stinton,[59] Ekem tries to circumvent it by suggesting a *ta panta* (good things) cosmic Christology.[60] He states, "A possible but debatable solution would be to postulate a, ta *panta* cosmic theology in which Christ primordial Lordship over all creation- and for that matter, African traditional religious systems—is affirmed."[61] Jesus, the *Okpelejen Wulormor*, to our estimation fits the *ta panta* (owns and fills all things) cosmic *archiereus* (high priest) (Heb 2:10; 9:11) described by Ekem. This fact is proven because the *Okpelejen* title, which is all-encompassing, fits the *ta panta* cosmic nature of the *archiereus*, who is the *Wulormor*. The gulf between Yesu the *Homowor Nuntsor* and the people is hereby filled by Jesus the *Okpelejen Wulormor*.

Indeed, a further discussion by Ekem on Heb 9:11–12 about the priests of the Akan, Ga and Anlo-Ewe ethnicities reveals a distinction among them as regards the Ga high priest. There are *akomfo, wontsemei*, and *tronunola* of the Akan, Ga, and Ewe, respectively, as priest, which do not satisfy adequately the position of the *archiereus*, viz., the high priest.[62] However, he posits a solution in the Ghanaian context:

> It is precisely at this point that the Ga *Wulormor* assumes special significance. Within the Ga state, the *Wulormor*, who functions as the High Priest = "Chief Traditional Priest," is, unlike the *akomfo, wontsemei* and *tronunola* in an entirely different category. He is neither possessed by Jemanworjii nor goes into ecstasy in order to deliver oracles. The *Wulormor* is the actual religious, political and spiritual leader of the Ga people. He is their king-maker and can even assume full political responsibility whenever the need arises. He intercedes and offers sacrifices to the Jemanworjii on behalf of his people. More significantly, the *Wulormor* functions as the spokesman of *Ataa-Naa Nyonmorr* = "Father-Mother God," the Ga Supreme Deity who is also the legitimate owner of the land. As a priest, prophet, and king-maker, the *Wulormor* is the custodian of the traditions of his people, and is expected to live above reproach. He wears white apparel as a symbol of purity.[63]

---

59. Waruta, "Prophet, Priest, Potentate," 181–83; see Stinton, *Jesus of Africa*.
60. Ekem, *Priesthood in Context*, 160–65.
61. Ekem, *Priesthood in Context*, 183.
62. Ekem, *Priesthood in Context*, 195.
63. Ekem, *Priesthood in Context*, 196.

There is, however, a caveat pertaining to the mortality and the absence of self sacrifice in the *Wulormor* scheme according to Ekem. This position may not hold, considering an earlier discussion that prominent Ga and Adangme priests died for their people. Moreover, it is believed that since they entered the sea by their own volition, they have the power to come back, which is affirmed by some rites performed. It has been discussed that these rites seem to be an eschatological hope and belief that the priest joins them and blesses them ultimately. However, he is right in criticizing the Ga translators for not using the title *Wulormor Nukpa* = "God's Chief *Wulormor*," rather than *Osorfonukpa*, which is quite restrictive in scope. The *Nukpa* (elder used as high) employed in the qualification tacitly shows that there may be others comparable, which the *Wulormor Nukpa* is the superior.

However, in the *ta panta* scheme, there can neither be a comparison nor a graduation for the *archiereus*. Thus, the application of the *Okpelejen* gives clearer meaning of the *archiereus* used in the Hebrews text. It also brings out clearly the deity of Jesus the Christ as fully God and fully human. The name *Okpelejen* makes the person and work of Christ truly Trinitarian because *Okpelejen* in itself is the title or the name of God, while perfectly fitting the *ta panta* suggested by Ekem.

His exegesis of the Ga translation of the tabernacle (*buu*) provides a unique framework within which cosmic Christology is concretized.[64] Therefore, the commentary Ekem provides for in the Mfantse and the English is authenticated by the use of the *Wulormornukpa* = *Ataa-Naa Nyonmorr Wulormor* as the *archiereus* who is the high priest.[65] The proposal of this work is that since God is *Ataa Naa Nyonmorr* and *Ataa Naa Nyonmor is Okpelejen*, the *Wulormornukpa*, which is *Ataa Naa Nyonmorr Wulormor*, should be called *Okpelejen Wulormor*.

Jesus the *Okpelejen Wulormor*

In this section, there is an examination of Jesus the *Okpelejen Wulormor* in the light of the theological criteria established in chapter 2 and applied in chapter 3 to examine the authenticity of other African theologies. Thus we ought to see the importance and role of an ultimate concern or relevance, biblical and ecclesiological identity, dialogue, the salvific event,

---

64. Ekem, *Priesthood in Context*, 196.
65. Ekem, *Priesthood in Context*, 200–203.

ecclesiological relevance, Trinitarian uniqueness, and eschatology in the theology of the *Okpelejen Wulormor*.

Ultimate concern is actually the reason for the discussion on the Jesus the *Okpelejen Wulormor*. As one looks at the contextual relevance, it is beyond any reasonable doubt that Jesus the *Okpelejen Wulormor* is relevant to the Ga people in view of the foregone discussion about *Wulormor*, *Kpele*, and *Homowor*. Jesus the *Okpelejen Wulormor* has been used, based upon the Ga religion, in its major forms such as the *Kpele*, and the *Homowor*, and the roles of the *Wulormor*, in the details of the categories. As shown by Ekem, it is relevant not only in the Ga context, but almost representative of the Ghanaian context, as he employs the Ga word *Wulormor* in Akan and Mfantse biblical texts. Furthermore, by establishing the inadequacies in African Christologies, it becomes very relevant in the African setting. The *Okpelejen Wulormor* is relevant to Reformed theological thinking, which has its roots to church tradition. It has the potential to illuminate the person and work of Christ in theology and the practice of the Christian life.

As per the biblical nature of Jesus, the *Okpelejen Wulormor*, we could safely posit that it is grounded in Scripture looking at the works of Douglas Waruta, John Calvin, and Karl Barth's, and Ekem's biblical elucidations. As to whether it fits the tradition of the church, we have already indicated that it is part of the church's tradition looking at Eusebius of Caesarea, Thomas Aquinas and Andreas Osiander. The Reformed Church has its theology firmly based upon the *munus triplex*; therefore, Jesus *Okpelejen Wulormor* belongs to the Gas and Africans on one hand, and on the other hand, traditional orthodoxy which is representative of the universal church.

When it comes to dialogue within the context, one should say that one has tried to engage the major categories of Ga *Kpele* and the *Homowor* festival, which in itself, develops part of the *Kpele* religious institution. In the course of the dialogue, categories of the Ga have shared more light on the *munus triplex* of Jesus Christ. Also, the work and person of Jesus the Christ has elucidated the Ga understanding of the religion and culture. To a large extent, this has been moderately and extensively achieved. Unlike Laryea's *Yesu Homowor Nuntsor*, which is more of the fulfillment type of dialogue, we have shown a mutual dialogue of the gospel with the *Kpele* religion of the Ga. This makes the title of *Okpelejen Wulormor*, not a fulfillment, but mutual theology of religions.

Jesus the *Okpelejen Wulormor* establishes priest-king-prophet office, which in all cases, demonstrates the earthly ministry of Jesus Christ, i.e., birth, life, death and also heavenly ministry, i.e., resurrection, ascension and Parousia. We have shown through the soteriology of Barth how the God-servant, servant-God and the Witness to the Truth achieved this. Also, it could be said that the *munus triplex*, as a way of identifying Christ as God-human and his work as triune, is based upon Barth's Christology and soteriology. This makes Jesus the *Okpelejen Wulormor* Trinitarian, eschatological and ecclesiologically relevant in view of Barth's work, which we have incorporated into the dialogue with the Ga religion and customs. Since the *Wulormor* is the mediator of the people and the reconciler to their deity and God, and points to the person, and work of Christ; the *Okpelejen Wulormor* truly satisfies the criteria.

Conclusion

In the final part of this book, the attempt has been made to resolve the problem by introducing the *Okpelejen Wulormor*, an original theology of Kpelelogy from the Ga ethnic group in the southern part of Ghana. It has sought to throw more light on the person and work of Jesus Christ. The assessment of the *Okpelejen Wulormor* by the available theological criteria, I think, strongly indicates that it may be more adequate, as it satisfactorily addresses the critical christological issues. Moreover, the problem posed by the inadequacy of African Christologies is effectively resolved by the *Okpelejen Wulormor* in chapter 6.

Notwithstanding the above, one of the crucial issues, which is scriptural and has Christian traditional foundations is accomplished as the *Okpelejen* engages the *munus triplex* of John Calvin, Karl Barth and John Ekem in chapter 7. The African perspective of Douglas Waruta was also critically engaged. Furthermore, even though the foundation of the *Okpelejen Wulormor* is rooted firmly in some patristic, Thomistic, Lutheran, Reformed, and African Christologies, this work has endeavored to express its uniqueness as follows:

1. *Okpelejen Wulormor* holds in tension the fulfillment and mutual theology of religious positions, which embraces Calvinistic partial replacement and goes beyond it.
2. *Okpelejen Wulormor* presents us with Jesus Christ who is known from both above and below, as against tradition which separates the

two. This stance provides the *Okpelejen Wulormor* the capacity to deal with African spiritual problems as well as the physical problems which they confront daily.

3. Again, it gives the capacity to ensure that personal faith is intertwined with religious and cultural life as well as politics, socioeconomic issues and ecology and issues of futurism with a great sense of responsibility and meaningfulness. For example, I have dealt with justification, sanctification, and vocation upon which the Christian life is experienced devotionally and personally but at the same time, with the responsibility of participating in the work of God in the world as a whole to end the human predicament.

4. *Okpelejen Wulormor* does not present Jesus Christ in the *munus triplex* as an abstraction but as a concrete or living reality.

5. Douglas Waruta's African perspective did not succeed to present a concrete undivided *munus triplex*, which the *Okpelejen Wulormor* represents.

6. The *Okpelejen Wulormor* joins inculturation and liberation Christologies together into what is called the *cultura-libero* African Christology, and beyond it into the new, called Kpelelogy. This point is very true of Jesus the Christ, since *Okpelejen Wulormor* is a cosmic figure that deals with issues beyond religio-cultural issues while addressing socioeconomic and political issues.

7. By virtue of the capacity of the *Okpelejen Wulormor* it has both local and universal appeal. At least in Ghana, Ekem has shown that the *Wulormor* is preferred to the Akan and Ewe concepts of priesthood. And it has connected well with the concept of the *munus triplex* in traditional theology.

8. By virtue of its all-encompassing nature, the *Okpelejen Wulormor* is able to effectively address issues of oppression, including the disabled, the poor, women, blacks, creation etc. It seeks to address the predicament of the whole of God's creation holistically.

9. Although this work confirms the work of Ekem by the common usage of the *Wulormor* as the name of Jesus, the preferred usage of the title "*Okpelejen*" as against Ekem's "*Nukpa*," makes this work unique.

Conclusion

AT THE END OF this introductory work of African Christian theology, I have made the attempt to define African Christian theology as the interpretation of the Christian faith of Africans in the light of the revelation of God through Jesus Christ in the power of the Holy Spirit to them.

I have endeavored to show that African Christian theology like any other theology is contextual. Yet in the African sense, it is Kpelelogical in view of the holistic worldview of Africans and their encounter with Jesus Christ who reveals God's love to them in the Holy Spirit. This holistic view of reality implies that African Christian theology is then subject of becoming essentially that which naturally flows into the doing of theology. The being of the African is in terms of the pre-Christian being that is inextricably immersed in the milieu of politics, religion and culture, and socioeconomic realities and of other realities of the natural environment, and health and history and so forth. This ontological mode is initially rejected but accepted and refined and utilized by the divine presence revealed through the Son by grace through faith in the power of the Holy Spirit in what we now term as Kpelelogy.

And because African Christian theology is able to deal with issues in holistic terms, there is the tendency of embracing seemingly contradictory elements together. For example, embracing elements of empiricism in history, ethnography and archeology and the pure sciences and technology on one hand together with pure rationalism, analytic thought in philosophy and the social sciences and psychology and arts and culture, aesthetics and ethics and anthropology and faith or religion and so forth on the other hand. These are seemingly contradictory elements, which none of the individual studies themselves may want interference from each other, and rightly so, to prevent absurdity. For example, pure science as a matter of principle will not entertain any iota of subjectivism such as in embracing a Werberian social analysis or faith. Yet African Christian theology as a Kpelelogical theology embraces all these realities in a whole and meaningfully via a theonomous reflection.

This Kpelelogical propensity I have explained is what is known as the paradoxical principle. And this paradoxical principle is that which is very akin to Africa as we look back to Origen and his enormous enigmatic theological contribution to the church of Christ in the world. Similar references have been given with regards to Tertullian and Saint Augustine in their espousal of Christian doctrine. And as these fathers remain pillars of traditional theology it ought to be stated that no comprehension of Christian thought could be gained if their paradoxical mode of thought is not fully grasped.

And today in African Christianity, the paradoxical mode of thought is deeply ingrained in the religion and culture of the people. This is reflected in the manner in which Pentecostalism and Charismaticism has presented the gospel consistently. I have sought to use Bishop David O. Oyedepo as an example of African Christian experience and expression as well as his own explanation to buttress the point. I also showed that this paradoxical thought is fundamental to traditional theology in the West citing in particular, Paul Tillich regarding his teaching of Protestant faith.

Thus, we conclude that Kpelelogical theology is fundamentally paradoxical just as traditional theology is. And that African Kpelelogical understanding is a bedrock to understanding the whole of Christian theology itself.

Now what then is the ontological Kpelelogical method? I have shown that a Kpelelogical method is not a natural theology, because as a rule, its starting point of reflection is based upon faith encountered through the revelation of God through grace in Jesus Christ in the Spirit. This subjective experience we should remember takes on board all of the existential realities of the African which also at the same time are the sources of questions regarding the African predicament. Naturally, this mode of being theological leads to seeking to understand more from the objective sense of the historical account of Jesus Christ in the Bible, as well as other prophetic declarations and other writings in the Bible.

Furthermore, it has come to light that African Christian theology ought to be biblical or based upon a sound interpretation of Scripture. It embraces the use of all biblical tools of interpretation, including form criticism, historical critical method, and all postcolonial tools of interpretation and the hermeneutics of suspicion and trust. By this African

Christian theology takes the symbolisms, the historical and social and cultural and religious and political and economic contexts of biblical narrative seriously. It thus avoids literalistic interpretations of Scripture that may lead to fundamentalism. At the same time it stays within bounds of traditional interpretation. All of these have been discussed in the first part of this book.

In part 2 of this book, I have discussed how the Kpelelogical method is different from praxis, and also different from both the kerygmatic and apologetic methods of Karl Barth and Paul Tillich, respectively, and no matter how nuanced it is. In this, there is a dynamic tension between the encounter with the Christian message and the existential questions being raised. Thus, in this mode, either side of the poles could at any point in time be the starting point. The African Christian mind has no qualms at all at the paradoxical mode because theonomously, there is a lot of sense and whichever pole starts the conversation is based upon the theonomous meaning engendered at that mode of being theological. Furthermore, it shows that the Kpelelogical sense is not bereft of praxis stemming from the understanding that a Kpelelogical theology is ontological. From this ontological mode, preaching, teaching and prophecy and the songs and the aesthetics and the ethics and the worship and prayers and dance and Christian character emerge from the African Christian and the African Christian churches as modes of reflection.

Nonetheless, in this book, the self-criticism of African Christian theology shows that African Christian reflection ought to move from those autonomous modes of reflection into heteronomous reflections that will bring a proper interpretation of the Christian faith in the African context. This active engagement is to forestall any future development and growth and the challenges that may accompany it. It is to present to the churches a proper understanding that may be a guide for the present and the future.

I have also shown further that in the good attempts at bringing into reality, African theological thought, some fundamental inadequacies emerged. The absence of a Trinitarian explication of theology that ought to emanate from the African experience of the triune God and thorough application of the salvific event showed the "reactionary" manner in which those theologies emerged. The ideological position which tended to draw African Christian theology into the realms of totalitarianism and utopianism did not help particularly the emerging Pentecostal and Charismatic churches and Protestant churches though a different story could be told of the Roman Catholic churches. And this, as I showed in this book, was due to the lacking eschatological element. And I contend that all these inadequacies are also due to the lacking method or unfavorable methods used.

A Kpelelogical theology fundamentally avoids dichotomization into inculturation and liberation. In fact it does not only present a paralysis of it,[1] it replaces it altogether with the paradoxical Kpelelogy that makes it possible to look at the African reality in holistic terms. Indeed, it engenders the expansion of African Christian theology into a holistic frame that ought to embrace all elements of human existence beyond the realm of *cultura-libero* category discussed in this book. It reveals why African Christian theology cannot be reduced to ethnographical studies in spite of the fact that the latter is indispensable in understanding theology in Africa. Yet, it is plain that theology is not ethnography. And it is ultimately crucial to state that African Christian theology needs to be brought into the front burner in view of the present predicament of our world of castes, pandemics and religions and environmental problems and scientific advancements and their consequences on faith, society and the whole of God's creation.

And in doing this, it came to light that in giving a lot of attention to present situations in Africa and the world as a whole, the traditional themes found in the creeds must not be ignored. Consequently, doing theology in Africa as a complete detachment from the Christian heritage is impossible. Ecumenical engagements in terms of the particular and the universal claims of Christian faith is thus the way forward. Traditional Christian theology as a Christian heritage be it from the Eastern Orthodox Church or the Western Church ought to be engaged without any shying away.

Furthermore, a Kpelelogical theology of Africa itself serves as a corrective to the parochialism associated once upon a time with Western theology. Similarly, it points out the weakness in contemporary African Christian theology as the parochialism that ultimately distorts the Christian message. Thus, even in Africa, theology ought to move out of its self-isolation, particularly its tribal theological scheming, and embrace with openness other crucial realities of existence. Mention has been made regarding the need to embrace realities that move beyond the realm of inculturation and liberation. Even, in those same realms, theologies dealing

---

1. Martey, *African Theology*, 122–37.

with poverty, caste or race, and gender and class must be deepened. So that issues of science and technology, environment and the religions, especially Islam and the New Religious Movements and ethics are brought on board.

Therefore, in part 3, I endeavored to present a Kpelelogical theology from the Ga context in Ghana in a manner that addresses all the understanding and principles upon which African Christian theology ought to be built. A special consideration is taken of the particular context which in this case is represented by the *Homowor* festival. The *Homowor* festival is also set within the Ga traditional and religious institution known as the *Kpele* Religious Institution. The description of this institution of *Kpele* works fundamentally as kpelelogy which also is the background for the Kpelelogical theology itself.

Moreover, the role of the Ga *Wulormor* in his threefold office is revealed as priest, king and prophet in the kpelelogical context of the Ga people of Ghana. This office of the *Wulormor* is interpreted based on the fact that he presides over the whole of the *Homowor* festival which stands for the holistic redemption of the people.

Finally, continuing from where I discovered that Philip Laryea declared Jesus as the *Homowor Nuntsor* (the Lord who drives away hunger), I deemed it is more appropriate to render that position to the *Okpelejen Wulormor*. Hence Jesus Christ is the all-encompassing or cosmic God who is priest, king and prophet (*ta panta archiereus* who is more than a priest, king and prophet). Ultimately, this discussion ends with the analytical engagement with John Calvin and Karl Barth, who employ the *munus triplex* to explain the person and works of Jesus Christ. The cosmic Jesus Christ is thus truly represented by the *Okpelejen Wulormor* as it elucidates the traditional theological position as the Lord who is with us and for all of us but beyond us all.

Again, it is only in the *Okpelejen Wulormor* (Son) that the perfect love of *Ataa Naa Okpelejen Nyonmor* (Father) is revealed to us in the *Okpelejen Mumor Kronkron* (Holy Spirit). Thus, there cannot be any discrimination in the *Okpelejen Wulormor* insofar as God stands against all, for all, with all and above all. In *Okpelejen Wulormor* all love is made perfect and at the eschaton, all these shall be realized against us, for us, with us and in us and above us.

Bibliography

Achebe, Chinua. *Things Fall Apart*. Oxford: Heinemann, 1958.
Adams, James Luther. *Paul Tillich's Philosophy of Culture, Science and Religion*. New York: Schocken, 1965.
Adjei, Nii Mensah. "*Nyonmor* (God) in Ga Tradition and Christian Mission: An Exploration of the Historical Relationship between the Religious Tradition of the Ga of South Eastern Ghana and Bible Translation and Its Implications for Ga Christian Theology." MTh thesis, University of KwaZulu-Natal, 2006.
African Development Bank. "The Middle of the Pyramid: Dynamics of the Middle Class in Africa." *Market Brief*, April 6, 2011.
Akinade, Akintande E. "African Christianity in the Twentieth Century." In *History of Global Christianity*, vol. 3, *History of Christianity in the 20th Century*, edited by Jen Holger Schjouring et al., translated by David Orton, 343–55. Leiden: Brill, 2018.
Akrong, Abraham. "Pre-monarchial Political Leadership among the Gas, with Special Reference to the People of La." *Research Review Supplement* 17 (2006) 137–47.
———. "Salvation in African Christianity." *Legon Journal of Humanities* 12 (1999–2001) 1–29.
Amarkwei, Charles. *The Christian Life in a Postmodernist World*. Tema, Ghana: Digibooks, 2018.
———. *Paul Tillich and His System of Paradoxical Correlation: Forging a New Way for Science and Theology Relations*. Eugene, OR: Wipf and Stock, 2020.
———. "Sacrament and Symbolism: The African Dimension in the Development of the Sacraments of Baptism and Eucharist." *Trinity Journal of Church and Theology* 18 (2016) 102–18.
Amoah, Elizabeth, and Mercy Amba Oduyoye. "The Christ for African Women." In *With Passion and Compassion: Third World Women Doing Theology*, edited by Virginia Fabella and Mercy Amba Oduyoye, 35–36. Maryknoll: Orbis, 1989.
Anselm. *Cur Deus Homo: To Which Is Added a Selection from His Letters*. Buffalo, WY: Creative Media Partners, 2018.
Aquinas, Thomas. *Summa Theologica*. New York: Benziger, 1948.
Asamoah-Gyadu, Kwabena J. *African Charismatics: Current Development within the Independent Indigenous Pentecostalism in Ghana*. Leiden: Brill, 2005.
———. "Christianity and Sports: Religious Functionaries and Charismatic Prophets in Ghana Soccer." *Studies in World Christianity* 21. 3 (2015) 239–59.
———. *Contemporary Pentecostal Christianity: Interpretations from an African Context*. Forewords by Allan Anderson and Nimi Wariboko. Akropong-Akuapem, Ghana: Regnum Africa, 2013.

———. "Pulling Down Strongholds: Evangelism, Principalities and Powers and the African Pentecostal Imagination." In *International Review of Mission* 96 (2007) 305–17.

———. "Religious Pluralism and Religious Education." *Religious Education* 105 (2010) 238–44.

———. *Taking Territories and Raising Champions: Contemporary Pentecostalism and the Changing Face of Christianity in Africa, 1980–2010*. Inaugural lecture in commemoration of promotion to the position of full professor. Accra, Ghana: Asempa, 2010.

———. "Therapeutic Strategies in African Religions: Health, Herbal Medicines and Indigenous Christian Spirituality." *Studies in World Christianity* 20 (2014) 70–90.

Asante, Emmanuel. *Towards an African Theology of the Kingdom of God: The Kinship of Onyame*. New York: Mellen University Press, 1995.

Augustine of Hippo. *The Trinity (De Trinitate)*. Edited by J. E. Rotelle. Introduction, translation, and notes by Edmund Hill. New York: New City, 2002.

Awoonor, Kofi. *The Africa Predicament: Collected Essays*. Accra, Ghana: Sub-Saharan, 2006.

Azumah, John Alembillah. *The Legacy of Arab-Islam in Africa: A Quest for Inter-religious Dialogue*. Oxford: Oneworld, 2001.

———. *My Neighbor's Faith: Islam Explained for Christians*. Grand Rapids: Zondervan, 2008.

Azumah, John Alembillah, and Lamin Sanneh, eds. *The African Christian and Islam*. Carlisle, UK: Langham, 2013.

Baik, Chung-Hyun. *The Holy Trinity—God for God and God for Us*. Eugene, OR: Pickwick, 2011.

Barrett, David B. *Schism and Renewal in Africa: An Analysis of Six Thousand Contemporary Religious Movements*. Oxford: Oxford University Press, 1968.

Barth, Karl. *Church Dogmatics*. London: SCM, 1949.

———. *Church Dogmatics*. Translated by Geoffrey William Bromiley. Edited by Geoffrey William Bromiley and Thomas Forsyth Torrance. Vol. 1. 4 vols. Edinburg: T. & T. Clark, 1956.

———. *Dogmatics in Outline*. Translated by G. T. Thomson. New York: Harper & Row, 1959.

Battle, Michael. *Reconciliation: The Ubuntu Theology of Desmond Tutu*. Cleveland: Pilgrim, 1997.

Bediako, Kwame. *Christianity in Africa: The Renewal of a Non-Western Religion*. Edinburgh: Edinburgh University Press, 1995.

———. "Cry Jesus! Christian Theology and Presence in Modern Africa." *Vox Evangelica* 23 (1993) 7–25.

———. *Jesus in Africa: The Christian Gospel in African History and Experience*. Akropong-Akuapem, Ghana: Regnum Africa, 2000.

———. *Theology and Identity: The Impact of Culture upon Christian Thought in the Second Century and Modern Africa*. Oxford: Regnum, 1992.

Beeley, Christopher. *Gregory of Nazianzus on the Trinity and the Knowledge of God: In Your Light We Shall See Light*. Oxford: Oxford University Press, 2008.

Benkes, Jacques, and Mary-Anne Plaatjies van Huffel. "Towards a Theology of Development in the Uniting Reformed Church in Southern Africa (URCSA): Embodying Article 4 of the Belhar Confession." *Missionalia* 44 (2016) 224–40.

Bevans, Stephen B. "Inculturation and the Church's Mission: Theological and Trinitarian Foundations." In *Communities of Faith in Africa and the Africana Diapora: In Honour of Dr Tite Tienou with Additional Essays on World Christianity*, edited by Casely B. Essamuah and David K. Ngarniga, 214–31. Eugene, OR: Pickwick, 2013.

Bible Study and Prayer Fellowship. *Choruses We Love to Sing*. Accra, Ghana: Bible Study and Prayer Fellowship, 1986.

Bimwenyi, Oscar K. "The Origins of EATWOT." *Voices from the Third World* 4 (1981) 19–26.

Blanchard, John. *Does God Believe in Atheists?* Darlington, UK: Evangelical, 2000.

Boahen, Adu. *African Perspectives on Colonialism*. Baltimore: Johns Hopkins University Press, 1987.

Boesak, Allan Aubrey. *Black and Reformed: Apartheid, Liberation and the Calvinist Tradition*. Maryknoll: Orbis, 1984.

———. *Farewell to Innocence: A Socio-ethical Study on Black Theology and Black Power*. Maryknoll: Orbis, 1976.

Boff, Leonardo. *Jesus Christ Liberator*. Maryknoll: Orbis, 1981.

Bonhoeffer, Dietrich. *Letters and Papers from Prison*. New York: Macmillan, 1972.

Bonino, Jose Miquez. "Latin America." In *An Introduction to Third World Theology*, edited by John Parrat, 16–43. Cambridge: Cambridge University Press, 2004.

Bosch, David. "Convertss and Cross-Currents in South African Black Theology." *JRA* 3 (1974) 1–22.

———. *Transforming Missions: Paradigm Shifts in Theology of Mission*. Maryknoll: Orbis, 1991.

Bowker, John. "Christology." *Encyclopedia.com*, 1997. Originally from *The Concise Oxford Dictionary of World Religions*. https://www.encyclopedia.com/philosophy-and-religion/bible/bible-general/christology.

BRC Designs. "Gbemlilaa: The Beginning of the Teshie Homowo Festival." YouTube video, 1:45. Posted August 14, 2011. http://www.youtube.com/watch?v=vCNB-QoQ6Xk.

Bromiley, Geoffrey W. *Historical Theology: An Introduction*. Edinburgh: T. & T. Clark, 1978.

Brown, Mackenzie D. *Ultimate Concern: Tillich in Dialogue*. New York: Harper & Row, 1965.

Bruce, Myers J. M. "The Origin of the Gas." *Journal of the African Society* 27 (1927–1928) 69–76.

Brunner, Emil. *The Christian Doctrine of Creation and Redemption* trans., Olive Wyon Philadelphia: Westminster, 1952.

Bujo, Bénézet. *African Theology in Its Social Context*, translated by John O'Donohue. Nairobi: Paulines, 1992.

Calvin, John. *Institutes of the Christian Religion*. Library of Christian Classics 2.30—34.20. Edited by John T. McNeil. Translated by Ford Lewis Battles. Philadelphia: Westminster, 1960.

Carpentar, Joel. "New Evangelical Universities: Cogs in a World System or Players in a New Game?" In *Interpreting Contemporary Christianity: Global Processes and Local Identities*, edited by Ogbu Kalu and Alaine Low, 151–86. Grand Rapids: Eerdmans, 2008.

Carson, Donald A. *Christ and Culture Revisited*. Nottingham, England: Apollos, 2008.

Carter, Craig A. *Rethinking Christ and Culture: A Post-Christendom Perspective*. Grand Rapids: Brazos, 2006.

Chandran, Russell J. "A Methodological Approach to Third World Theology." In *Irruption of The Third World: Challenge to Theology*, edited by Virginia Fabella and Sergio Torres, 79–86. Maryknoll: Orbis, 1983.

Chike, Chigor. "Proudly African, Proudly Christian: The Roots of Christologies in an African Worldview." *Black Theology: An International Journal* 6 (2008) 221–40.

Clark, Peter B. *West Africa and Christianity: A Study of Religions Development from the 15th to the 20th Century*. London: Edward Arnold, 1986.

Crowder, Michael. *West Africa under Colonial Rule*. London: Hutchinson, 1968.

Dickson, Kwesi. *Theology in Africa*. Maryknoll: Orbis, 1984.

Diop, Cheikh Anta. *Civilization or Barbarian: An Authentic Anthropology*. Edited by Harold J. Salemson and Marjolijn de Jagar. Translated by Yaa-Lengi Meemy Ngeni. New York: Lawrene Hill, 1991.

———. *The Cultural Unity of Black Africa: The Domains of Matriarchy and Patriarchy in Classical Antiquity*. London: Karnak House, 1989.

———. *Nations Nègres et Culture*. Paris: Prèsence Africaine, 1979.

Diop, Dialo. "Africa: Mankind's past and Future." In *African Renaissance* edited by Malegapam William Maccgoba. Prologue by Thabo Mbeki, 3–10. Capetown: Mafube and Tafalberg, 1999.

Dougal, John. W. C. *Christians in the African Revolution: The Duff Missionary Lectures, 1962*. Edinburgh: Saint Andrew, 1963.

Dsane, Mark. "Homowo Teshie 2011 (New)." YouTube video, 9:05. Posted September 4, 2011. http://www.youtube.com/watch?v=AffVjiyJmPQ&feature=related.

Dube, Musa. "Diving Ruth for International Relations." In *Other Ways of Reading: African Women and the Bible*, edited by Musa Dube, 179–95. Atlanta: Fereva, 2001.

———. *Postcolonial Feminist Interpretation of the Bible*. Saint Louis: Chalice, 2012.

Dunn, James D. G. *Jesus Remembered: Christianity in the Making*. Vol. 1. 3 vols. Grand Rapids: 2003.

———. *Theology of Paul the Apostle*. Grand Rapids: Wm. B. Eerdmans, 2006.

Editors of Encyclopaedia Britannica. "Imhotep: Egyptian Architect, Physician, and Statesman." *Encyclopedia Britannica*. November 11, 2019. https://www.britannica.com/biography/Imhotep.

Ekem, John David Kwabena. *Early Scriptures of the Gold Coast (Ghana): The Historical, Linguistic, and Theological Settings of the Ga, Twi, Mfantse, and Ewe Bibles*. London: St Jerome, 2011.

———. *Priesthood in Context: A Study of Priesthood in Some Christian and Primal Communities of Ghana and its Relevance for Mother-Tongue Biblical Interpretation*. Accra, Ghana: SonLife, 2009.

Ela, Jean-Marc, and René Luneau. *Voici le temps des heritiers*. Paris: Karthala, 1981.

Emmet, Dorothy M. "Epistemology and the Idea of Revelation." In *The Theology of Paul Tillich*, edited by Charles W. Kegley and Robert W. Bretall, 212–14. New York: Macmillan, 1952.

Evans, James H., Jr. "Eschatology, White Supremacy and the Beloved Community." In *Reconstructing Christian Theology*, edited by Rebbecca S. Chopp and Mark Lewis Taylor, 346–73. Minneapolis: Fortress, 1994.

Falk, Peter. *The Growth of the Church in Africa*. Grand Rapids: Zondervan, 1979.

Ferm, Dean William. *Third World Liberation Theologies: An Introductory Survey*. Maryknoll: Orbis, 1986.

Bibliography

Feuerbach, Ludwig Andreas. *The Essence of Christianity*. Translated by George Eliot. Mineola, NY: Dover, 2008.

Fiedler, NyaGondwe Rachel. *A History of the Circle of Concerned African Women Theologians, 1989–2007*. Malawi: Mzuni, 2017.

Field, Magaret J. *Religion and Medicine of the Ga People*. London: Oxford University Press, 1937.

Fiorenza, Elizabeth S. *In Memory of Her: A Feminist Theological Reconstruction of Christian Origins*. New York: Crossroads, 1984.

Frederiks, Martha. "Congruency, Conflict or Dialogue: Lamin Sanneh on the Relation between Gospel and Culture." *Exchange* 24 (1995) 123–34.

Frei, Hans. *The Identity of Jesus Christ*. Philadelphia: Fortress, 1984.

Gadamer, Hans-Georg. *Truth and Method*. Translated by Joel Weinshiemer and Donald G. Marshall. London: Continuum, 1989.

Garlock, Ruthanne. *Fire in His Bones: The Story of Benson Idahosa*. Plainfield, NJ: Logos International, 1981.

Gecaga, Margaret G. "Creative Stewardship for a New Earth." In *Theology of Reconstruction: Exploratory Essays*, edited by Mary Getui and Emmanuel Obeng, 28–49. Nairobi: Acton, 1999.

Geiss, Immanuel. *The Pan-African Movement*. New York: Africana, 1974.

Gifford, Paul. *Ghana's New Christianity: Pentecostalism in a Globalizing African Economy*. Bloomington: University of Indiana Press, 2004.

Gifford, Paul, and J. Kwabena Asamoah-Gyadu. "Enlarging Christian Coasts: Pentecostalism and Higher Education in Sub-Saharan Africa." In *Communities of Faith in Africa and the Africana Diapora: In Honour of Dr Tite Tienou with Additional Essays on World Christianity*, edited by Casely B. Essamuah and David K. Ngarniga, 8–17. Eugene, OR: Pickwick, 2013.

Gill, Robin. *Theology and Social Structure*. Oxford: Mowbray, 1977.

Goba, Bonganjalo. *An Agenda for Black Theology: Hermeneutics for Social Change*. Johannesburg: Skotaville, 1988.

Gonzales, Justo L. *The Story of Christianity: The Early Church to the Reformation*. Vol. 1. 2 vols. San Francisco: Harper & Row, 1984.

Gqubule, Simon. "Theologie Noire Sud-africaine." *Spiritus* 20 (1979) 105–9.

Grenz, Stanley J. *The Matrix of Christian Theology: The Social God and the Relational Self; A Trinitarian Theology of the Imago Dei*. Louisville: Westminster John Knox, 2001.

Gupta, Avijit. *Ecology and Development in the Third World*. Canada: Routledge 1988.

Gyekye, Kwame. *African Cultural Values: An Introduction*. Accra, Ghana: Sankofa, 1996.

———. *The Unexamined Life: Philosophy and the African Experience*. Legon, Ghana: Sankofa, 1988.

Hamilton, Kenneth. "Paul Tillich." In *Creative Minds in Contemporary Theology*, edited by Philip Edgcumbe Hughes, 452–54. Grand Rapids: Eerdmans, 1969.

Haar, Gerrie ter. "Standing Up for Jesus: A Survey of New Development in Christianity in Ghana." *Exchange* 23 (1994) 221–40.

Hastings, Adrian. *The Church in Africa, 1450–1950*. Edited by Henry Chadwick and Owen Chadwick. Oxford: Clarendon, 1994.

———. *A History of Christianity, 1950–1975*. Cambridge: Cambridge University Press, 1979.

Henderson-Quartey, David K. *The Ga of Ghana: History and Culture of a West African People*. London: Henderson-Quartey, 2001.

Bibliography

Hopkins, Dwight N. *Being Human Race, Culture and Religion*. Minneapolis: Fortress, 2005.

———. *Black Theology: USA and South Africa; Politics, Culture and Liberation*. Maryknoll: Orbis, 1989.

Horton, Walter M. "Tillich's Role in Contemporary Theology." In *The Theology of Paul Tillich*, edited by Charles W. Kegley and Robert W. Bretall, 26–29. Library of Living Theology 1. New York: Macmillan, 1952.

Idowu, Bolaji E. *African Traditional Religion*. New York: Orbis, 1973.

Iliffe, John. *Africans: The History of a Continent*. Cambridge: Cambridge University Press, 1995.

Isichei, Elizabeth. *A History of African Societies to 1870*. Cambridge: Cambridge University Press, 1997.

———. *A History of Christianity in Africa: From Antiquity to the Present*. Grand Rapids: Eerdmans, 1995.

Jackson, Tom. "Africa's Many Middle Class and Why It Matters." *NewAfrican*, December 26, 2016.

James, George G. M. *Stolen Legacy: Greek Philosophy Is Stolen Egyptian Philosophy*. Bensenville, IL: Lushena, 2014.

Jansen, John F. *Calvin's Doctrine of the Work of Christ*. London: Clarke, 1956.

Jenkins, Philip. *The Next Christendom: The Coming of Global Christianity*. Oxford: Oxford University Press, 2002.

Joy News. "Ga Chief Priest Unhappy with Media Reports." *Joy Online*, January 21, 2008. https://www.myjoyonline.com/news/ga-chief-priests-unhappy-with-media-reports/.

Kabasele, François Lumbala. "Christ as Ancestor and Elder Brother." In Schreiter, *Many Faces of Jesus in Africa*, 116–27.

———. "Christ as Chief." In Schreiter, *Many Faces of Jesus in Africa*, 103–15.

Kagabo, Liboire. "Alexis Kagame: The Trail of an African Theology" in *African Theology in the 21st Century: The Contribution of the Pioneers*, edited by Benezet Bujo and Juvenal Ilunga Muya, translated by Sylvano Borruso, 13–44. Kenya: Paulines, 2006.

Kalu, Ogbu K. *African Pentecostalism: An Introduction*. Oxford: Oxford University Press, 2008.

———. *Power, Poverty and Prayer: The Challenges of Poverty and Pluralism in African Christianity, 1960-996*. Frankfurt: Lang, 2000.

Kamau-Goro, Nicholas. "Rejection or Reappropriation? Christian Allegory and the Critique of Postcolonial Public Culture in the Early Moods of Nugi wa Thiongó." In *Christianity and Public Culture in Africa*, edited by Harri Englund, 67–85 Athens: Ohio University Press, 2011.

Kelly, John Norman Davidson. *Early Christian Doctrines*. San Francisco: Harper & Row, 1978.

Kibongi, Raymond Buana. "Priesthood." In *Biblical Revelation and African Beliefs*, edited by Kwesi Dickson and Paul Ellingworth, 47–56. London: Lutterworth, 1969.

Kierkegaard, Søren. *Philosophical Fragments*. Princeton: Princeton University Press, 1942.

Kilson, Marion. *African Urban Kinsmen: The Ga of Central Accra*. London: Hurst, 1974.

———. *Kpele Lala: Ga Religious Songs and Symbols*. Cambridge: Harvard University Press, 1971.

Bibliography

Kolie, Cece. "Jesus as Healer." In Schreiter, *Many Faces of Jesus in Africa*, 128–50.
Koo, Choon-Seo. *Doing Christology in Asian Context*. South Korea: Handl, 2011.
Knitter, Paul. *Introducing Theologies of Religion*. Maryknoll: Orbis, 2002.
Kraemer, Hendrik. *The Christian Message in a Non-Christian World*. New York: Harper, 1938.
Krüger, René. "The Biblical and Theological Significance of the Accra Confession: A Perspective from the South." *Reformed World* 55 (2005) 226–33.
Kuma, Afua. *Kwaebirentuw Ase Yesu: Afua Kuma Ayeyi ne Mpaebo* [Jesus of the Deep Forest: Afua Kuma Praises and Prayers]. Accra, Ghana: Asempa, 1980.
Kunihyop, Samuel Waje. *African Christian Theology*. Grand Rapids: Zondervan, 2012.
Küster, Volker. *The Many Faces of Jesus Christ: Intercultural Christology*. Translated by John Bowden. London: SCM, 2001.
La Due, William J. *Jesus among the Theologians*. Harrisburg, PA: Trinity International, 2001.
LaCugna, Mowry C. *God for Us: The Trinity and Christian Life*. New York: HarperCollins, 1991.
Larbi, Emmanuel Kingsley. *Pentecostalism: The Eddies of Ghanaian Christianity*. Accra, Ghana: CPCS, 2001.
Laryea, Philip Tetteh. *Ephraim Amu: Nationalist, Poet and Theologian (1899–1995)*. Foreword by J. H. K. Nketia. Akropong-Akuapem, Ghana: Regnum Africa, 2012.
———. *Yesu Homowor Nuntsor: Nikasemor ni koor bor ni Kristofoi Naa Yesu yer Gamei Akusumfeemɔ kɛ Blema Sajii Amli* [Jesus, Lord of the Homowor: A Study about How the Ga People Appreciate Jesus in the Context of Their Traditions and History]. Akropong-Akuapem, Ghana: Regnum Africa, 2004.
Lebreton, Jules. "The Logos." *New Advent* (1910). http://www.newadvent.org/cathen/09328a.htm.
Lee, Jung Young. *Ancestor Worship and Christianity in Korea*. New York: Mellen, 1988.
———. *An Emerging Theology in World Perspective: Commentary on Korean Minjung Theology*. Mystic, CT: Twenty-Third, 1988.
———. *Korean Shamanistic Rituals*. The Hague, Netherlands: Mouton, 1981.
———. *Patterns of Inner Process*. Secaucus, NJ: Citadel, 1976.
Lives of Saints. "St. Anselm of Canterbury, Archbishop, Doctor of the Church." https://www.ewtn.com/catholicism/library/st-anselm-of-canterbury-archbishop doctor-of-the-church-5190.
Lowe, Walter. "Christ and Salvation." In *Christian Theology: An Introduction to Its Traditions and Tasks*, edited by in Hodgson Peter C. and Robert H. King, 222–48. Philadelphia: Fortress, 1985.
MacRobert, Ian. "The Black Roots of Pentecostalism." In *Pentecost, Mission and Ecumenism: Essays on Intercultural Theology*, edited by Jan A. B. Jongeneel, 73–84. Frankfurt: Lang, 1992.
Magesa, Laurenti. "Christ the Liberator and Africa Today." In Schreiter, *Many Faces of Jesus in Africa*, 151–63.
Maimela, Simon. *Modern Trends in Theology*. Braamfontein: Skotaville, 1990.
Maluleke, Tinyiko. "Half a Century of African Christian Theologies: Elements of the Engaging Agenda for the Twenty-First Century." *Journal of Theology for Southern Africa* 99 (1997) 4–23.
Martey, Emmanuel. "An African Examines Trends in Asian Christian Theology." *Trinity Journal of Church and Theology* 6 (1996) 24–36.

———. *African Theology: Inculturation and Liberation*. New York: Orbis, 1993.

———. "African Theology and Latin American Liberation Theology: Initial Differences within the Context of EATWOT." *Trinity Journal of Church and Theology* 5 (1995) 45–59.

Mazorewa, Gwinyai H. *The Origin and Development of African Theology*. Maryknoll: Orbis, 1985.

Mbilla, Johnson. "Election 2020: Religious Leaders Cautioned against Divisive Comments." *Joy Online*, December 5, 2020. https://www.myjoyonline.com/election-2020-religious-leaders-cautioned-against-divisive-comments/.

———. "Let's Stop Politicizing Religion to Promote Peace." *Business Ghana*, October 12, 2019. http://businessghana.com/site/news/General/197959/Let-s-stop-politicising-religion-to-promote-peace-Dr-Mbilla.

Mbiti, John S. *African Religions and Philosophy*. Oxford: Heinemann, 1990.

———. "African Theology." In *Dictionary of the Ecumenical Movement*, edited by Nicholas Lossky et al., 977–80. Geneva: WCC, 1991.

———. "An African Views American Black Theology." In *Black Theology: A Documentary History, 1966–1979*, edited by James H. Cone and Gayraud S. Wilmore, 379–84. Maryknoll: Orbis, 1993.

———. *Concepts of God in Africa*. London: SPCK, 1970.

———. *New Testament Eschatology in an African Background*. Oxford University Press, 1971.

———. "Some African Concepts of Christology." In *Christ and the Younger Churches*, edited by G. Vicedom, 51–62. London: SPCK, 1972.

McCormick, Matt. "Immanuel Kant: Metaphysics." *Internet Encyclopedia of Philosophy*. 2005. http://www.iep.utm.edu/Kantmeta.

McCulloh, Gerald W. *Christ's Person and Life-Work in the Theology of Albrecht Ritschl with Special Attention to "Munus Triplex."* Lanham, MD: University Press of America, 1990.

McGrath, Alister E. *Scientific Theology: Theory*. Vol. 3. 3 vols. London: T. & T. Clark, 2003.

McWilliams, W. *The Passion of God: Divine Suffering in Contemporary Protestant Theology*. Atlanta: Mercer University Press, 1985.

Migliore, Daniel. *Faith Seeking Understanding*. Grand Rapids: Eerdmans, 2004.

Moloney, Raymond. "African Christology." *Theological Studies* 48 (1987) 505–15.

Moltmann, Jürgen. *The Coming of God: Christian Eschatology*. Translated by Magaret Kohl. Minneapolis: Fortress, 1996.

———. *The Crucified God*. New York: Harper & Row, 1974.

———. *The Crucified God: The Cross of Christ as the Foundation and Criticism of Christian Theology*. Translated by R. A. Wilson and John Bowden. Minneapolis: Fortress, 1993.

———. *The Trinity and the Kingdom: The Doctrine of God*. Translated by Magaret Kohl. Minneapolis: Fortress, 1993.

———. *The Way of Jesus Christ: Christology in Messianic Dimensions*. London: SCM, 1990.

Moyo, Ambrose Mavingire. "Material Things in African Society: Implications for Christian Ethics." In *Moral and Ethical Issues in African Christianity: A Challenge for African Christianity*, edited by Mugambi Jesse N. K. and Nasimiyu-Wasike, Anne, 49–58. Nairobi: Acton, 1999.

Mudimbe, Valentin-Yves. *The Idea of Africa*. Indianapolis: Indiana University Press, 1994.

Mugabe, Henry J. "Christology in African Context." *Review and Expositor* 88 (1991) 343–55.

Mugambi, Jesse N. K., and Laurenti Magesa. *Jesus in African Christianity: Experimentation and Diversity in African Christology*. Nairobi: Initiatives 1989.

———. "Theological Method in African Christianity." In *Theological Method and Aspects of Working in African Christianity*, edited by Mary N. Getui, 5–40. African Christianity series. Nairobi: Action, 1998.

Mveng, Englebert. "Only a Monologue of the Poor and Those Left Out of Accounts: A Cultural Response to Doing Theology in a Divided World." In *Doing Theology in a Divided World*, edited by V. Fabella and S. Torres, 72–75. Maryknoll: Orbis, 1985.

Namisiyu-Wasike, Anne. "Christology and an African Woman's Experience." In *Jesus in African Christianity: Experimentation and Diversity in African Christology*, edited by. J. N. K. Mugambi and Laurenti Magesa, 123–35. Nairobi: Initiatives, 1989.

Nelson, Douglas J. "For Such a Time as This: The Story of Bishop William Seymour and the Azuza Street Revival." PhD diss., University of Birmingham, 1981.

Neve, Juergen Ludwig. *A History of Christian Thought*. Vol. 1. 2 vols. Philadelphia: United Lutheran Publication House, 1943.

Niebuhr, Richard R. *Schleiermacher on Christ and Religion*. New York: Scribner, 1964.

Nkrumah, Kwame. *Consciencism: Philosophy and Ideology for Decolonization*. London: Panaf, 1970.

———. "Full Text: First Independent Speech by Kwame Nkrumah." Accra, Ghana, March 5, 1957. *Joy Online*, posted September 21, 2018. https://www.myjoyonline.com/text-kwame-nkrumahs-famous-independence-day-speech/..

Nyamiti, Charles. "African Christologies Today" In Schreiter, *Many Faces of Jesus in Africa*, 3–23.

Obeng, Emmanuel Adow. "Synthetic and Praxis models in African Theology." In *African Christianity Series*, 41–54. Nairobi: Action, 1998.

Oden, Thomas C. *How Africa Shaped the Christian Mind: Rediscovering the African Seabed of Western Christianity*. Downers Grove: InterVarsity, 2007.

Odotei, Irene. "External Influences on Ga Society and Culture." *Research Review NS* 7 (1991) 61–71.

———. "The Ga and Their Neighbour." PhD diss., University of Ghana, Legon, 1972.

———. "What Is in a Name? The Social and Historical Significance of Ga Names." *Institute of African Studies Research Review* 5 (1989) 34–51.

Oduyoye, Mercy Amba. *Beads and Strands: Reflections of an African Woman on Christianity in Africa*. Ghana and Cameroun: Regnum Africa and Clé, 2002.

———. *Hearing and Knowing: Theological Reflections on Christianity in Africa*. Maryknoll: Orbis, 1986.

———. Kanyoro Musimbi R. A. *The Will to Arise: Women, Tradition and the Church in Africa*. Maryknoll: Orbis, 1995.

Ogden, Schubert M. *The Point of Christology*. New York: Harper & Row, 1982.

Okure, Teresa. "Women in the Bible." In *With Passion and Compassion: Third World Women Doing Theology-Reflections from the Women's Commission of the Ecumenical Association of Third World Theologians*, edited by Virginia Fabella and Mercy Amba Oduyoye, 47–59. Maryknoll: Orbis, 1989.

Olela, Henri. "The African Foundations of Greek Philosophy." In *African Philosophy: An Anthology*, edited by Emmanuel Chukwudi Eze, 43–49. Malden, MA: Blackwell, 1998.

Omenyo, Cephas N. "Charismatic Churches in Ghana and Contextualization." *Exchange* 31 (2002) 252–77.

———. *Pentecost Outside Pentecostalism: A Study of the Development of Charismatic Renewal in Mainline Churches in Ghana*. Zoetermeer, Netherlands: Uitgeverij Boekencentrum, 2002.

Oosthuizen, Gerhardus Cornelis. *Post Christianity in Africa: A Theological and Anthropological Study*. Grand Rapids: Eerdmans, 1968.

Opoku, Kofi Asare. *West African Traditional Religion*. Singapore: PEP, 1978.

Origen. *Contra Celsum*. Cambridge University Press, 1980.

———. "*De Principiis*: On the Incarnation of Christ." Christian Classics Ethereal Library. N.d. https://www.ccel.org/ccel/schaff/anf04.vi.v.iii.vi.html.

Oruka, Odera H. "Four Trends in Current African Philosophy." In *Trends in Contemporary African Philosophy*, edited by Oruka H. Odera, 13–22. Nairobi: Shirikon, 1990.

Osabu-Kle, Daniel Tetteh. "The Ga People and the Homowo Festival." Accessed February 21, 2012. https://carleton.ca/africanstudies/wp-content/uploads/Ga-People-and-Homowo-Festival.pdf.

Ositelu, Gabriel, II, et al. *African Initiatives in Christianity: The Growth, Gifts and Diversities of Indigenous African Churches; A Challenge to the Ecumenical Movements*. Geneva: World Council of Churches, 1998.

Outlaw, Lucius. "African, African American, Africana Philosophy." In *African Philosophy*, edited by Emmanuel Chuwudi Eze, 25–39. Oxford: Blackwell, 1998.

Oyedepo, David O. *Anointing for Exploits*. Ikeja, Nigeria: Dominion, 2005.

———. "Bishop Oyedepo Unveiling the Stronghold of Faith." YouTube video, 1:14:08. Posted July 1, 2016. https://www.youtube.com/watch?v=nRfupav9wPE.

Ozanne, Paul. "Ladoku: An Early Town Near Prampram." *Ghana Notes and Queries* 7 (1965) 6–7.

Pannenberg, Wolfhart. *Jesus, God and Man*. 2nd ed. Translated by Lewis Wilkins and Duane Priebe. Philadelphia: Westminster, 1977.

———. *Systematic Theology*. Translated by Geoffrey Bromiley. 3 vols. Grand Rapids: Eerdmans, 1991–98.

Parratt, John. *A Guide to Doing Theology*. London: SPCK, 1996.

———. Introduction to *An Introduction to Third World Theologies*, edited by John Parratt, 1–15. Cambridge: Cambridge University Press, 2004.

———. *Reinventing Christianity: African Theology Today*. Grand Rapids: Eerdmans, 1995.

Parrinder, Geoffrey E. *African Traditional Religion*. London: Sheldon, 1962.

Parsons, Robert T. *The Churches and Ghana Society, 1918–1955: A Survey of the Work of Three Protestant Mission Societies and the African Churches Which They Established in Their Assistance to Societary Development*. Leiden: Brill, 1963.

Pearson, Birger A. *Gnosticism, Judaism, and Egyptian Christianity*. Minneapolis: Fortress, 1990.

Peters, Ted. *God as Trinity: Relationality and Temporality in Divine Life*. Louisville: Westminster John Knox, 1993.

———. *God—the World's Future: Systematic Theology for a New Era*. 2nd ed. Minneapolis: Fortress, 2000.

———. *God the Worlds Future: Systematic Theology for a Postmodern Era*. Minneapolis: Fortress, 1992.

Pieris, Aloysius. *An Asian Theology of Liberation*. Maryknoll: Orbis, 1988.

Pobee, John S. *Kwame Nkrumah and the Church in Ghana (1949–1966)*. Accra, Ghana: Asempa, 1988.

———. *Toward an African Theology*. Nashville: Abingdon, 1979.

Quartey-Papafio, Arthur Boi. "The Native Tribunals of the Accra of Gold Coast." *Journal of the African Society* 10 (1911) 320–30.

Race, Alan. *Christians and Religious Pluralism*. Maryknoll: Orbis, 1982.

Rashidi, Runocco. *Introduction to the Study of African Classical Civilizations*. London: Karnak House, 1992.

Rayan, Samuel. "The Irruption of the Third World: A Challenge to Theology." *Vidyajyoti* 46 (1982) 106–27.

Reed, Rodney L., and Gift Mtukwa. "Christ Our Ancestor: African Christology and the Danger of Contextualization." *Wesleyan Journal of Theology* 45 (2010) 144–63.

Reindorf, Carl Christian. *History of the Gold Coast and Asante*. Legon: Ghana University Press 2007.

Rieger Joeg. *Christ and Empire: From Paul to Post Colonial Times*. Minneapolis: Fortress, 2007.

Ritschl, Albrecht. *The Christian Doctrine of Justification and Sanctification*. Translated and edited by H. R. Mackintosh and A. B. Macaulay. Clifton, NJ: Reference Book, 1966.

Romer, Ludewig Ferdinand. *A Reliable Account of the Coast of Guinea*. Translated and edited by Selena Axelrod Winsnes. Oxford: Oxford University Press, 2000.

Ross, Kenneth R. "Nicene Methodology and the Christological Task in Africa Today." Paper delivered at the Centre for the Study of Christianity in the Non-Western World, University of Edinburgh, December 3, 1996.

Roukema, Riemer. *Gnosis and Faith in Early Christianity: An Introduction to Gnosticism*. London: SCM, 1998.

Sadler, Greg. "St Anselm of Canterbury (1033–1109)." *Internet Encyclopedia of Philosophy*. 2006. http://www.iep.utm.edu/Anselm.

Sanneh, Lamin O. *Beyond Jihad: The Pacifist Tradition in West African Islam*. New York: Oxford University Press, 2016.

———. *Disciples of All Nations: Pillars of World Christianity*. Oxford: Oxford University Press, 2008.

———. *Translating the Message: The Missionary Impact on Culture*. Maryknoll: Orbis, 1989.

———. *West African Christianity: The Religious Impact*. Maryknoll: Orbis, 1983.

Sanon, Anselme T. "Jesus, Master of Initiation." In *Faces of Jesus in Africa*, edited by Robert J. Schrieter, 85–102. Maryknoll: Orbis, 1991.

Schleiermacher, Friedrich. *The Christian Faith*. Translated by Hugh Ross MacKintosh. Edited by James S. Stewart. Edinburgh: T. & T. Clark, 1999.

Schreiter, Robert J., ed. *Faces of Jesus in Africa*. Maryknoll: Orbis, 1995.

———. *The New Catholicity: Theology between the Global and the Local*. Maryknoll: Orbis, 1999.

Sertima, Ivan Van. "The Lost Sciences of Africa: An Overview." In *African Renaissance*, edited by William Malegapam Maccgoba, 305–30. Cape Town: Mafube and Tafalberg, 1999.

Setiloane, Gabriel M. "Where Are We in African Theology?" In *Theology en Route*, edited by Appiah Kubi, and Sergio Torres, 59–66. Maryknoll: Orbis, 1979.

Shank, David A. *The "Black Elijah" of West Africa*. Abridged by Jocelyn Murray. Leiden: Brill, 1998.

Shiva, Vandana. "Earth Democracy, Living Democracy." *Reformed World* 54 (2004) 115–26.

Shorter, Aylward. *Jesus and the Witchdoctor*. New York: Orbis, 1985.

Smith, James K. A. *Who's Afraid of Postmodernism? Taking Derrida, Lyotard, and Foucault to Church*. Grand Rapids: Baker Academic, 2006.

Sobrino, John. *Christ the Liberator: A View from the Victims*. Maryknoll: Orbis, 2001.

Souga, Thérèsa. "The Christ Event from the Viewpoint of African Women: A Catholic Perspective." In *With Passion and Compassion: Third World Women Doing Theology*, edited by Virginia Fabella and Mercy Amba Oduyoye, 22–29. Maryknoll: Orbis, 1989.

Stinton, Diane S. *Jesus of Africa: Voices of Contemporary African Christology*. Maryknoll: Orbis, 2004.

Stroup, George W. "The Relevance of the *Munus Triplex* for Reformed Theology and Ministry." *Austin Seminary Bulletin* 98 (1983) 12–32.

Sugirtharajah, Rasiah S. *Asian Biblical Hermeneutics and Postcolonialism: Contesting the Interpretations*. Sheffield, UK: Sheffield Academic, 1999.

———. *Asian Faces of Jesus*. Maryknoll: Orbis, 1993.

Tang, Edmond. "East Asia." In *An Introduction to Third World Theology*, edited by John Parrat, 74–104. Cambridge: Cambridge University Press, 2004.

Tappa, Louis. "The Christ Event from the Viewpoint of African Women: A Protestant Perspective." In *With Passion and Compassion: Third World Women Doing Theology*, edited by Virginia Fabella and Mercy Amba Oduyoye, 30–34. Maryknoll: Orbis, 1989.

Taylor, John. V. *The Growth of the Church in Buganda*. London: SCM, 1958.

Tillich, Paul. *A Complete History of Christian Thought*. Edited by Carl E. Braaten. New York: Harper & Row, 1968.

———. *The Courage to Be*. New Haven: Yale University Press, 1952.

———. *The Eternal Now*. New York: Scribner, 1963.

———. *Systematic Theology*. Vol. 1, *Reason and Revelation; Being and God*. Chicago: University of Chicago Press 1951.

———. *Systematic Theology*. Vol. 2, *Existence and the Christ*. Chicago: University of Chicago Press, 1957.

———. *Systematic Theology*. Vol. 3, *Life and the Spirit, History and the Kingdom of God*. Chicago: University of Chicago Press, 1963.

Torres, Sergio. "The Irruption of the Third World." In *Irruption of the Third World: Challenge to Theology*, edited by Virginia Fabella and Sergio Torres, 3–15. Maryknoll: Obis, 1983.

Torres, Sergio, and John Eagleson, eds. *The Challenge of the Basic Christian Communities: Papers from the International Ecumenical Congress of Theology, February 20–March 2, 1980, Sao Paolo, Brazil*. Translated by John Druny. Maryknoll: Orbis, 1988.

Turner, Harold W. "The Primal Religions of the World and Their Study." In *Australian Essays in World Religions*, edited by Victor Hayes, 1–15. Bedford Park: Australian Association for World Religions, 1977.

Tutu, Desmond. "Black Theology / African Theology: Soul Mates or Antagonists?" In *Black Theology: A Documentary History, 1966–1979*, edited by James H. Cone and Gayraud S. Wilmore, 483–91. Maryknoll: Orbis, 1993.

———. *A Voice of One Crying in the Wilderness*. London: Mowbray, 1982.

Ukpong, Justin. "The Emergence of African Theologies." *Theological Studies* 45 (1984) 523.

Walls, Andrew. *The Missionary Movement in Christian History: Studies in the Transmission of Faith*. Maryknoll: Orbis, 1996.

Ward, Kevin. "African Christianity in the Twentieth Century—Part Two." In *History of Global Christianity*, vol. 3, *History of Christianity in the 20th Century*, edited by Jen Holge Schjouring et al., translated by David Orton, 364–65. Leiden: Brill, 2018.

Ward, William Ernest Frank. *A Short History of the Gold Coast*. London: Longman, 1935.

Wariboko, Nimi. *Nigerian Pentecostalism*. Vol. 62, *Rochester Studies in African History and the Diaspora*. Rochester, NY: University of Rochester Press, 2014.

Waruta, Douglas W. "Who Is Jesus Christ for Africans Today? Prophet, Priest, Potentate." In Schreiter, *Many Faces of Jesus in Africa*, 52–64.

Welsh-Asante, Kariamu. *World of Dance: African Dance*. 2nd ed. Foreword by Jacques D'Ambois. Edited by Elizabeth A. Hanley. New York: Chelsea House, 2010.

Wendell, Thomas. *On the Resolution of Science and Faith*. New York: Island, 1946.

Wilkerson, Isabel. *Caste: The Origins of Our Discontents*. New York: Penguin Random House, 2020.

William, Kent. "St. Anselm." *New Advent*. 1907. http://www.newadvent.org/cathen/01546a.htm.

Williams, Kingsley C. *Achimota: The Early Years (1924–1948)*. London: Longmans, 1962.

Wolfers, Michael. "Thomas Hodgkin: Some Lost Pages of History." In *Revisiting African Studies in a Globalized World—Institute of African Studies, University of Ghana 50th Anniversary Conference*, edited by Albert Awedobu et al., 95–105. Sakumono, Ghana: Smartline, 2017.

World Alliance of Reformed Churches (WARC). "Covenanting for Justice: The Accra Confession." *Reformed World, Reformed Faith and the Rejection of Economic Injustice: Essays on Practising the Accra Confession* 55 (2005) 226–33.

Yong, Bok Kim. "Messiah and Minjung: Discerning Messianic Politics over against Political Messianism." In *Minjung Theology*, edited by Christian Conference of Asia, Commission on Theological Concerns, 893–912. New York: Orbis, 1983.

Zizioulas, John D. *Being a Communion: Studies in Personhood and the Church, Contemporary Green Theologies*. Crestwood, NY: Saint Vladimir's Seminary Press, 1985.

———. "Human Capacity and Human Incapacity: A Theological Exploration of Personhood." *Scottish Journal of Theology* 28 (1975) 401–8.

www.ingramcontent.com/pod-product-compliance
Lightning Source LLC
Chambersburg PA
CBHW050345230426
43663CB00010B/1995